Africa

lonely planet

phrasebooks

Africa phrasebook
1st edition – June 2007

Published by
Lonely Planet Publications Pty Ltd ABN 36 005 607 983
90 Maribyrnong St, Footscray, Victoria 3011, Australia

Lonely Planet Offices
Australia Locked Bag 1, Footscray, Victoria 3011
USA 150 Linden St, Oakland CA 94607
UK 72–82 Rosebery Ave, London, EC1R 4RW

Cover illustration
Jammin' by Wendy Wright

ISBN 978 1 74059 692 3

text © Lonely Planet Publications Pty Ltd 2007
cover illustration © Lonely Planet Publications Pty Ltd 2007

10 9 8 7 6 5 4 3 2

Printed through the Bookmaker International Ltd
Printed in China

acknowledgments

This book is based on existing editions of Lonely Planet's phrasebooks as well as new content. It was developed with the help of the following people:

- Wilna Liebenberg for the Afrikaans chapter
- Daniel Aboye Aberra for the Amharic chapter
- Shalome Knoll for the Arabic chapter
- Michael Janes for the French chapter
- Izabela Will for the Hausa chapter
- Vololona Rasolofoson for the Malagasy chapter
- Robert Landon for the Portuguese chapter
- Chenjerai Shire for the Shona chapter
- Martin Benjamin for the Swahili chapter
- Fiona McLaughlin for the Wolof chapter
- Harrison Adeniyi for the Yoruba chapter
- Russell Kaschula and Thanduxolo Fatyi for the Xhosa chapter
- Derek Gowlett for the Zulu chapter

Thanks also to thank Jean-Pierre Masclef (French) and Yukiyoshi Kamimura (Portuguese) for additional language expertise.

Lonely Planet Language Products

Publishing Manager: Chris Rennie
Commissioning Editors: Karin Vidstrup Monk (assisted by Branislava Vladisavljevic) & Rachel Williams
Editor: Vanessa Battersby
Assisting Editors: Branislava Vladisavljevic & Francesca Coles
Managing Editor: Annelies Mertens

Layout Designer: Margie Jung, Jacqueline Mcleod & Pablo Gastar
Managing Layout Designer: Sally Darmody
Cartographer: Wayne Murphy
Series Designer & Illustrations: Yukiyoshi Kamimura
Title Illustration: Wendy Wright

contents

CONTENTS

4

LANGUAGE MAP

Africa

NORTH ATLANTIC OCEAN

INDIAN OCEAN

Mediterranean Sea

Red Sea

Gulf of Aden

Gulf of Guinea

Portugal
Madeira (Portugal)
Canary Islands (Spain)
Spain
Italy
Greece
Turkey
Cyprus
Lebanon
Israel & the Palestinian Territories
Jordan
Syria
Iraq
Armenia
Azerbaijan
Turkmenistan
Iran
Qatar
U.A.E.
Oman
Saudi Arabia
Yemen
Socotra (Yemen)

MOROCCO ⊗ Rabat
ALGERIA ⊗ Algiers
TUNISIA ⊗ Tunis
LIBYA ⊗ Tripoli
EGYPT ⊗ Cairo
MAURITANIA ⊗ Nouakchott
MALI ⊗ Bamako
NIGER ⊗ Niamey
CHAD ⊗ Ndjamena
SUDAN ⊗ Khartoum
ERITREA ⊗ Asmara
DJIBOUTI ⊗ Djibouti
SOMALIA ⊗ Mogadishu
ETHIOPIA ⊗ Addis Ababa
KENYA ⊗ Nairobi
UGANDA ⊗ Kampala
SENEGAL ⊗ Dakar
THE GAMBIA ⊗ Banjul
GUINEA-BISSAU ⊗ Bissau
GUINEA ⊗ Conakry
SIERRA LEONE ⊗ Freetown
LIBERIA ⊗ Monrovia
CÔTE D'IVOIRE ⊗ Yamoussoukro
BURKINA FASO ⊗ Ouagadougou
GHANA ⊗ Accra
TOGO ⊗ Lomé
BENIN ⊗ Cotonou
NIGERIA ⊗ Abuja
CAMEROON ⊗ Yaoundé
EQUATORIAL GUINEA ⊗ Malabo
GABON ⊗ Libreville
SÃO TOMÉ & PRÍNCIPE
CENTRAL AFRICAN REPUBLIC ⊗ Bangui

Nile
Niger
Chad
Lake Tana
Blue Nile
White Nile

Victoria ⊛
SEYCHELLES

MAURITIUS
Port Louis ⊛
St-Denis ⊛
RÉUNION

COMOROS
Moroni ⊛ ⊛ Mamoudzou
MAYOTTE
MADAGASCAR
Antananarivo ⊛

Pemba
Zanzibar
Mafia

Mozambique (Channel)

Nairobi ⊛
Dodoma ⊛
TANZANIA

MALAWI
Lilongwe ⊛
MOZAMBIQUE

Lusaka ⊛
ZAMBIA
Harare ⊛
ZIMBABWE
Maputo ⊛
Mbabane ⊛ ⊛ SWAZILAND
Tshwane
(Pretoria) ⊛
Maseru ⊛ LESOTHO

CONGO DEMOCRATIC RWANDA
REPUBLIC BURUNDI
OF CONGO
(ZAÏRE)
Brazzaville ⊛
Kinshasa ⊛

BOTSWANA
Gaborone ⊛
Bloemfontein ⊛
SOUTH
AFRICA

ANGOLA

Luanda ⊛

NAMIBIA
Windhoek ⊛

Cape Town ⊛

SOUTH
ATLANTIC
OCEAN

0   500 mi
0   1000 km

Note: Language areas are
approximate only. For more detail
see the relevant introduction.

Afrikaans
Amharic
Arabic
French

Hausa
Malagasy
Portuguese
Shona

Swahili
Wolof
Xhosa

Yoruba
Zulu

africa – at a glance

In addition to its many other attractions, Africa offers incredible linguistic diversity. Most African languages belong to one of the following four language families: Afro-Asiatic, Nilo-Saharan, Niger-Congo (with the Bantu languages as the major branch) and Khoisan. In addition, the languages of Madagascar belong to the Austronesian language family. Even though the number of languages spoken in Africa is huge (around 1000), most of them have less than a million speakers. On the other hand, more prominent languages usually also serve as regional lingua francas – such as Swahili in East Africa. Luckily for English speakers, most African languages use Roman script and there's a general correspondence between the pronunciation and the written form of words.

Arabic has a particularly important status in the north and northeast of the continent, due to its proximity to the Middle East and the Arab conquests of North Africa from the 7th century. Among the African languages, Amharic is linguistically closest to Arabic, as they both belong to the Semitic group of the Afro-Asiatic family. In addition, they're both script languages, but the two scripts are quite different.

Due to the 19th-century European colonisation of Africa, a few European languages (particularly English, French and Portuguese) are still influential in various African countries and even share official status with native African languages. English is predominantly represented in the east and the south, French in the north and the west, and Portuguese in the east and the west of the continent.

A unique linguistic feature of Africa is Afrikaans, which belongs to the Germanic branch of the Indo-European language family. It was created as a result of the 17th-century Dutch colonisation of the south of the continent. Although still very similar to Dutch, Afrikaans is now considered a language in its own right.

did you know?

- The African Union (AU) was established in 2000 by the adoption of the Constitutive Act at the Lome Summit (Togo). It developed from the African Economic Community and the Organisation of African Unity. It has 53 member states, covering the entire continent except for Morocco. The AU is governed by the Assembly of Heads of State and Government and the Pan-African Parliament.
- The home of the AU is Addis Ababa in Ethiopia. The AU anthem is the song 'Let Us All Unite and Celebrate Together'. The AU flag combines green, yellow and gold colours, with the emblem showing the African continent in the middle.
- The official languages of the AU are all African languages, as well as Arabic, English, French and Portuguese. The African Academy of Languages (founded in 2001) strives to preserve African languages and promote their use among the African people.

Afrikaans

pronunciation

Vowels		Consonants	
Symbol	**English sound**	**Symbol**	**English sound**
a	run	b	bed
aa	father	ch	cheat
ai	aisle	d	dog
aw	law	f	fun
ay	say	g	go
e	bet	h	hat
ee	see	k	kit
eu	nurse	kh	as the 'ch' in the Scottish *loch*
ew	ee with rounded lips	l	lot
ey	as in bet, but longer	m	man
i	hit	n	not
o	pot	ng	ring
oh	cold	p	pet
oo	poor	r	run (trilled)
oy	toy	s	sun
u	put	sh	shot
uh	ago	t	top
In this chapter, the Afrikaans pronunciation is given in blue after each phrase.		v	very
		w	win
		y	yes
Each syllable is separated by a dot, and the syllable stressed in each word is italicised. For example:		z	zero
		zh	pleasure
Dankie. dang·kee			

introduction

You don't need to look hard for evidence of Afrikaans in English: *aardvark*, the name of a termite-eating mammal native to Africa, is one of the first words in any English dictionary. English has also borrowed the Afrikaans words *commando* and *trek*, among others. Afrikaans (*Afrikaans* a·free·kans) belongs to the Germanic branch of the Indo-European language family – just like English. It's closely related to the 17th-century Dutch brought to South Africa from 1652 onward, when The Dutch East India Company established the first European settlement at the Cape of Good Hope. Afrikaans derives from the dialect that developed among these settlers, most of whom were from the Netherlands. Until the late 19th century, Afrikaans was considered a Dutch dialect and was known as 'Cape Dutch' – in fact, it wasn't until 1925 that it became one of the official languages of South Africa. Today, it's the first language of some six million people, and is spoken in Botswana, Malawi, Namibia and Zambia as well as South Africa.

afrikaans (native language)   **afrikaans** (generally understood)

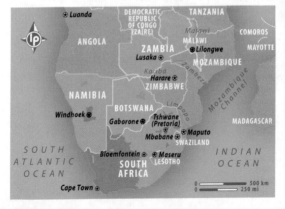

language difficulties

Do you speak English?		
Praat jy Engels?		praat yay *eng*·ils
Do you understand?		
Verstaan jy?		vir·*staan* yay
I (don't) understand.		
Ek verstaan (nie).		ek vir·*staan* (nee)
Could you please ...?	*Kan jy asseblief ...?*	kan yay a·si·*bleef* ...
repeat that	*dit herhaal*	dit her·*haal*
speak more slowly	*stadiger praat*	*staa*·di·khir praat
write it down	*dit neerskryf*	dit *neyr*·skrayf

time, dates & numbers

What time is it?	*Hoe laat is dit?*	hu laat is dit
It's one o'clock.	*Dis een-uur.*	dis *eyn*-ewr
It's (two) o'clock.	*Dis (twee-)uur.*	dis (*twey*·)ewr
Quarter past (one).	*Kwart oor (een).*	kwart oor (eyn)
Half past (one).	*Half (twee).*	half (twey)
Quarter to (eight).	*Kwart voor (agt).*	kwart voor (akht)
At what time ...?	*Hoe laat ...?*	hu laat ...
At ...	*Om ...*	om ...
It's (15 December).	*Dis (vyftien Desember).*	dis (*fayf*·teen dey·*sem*·bir)

yesterday	*gister*	*khis*·tir
today	*vandag*	fin·*dakh*
tomorrow	*môre*	*mo*·ri

Monday	*Maandag*	*maan*·dakh
Tuesday	*Dinsdag*	*dins*·dakh
Wednesday	*Woensdag*	*wuns*·dakh
Thursday	*Donderdag*	*don*·ir·dakh
Friday	*Vrydag*	*vray*·dakh
Saturday	*Saterdag*	*sa*·tir·dakh
Sunday	*Sondag*	*son*·dakh

AFRIKAANS – language difficulties

12

numbers

0	nul	*neul*		16	sestien	*ses*-teen
1	een	*eyn*		17	sewentien	*sey*-vin-teen
2	twee	*twey*		18	agtien	*akh*-teen
3	drie	*dree*		19	negentien	*ney*-khin-teen
4	vier	*feer*		20	twintig	*twin*-tikh
5	vyf	*fayf*		21	een en twintig	*eyn* en *twin*-tikh
6	ses	*ses*		22	twee en twintig	*twey* en *twin*-tikh
7	sewe	*see*-vi		30	dertig	*der*-tikh
8	agt	*akht*		40	veertig	*feyr*-tikh
9	nege	*ney*-khi		50	vyftig	*fayf*-tikh
10	tien	*teen*		60	sestig	*ses*-tikh
11	elf	*elf*		70	sewentig	*sey*-vin-tikh
12	twaalf	*twaalf*		80	tagtig	*takh*-tikh
13	dertien	*der*-teen		90	negentig	*ney*-khin-tikh
14	veertien	*feyr*-teen		100	honderd	*hon*-dirt
15	vyftien	*fayf*-teen		1000	duisend	*day*-sint

border crossing

English	Afrikaans	Pronunciation
I'm here ...	*Ek is hier ...*	ek is heer ...
in transit	*onderweg*	on-dir-*wekh*
on business	*vir besigheid*	fir *bey*-sikh-hayt
on holiday	*met vakansie*	met fi-*kan*-see
I'm here for ...	*Ek is hier vir ...*	ek is heer fir ...
(10) days	*(tien) dae*	(teen) *daa*-i
(three) weeks	*(drie) weke*	(dree) *vey*-ki
(two) months	*(twee) maande*	(twey) *maan*-di

I'm going to (Johannesburg).
Ek gaan na (Johannesburg).   ek khaan naa (yu-*ha*-nis-birkh)

I'm staying at the (Ritz).
Ek bly in die (Ritz).   ek blay in dee (rits)

tickets

A ... ticket (to Cape Town), please.	Een ... kaartjie (na Kaapstad), asseblief.	eyn ... *kaar*·kee (naa *kaap*·stat) a·si·*bleef*
one-way	eenrigting	eyn·rikh·ting
return	retoer	ri·*tur*
I'd like to ... my ticket, please.	Ek wil my kaartjie, asseblief ...	ek vil may *kaar*·kee a·si·*bleef* ...
cancel	kanselleer	kan·si·*leyr*
change	verander	fir·*an*·dir
collect	afhaal	*af*·haal

I'd like a (non)smoking seat, please.
Ek wil asseblief 'n (nie-)rook-sitplek hê.   ek vil a·si·*bleef* i (nee·)rook·*sit*·plek he

Is there a toilet/air conditioning?
Is daar 'n toilet/lugreëling?   is daar i toy·*let*/likh·rey·ling

How long does the trip take?
Hoe lank neem die reis?   hu langk neym dee rays

Is it a direct route?
Is dit 'n direkte roete?   is dit i *dee*·rek·ti *ru*·ti

transport

Where does flight (MN367) arrive?
Waar kom vlug (MN367) aan?   vaar kom flikh (em en dree ses *sey*·vi) aan

Where does flight (MN367) depart?
Waar vertrek vlug (MN367)?   vaar fir·*trek* flikh (em en dree ses *see*·vi)

How long will it be delayed?
Hoe lank sal dit vertraag word?   hu langk sal dit fir·*traakh* vort

Is this the ...	Is dit die ...	is dit dee ...
to (Durban)?	na (Durban)?	naa (*dir*·ban)
boat	boot	boot
bus	bus	bis
plane	vliegtuig	*flikh*·tayg
train	trein	trayn

How much is it to …?
Hoeveel kos dit na …?   hu·fil kos dit naa …

Please take me to (this address).
Neem my asseblief na (hierdie adres).   neym may a·si·*bleef* naa (*heer*·dee a·*dres*)

I'd like to hire a car/4WD (with air conditioning).
Ek wil 'n motor/4-by-4   ek vil i *moo*·tir/feer·bay·feer
(met lugreëling) huur.   (met *likh*·rey·ling) hewr

How much is it for (three) days/weeks?
Hoeveel kos dit vir (drie) dae/weke?   hu·fil kos dit fir (dree) *daa*·i/*vey*·ki

directions

Where's the (nearest) …?	Waar's die (naaste) …?	vaars dee (*naas*·ti) …
internet café	Internet-kafee	*in*·tir·net·ka·*fey*
market	mark	mark

Is this the road to (Cape Town)?
Is dit die pad na (Kaapstad)?   is dit dee pat naa (*kaap*·stat)

Can you show me (on the map)?
Kan jy my (op die kaart) wys?   kan yay may (op dee kaart) vays

What's the address?
Wat is die adres?   vat is dee a·*dres*

How far is it?
Hoe ver is dit?   hu fer is dit

How do I get there?
Hoe kom ek daar?   hu kom ek daar

Turn left/right.
Draai links/regs.   drai lings/rekhs

It's …	Dis …	dis …
behind …	agter …	*akh*·tir …
in front of …	voor …	foor …
near (to) …	naby …	*naa*·bay …
next to …	langs …	langs …
on the corner	op die hoek	op dee huk
opposite …	oorkant …	*oor*·kant …
straight ahead	reguit aan	*rekh*·ayt aan
there	daar	daar

accommodation

Where's a ...?	Waar's 'n ...?	vaars i ...
camping ground	kampeerplek	kam-peyr-plek
guesthouse	gastehuis	khas-ti-hays
hotel	hotel	hu-tel
youth hostel	jeugtuiste	yeykh-tays-ti

Can you recommend somewhere cheap/good?
Kan jy 'n goedkoop/goeie
plek aanbeveel?
kan yay i khut-koop/khoy-i
plek aan-bi-feyl

I'd like to book a room, please.
Ek wil 'n kamer bespreek, asseblief.
ek vil i kaa-mir bi-spreyk a-si-bleef

I have a reservation.
Ek het 'n bespreking.
ek het i bi-sprey-king

Do you have	Het jy	het yay
a ... room?	'n ... kamer?	i ... kaa-mir
single	enkel	eng-kil
double	dubbel	di-bil
twin	dubbelkamer met	di-bil-kaa-mir met
	twee enkelbeddens	twey eng-kil-be-dins

How much is it per night/person?
Hoeveel kos dit per nag/
persoon?
hu-fil kos dit pir nakh/
pir-soon

I'd like to stay for (two) nights.
Ek wil vir (twee) nagte bly.
ek vil fir (twey) nakh-ti blay

What time is check-out?
Hoe laat moet ek uit my
kamer wees?
hu laat mut ek ayt may
kaa-mir veys

Am I allowed to camp here?
Mag ek hier kampeer?
makh ek heer kam-peyr

banking & communications

I'd like to ...	Ek wil asseblief ...	ek vil a·si·bleef ...
arrange a transfer	'n oorplasing reël	i oor·plaa·sing reyl
cash a cheque	'n tjek wissel	i chek vi·sil
change a travellers cheque	'n reisigerstjek wissel	i ray·si·khirs·chek vi·sil
change money	geld ruil	khelt rayl
withdraw money	geld trek	khelt trek

I want to ...	Ek wil asseblief ...	ek vil a·si·bleef ...
buy a phonecard	'n foonkaart koop	i foon·kaart koop
call (Singapore)	(Singapoer) skakel	(seeng·ga·pur) skaa·kil
reverse the charges	'n kollekteeroproep maak	i ko·lek·teyr·op·rup maak
use a printer	'n drukker gebruik	i dri·kir khi·brayk
use the internet	die Internet gebruik	dee in·tir·net khi·brayk

How much is it per hour?
Hoeveel kos dit per uur? · hu·fil kos dit pir ewr

How much does a (three-minute) call cost?
Hoeveel kos 'n oproep (van drie minute)? · hu·fil kos i op·rup (fan dree mi·nee·ti)

(One rand/cent) per minute/hour.
(Een rand/sent) per minuut/uur. · (eyn rant/sent) pir mi·newt/ewr

tours

When's the next ...?	Wanneer is die volgende ...?	va·nir is dee fol·khin·di ...
day trip	dagrit	dakh·rit
tour	toer	tur

Is ... included?	Is ... ingesluit?	is ... in·khi·slayt
accommodation	verblyf	fir·blayf
the admission charge	die toegangsgeld	dee tu·khangs·khelt
food	kos	kos
transport	vervoer	fir·fur

How long is the tour?
Hoe lank is die toer?   hu langk is dee tur

What time should we be back?
Hoe laat sal ons terug wees?   hu laat sal ons trig veys

shopping

I'm looking for ...
Ek soek na ...   ek suk naa ...

I need film for this camera.
Ek het film vir my kamera nodig.   ek het *fi*·lim vir may *ka*·mi·ra *noo*·dikh

Can I listen to this?
Kan ek hierna luister?   kan ek *heer*·naa *lays*·tir

Can I have my ... repaired?
Kan ek my ... laat regmaak?   kan ek may ... laat *rekh*·maak

When will it be ready?
Wanneer sal dit rekh wees?   *va*·nir sal dit rekh veys

How much is it?
Hoeveel kos dit?   *hu*·fil kos dit

What's your lowest price?
Wat is jou laagste prys?   vat is yoh *laakh*·sti prays

I'll give you (five) rand.
Ek sal jou (vyf) rand gee.   ek sal yoh (fayf) rant khey

There's a mistake in the bill.
Daar's 'n fout op die rekening.   daars i foht op dee *rey*·ki·ning

It's faulty.
Dis stukkend.   dis *sti*·kint

I'd like a ..., please.	*Ek wil asseblief 'n ...*	ek vil a·si·*bleef* i ...
receipt	*kwitansie hê*	kwi·*tan*·see he
refund	*my geld terug hê*	may khelt trikh he
Do you accept ...?	*Aanvaar jy ...?*	aan·*faar* yay ...
credit cards	*kredietkaarte*	kri·*deet*·kaar·ti
debit cards	*debietkaarte*	di·*beet*·kaar·ti
travellers cheques	*reisigerstjeks*	ray·si·khirs·cheks

Could you …?	Kan jy …?	kan yay …
burn a CD from	'n CD van my	i *sey*-dey fan may
my memory card	geheuekaart brand	khi-*hee*-i-kaart brant
develop this film	hierdie film ontwikkel	*heer*-dee *fi*-lim ont-*vi*-kil

making conversation

Hello.	Hallo.	ha-*loh*
Good night.	Goeienag.	*khoy*-i-nakh
Goodbye.	Totsiens.	tot-*seens*

Mr	Meneer	mi-*neyr*
Mrs	Mevrou	mi-*froh*
Miss	Juffrou	*yi*-froh

How are you?
Hoe gaan dit?   hu khaan dit

Fine, and you?
Goed dankie, en jy?   khut *dang*-kee en yay

What's your name?
Wat's jou naam?   vats yoh naam

My name's …
My naam is …   may naam is …

I'm pleased to meet you.
Bly te kenne.   blay ti *ke*-ni

This is my …	Dit is my …	dit is may …
boyfriend	*kêrel*	*ke*-ril
brother	*broer*	brur
daughter	*dogter*	*dokh*-tir
father	*pa*	paa
friend	*vriend* m	freend
	vriendin f	freen-*din*
girlfriend	*meisie*	*may*-see
husband	*man*	man
mother	*ma*	maa
partner	*maat*	maat
sister	*suster*	*sis*-tir
son	*seun*	seyn
wife	*vrou*	froh

Here's my ...	Hier's my ...	heers may ...
What's your ...?	Wat's jou ...?	vats yoh ...
address	adres	a-*dres*
email address	e-posadres	ey-paws-a-*dres*
phone number	foonnommer	*foon*-no-mir

Where are you from?
Waarvandaan kom jy?   vaar-fan-daan kom yay

I'm from ...	Ek kom van ...	ek kom fan ...
Australia	Australië	oh-*stra*-lee-i
Canada	Kanada	*ka*-na-da
New Zealand	Nieu-Seeland	new-*sey*-lant
the UK	Brittanje	bri-*tan*-yi
the USA	die VSA	dee *fey*-es-aa

I'm (not) married.
Ek's (nie) getroud (nie).   eks (nee) khi-*troht* (nee)

Can I take a photo (of you)?
Kan ek 'n foto (van jou) neem?   kan ek i *foo*-tu (fan yoh) neym

eating out

Can you	Kan jy 'n ...	kan yay i ...
recommend a ...?	aanbeveel?	*aan*-bi-feyl
bar	kroeg	krukh
dish	gereg	khi-*rekh*
place to eat	eetplek	*eyt*-plek

I'd like ..., please.	Ek wil asseblief ... hê.	ek vil a-si-*bleef* ... he
the bill	die rekening	dee *rey*-ki-ning
the menu	die spyskaart	dee *spays*-kaart
a table for (two)	'n tafel vir (twee)	i *taa*-fil fir (twey)
that dish	daardie gereg	*daar*-dee khi-*rekh*

Do you have | Het julle | het *yi*-li
vegetarian food? | vegetariese kos? | fe-gee-*taa*-ree-si kos

20

Could you prepare a meal without ...?	Kan julle 'n maaltyd sonder ... bedien?	kan *yi*·li i *maal*·tayt *son*·dir ... bi·*deen*
eggs	eiers	*ay*·irs
meat stock	vleisaftreksel	*flays*·af·trek·sil
(cup of) coffee ...	(koppie) koffie ...	(*ko*·pee) *ko*·fee ...
(cup of) tea ...	(koppie) tee ...	(*ko*·pee) *tey* ...
with milk	met melk	met melk
without sugar	sonder suiker	*son*·dir *say*·kir
boiled water	kookwater	*kook*·vaa·tir

emergencies

Help!	Help!	help
Call ...!	Kry ...!	kray ...
an ambulance	'n ambulans	i am·bew·*lans*
a doctor	'n dokter	i *dok*·tir
the police	die polisie	dee pu·*lee*·see

Could you help me, please?
Kan jy my help, asseblief? kan yay may help a·si·*bleef*

I'm lost.
Ek is verdwaal. ek is fir·*dwaal*

Where are the toilets?
Waar is die toilette? vaar is dee toy·*le*·ti

I want to report an offence.
Ek wil 'n misdaad aanmeld. ek vil i *mis*·daat *aan*·melt

I have insurance.
Ek het versekering. ek het fir·*sey*·ki·ring

I want to contact my consulate/embassy.
Ek wil my konsulaat/ ek vil may kon·sew·*laat/*
ambassade kontak. am·ba·*saa*·di *kon*·tak

I've been ...	*Ek is ...*	ek is ...
assaulted	*aangerand*	*aan*-khi-rant
raped	*verkrag*	fir-*krakh*
robbed	*beroof*	bi-*roof*

I've lost my ...	*Ek het my ... verloor.*	ek het may ... vir-*loor*
My ... was/were stolen.	*My ... is gesteel.*	may ... is khi-*steyl*
bags	*bagasie*	bi-*khaa*-see
credit card	*kredietkaart*	kri-*deet*-kaart
handbag	*handsak*	*hant*-sak
jewellery	*juwele*	yu-*vee*-li
money	*geld*	khelt
passport	*paspoort*	*pas*-poort
travellers cheques	*reisigerstjeks*	*ray*-si-khirs-cheks
wallet	*beursie*	*beyr*-see

medical needs

Where's the nearest ...?	*Waar's die naaste ...?*	vaars dee *naas*-ti ...
dentist	*tandarts*	*tant*-arts
doctor	*dokter*	*dok*-tir
hospital	*hospitaal*	*hos*-pee-taal
pharmacy	*apteek*	ap-*teyk*

I need a doctor (who speaks English).
Ek het 'n dokter nodig (wat Engels praat).
ek het i *dok*-tir *noo*-dikh (vat *eng*-ils praat)

Could I see a female doctor?
Kan ek 'n vroulike dokter sien?
kan ek i *froh*-li-ki *dok*-tir seen

It hurts here.
Dis hier seer.
dis heer seyr

I'm allergic to (penicillin).
Ek's allergies vir (penisillien).
eks a-*ler*-khees fir (pi-ni-si-*leen*)

english–afrikaans dictionary

In this dictionary, words are marked as n (noun), a (adjective), v (verb), sg (singular), pl (plural), inf (informal) and pol (polite) where necessary.

A

accommodation *akkommodasie* a-kaw-maw-daa-see
adaptor *adaptor* i-*dep*-tir
after *na* naa
airport *lughawe* leukh-haa-vi
alcohol *alkohol* al-ku-hawl
all *alle* a-li
allergy *allergie* a-ler-*khee*
and *en* en
ankle *enkel* eng-kil
antibiotics *antibiotika* an-tee-*bee*-oo-tee-ka
anti-inflammatories *anti-inflammatoriese middels*
   an-tee-in-fla-ma-*too*-ree-si mi-dils
arm *arm* a-rim
aspirin *aspirien* as-pi-*reen*
asthma *asma* as-ma
ATM *OTM* oo-tey-em

B

baby *baba* baa-ba
back (body) *rug* reukh
backpack *rugsak* reukh-sak
bad *sleg* slekh
baggage claim *bagasiebewys* bi-khaa-see-bi-vays
bank *bank* bank
bathroom *badkamer* bat-kaa-mir
battery *battery* ba-ti-*ray*
beautiful *mooi* moy
bed *bed* bet
beer *bier* beer
bees *bye* bay-i
before *voor* foor
bicycle *fiets* feets
big *groot* khroot
blanket *kombers* kawm-*bers*
blood group *bloedgroep* blut-khrup
bottle *bottel* baw-til
bottle opener *botteloopmaker* baw-til-oop-maa-kir
boy *seun* seyn
brakes (car) *remme* re-mi

breakfast *ontbyt* awnt-*bayt*
bronchitis *bronchitis* brawn-*khee*-tis

C

café *kafee* ka-*fey*
cancel *kanselleer* kan-si-*leyr*
can opener *blikoopmaker* blik-oop-maa-kir
cash n *kontant* kawn-*tant*
cell phone *selfoon* sel-foon
centre n *sentrum* sen-treum
cheap *goedkoop* khut-koop
check (bill) *rekening* rey-ki-ning
check-in n *aanmeld* aan-melt
chest *bors* bawrs
child *kind* kint
cigarette *sigaret* see-kha-*ret*
city *stad* stat
clean a *skoon* skoon
closed *toe* tu
codeine *kodeïen* koo-dey-*heen*
cold a *koud* koht
collect call *kollekteeroproep* kaw-lek-*teyr*-awp-rup
condom *kondoom* kawn-*doom*
constipation *hardlywigheid* hart-*lay*-vikh-hayt
contact lenses *kontaklense* kawn-tak-len-si
cough n *hoes* hus
currency exchange *valutawinkel* va-*lew*-ta-ving-kil
customs (immigration) *doeane* du-*haa*-ni

D

dairy products *suiwelprodukte* soy-vil-pru-dik-ti
dangerous *gevaarlik* khi-*faar*-lik
date (time) *datum* daa-tim
day *dag* dakh
diaper *doek* duk
diarrhoea *diarree* dee-ha-*rey*
dinner *aandete* aant-ey-ti
dirty *vuil* vayl
disabled *gestremd* khi-*stremt*
double bed *dubbelbed* di-bil-bet

drink n *drankie* drang-kee
drivers licence *bestuurderslisensie* bi-*stewr*-dirs-li-sen-see
drug (illicit) *dwelm* dwe-lim

E

ear *oor* oor
east *oos* oos
economy class *ekonomiese klas* e-ku-*noo*-mee-si klas
elevator *hysbak* hays-bak
email n *e-pos* ey-paws
English (language) *Engels* eng-ils
exchange rate *wisselkoers* vi-sil-kurs
exit n *uitgang* ayt-khang
expensive *duur* dewr
eye *oog* ookh

F

fast *vinnig* fi-nikh
fever *koors* koors
finger *vinger* fing-ir
first-aid kit *noodhulpkissie* noot-hilp-ki-see
first class *eerste klas* eyr-sti klas
fish n *vis* fis
food *kos* kaws
foot *voet* fut
fork *vurk* firk
free (of charge) *gratis* khra-tis
fruit *vrugte* frikh-ti
funny *snaaks* snaaks

G

game park *wildtuin* vil-tayn
gift *geskenk* khi-skengk
girl *meisie* may-see
glass (drinking) *glas* khlas
glasses *bril* bril
gluten *gluten* glu-tin
good *goed* khut
gram *gram* khram
guide n *gids* khits

H

hand *hand* hant
happy *gelukkig* khi-*leu*-kikh

have *het* het
he *hy* hay
head *kop* kawp
headache *hoofpyn* hoof-payn
heart *hart* hart
heart condition *harttoestand* hart-tu-stant
heat n *hitte* hi-ti
here *hier* heer
high *hoog* hookh
highway *hoofpad* hoof-pat
homosexual n *homoseksueel* hoo-mu-sek-see-heyl
homosexual a *homoseksuele* hoo-mu-sek-see-hey-li
hot *warm* va-rim
hungry *honger* hawn-gir

I

I *ek* ek
identification (card) *identifikasie* ee-den-ti-fee-*kaa*-see
ill *siek* seek
important *belangrik* bi-*lang*-rik
internet *Internet* in-tir-net
interpreter *tolk* tawlk

J

job *werk* verk

K

key *sleutel* sley-til
kilogram *kilogram* kee-lu-khram
kitchen *kombuis* kom-*bays*
knife *mes* mes

L

laundry (place) *wassery* va-si-*ray*
lawyer *prokureur* praw-keu-*rewr*
left-luggage office *bagasiekantoor* ba-*kha*-see-kan-toor
leg *been* beyn
lesbian n *lesbiër* les-bee-ir
lesbian a *lesbies* les-bees
less *minder* min-dir
letter (mail) *brief* breef
like v *hou van* hoh fan
lost-property office *verlore goedere kantoor*
vir-*loo*-ri khu-di-ri kan-*toor*

love (romantic) ∨ *lief hê* leef he
lunch *middagete* mi-dakh-ey-ti

M

man *man* man
matches *vuurhoutjies* vewr-hoh-kees
meat *vleis* vlays
medicine *medisyne* mi-di-say-ni
message *boodskap* boot-skap
mobile phone *selfoon* sel-foon
month *maand* maant
morning *oggend* aw-khint
motorcycle *motorfiets* moo-tir-feets
mouth *mond* mawnt
movie *fliek* fleek
MSG *MSG* em es khey
museum *museum* mee-zeym
music *musiek* meu-seek

N

name *naam* naam
napkin *servet* sir-vet
nappy *doek* duk
national park *nasionale park* na-shu-naa-li park
nausea *naarheid* naar-hayt
neck *nek* nek
new *nuut* newt
news *nuus* news
newspaper *koerant* ku-rant
night *nag* nakh
nightclub *nagklub* nakh-kleup
noisy *raserig* raa-si-rikh
nonsmoking *nie-rook* nee-rook
north *noord* noort
nose *neus* neys
now *nou* noh
number *nommer* naw-mir
nuts *neute* ney-ti

O

oil (engine) *olie* oo-lee
OK *goed* khut
old *oud* oht
open a *oop* oop
outside *buite* bay-te

P

package *pakkie* pa-kee
pain *pyn* payn
paper *papier* pa-peer
park (car) ∨ *parkeer* par-keyr
passport *paspoort* pas-poort
pay *betaal* bi-taal
pen *pen* pen
petrol *petrol* pe-trawl
pharmacy *apteek* ap-teyk
plate *plaat* plaat
postcard *poskaart* paws-kaart
post office *poskantoor* paws-kan-toor
pregnant *swanger* swang-ger

Q

quiet *stil* stil

R

rain n *reën* reyn
razor *skeermes* skeyr-mes
registered mail *geregistreerde pos*
    khi-re-khi-streyr-di paws
rent ∨ *huur* hewr
repair ∨ *herstel* her-stel
reservation *bespreking* bi-sprey-king
restaurant *restaurant* res-toh-rant
return ∨ *terugkeer* ti-reukh-keyr
road *pad* pat
room *kamer* kaa-mir

S

sad *hartseer* hart-seyr
safe a *veilig* fay-likh
sanitary napkin *sanitêre doekie* sa-nee-te-ri du-kee
seafood *seekos* sey-kaws
seat *sitplek* sit-plek
send *stuur* stewr
sex *seks* seks
shampoo *sjampoe* sham-pu
share (a dorm, etc) *deel* deyl
shaving cream *skeerroom* skeyr-room
she *sy* say
sheet (bed) *laken* laa-kin

shirt *hemp* hemp
shoes *skoene* sku-ni
shop n *winkel* ving-kil
shower n *stort* stawrt
skin *vel* fel
skirt *romp* rawmp
sleep v *slaap* slaap
small *klein* klayn
smoke (cigarettes) v *rook* rook
soap *seep* seyp
some *'n paar* i paar
soon *gou* khoh
sore throat *seer keel* seyr keyl
south *suid* sayt
souvenir shop *soewenierwinkel* su-vi-neer-ving-kil
speak *praat* praat
spoon *lepel* ley-pil
stamp *seël* seyl
stand-by ticket *bystandkaartjie* bay-stant-kaar-kee
station (train) *stasie* staa-see
stomach *maag* maakh
stop v *stop* stawp
stop (bus) n *halte* hal-ti
street *straat* straat
student *student* stu-dent
sunscreen *sonskerm* sawn-ske-rim
swim v *swem* swem

T

tampons *tampons* tam-pawns
teeth *tande* tan-di
telephone n *telefoon* te-li-foon
television *televisie* te-li-vee-see
temperature (weather) *temperatuur* tem-pi-ra-tewr
tent *tent* tent
that (one) *daardie* daar-dee
they *hulle* heu-li
thirsty *dors* dawrs
this (one) *hierdie* heer-dee
throat *keel* keyl
ticket *kaartjie* kaar-kee
time n *tyd* tayt
tired *moeg* mukh
tissues *tissues* tee-shus
today *vandag* van-dakh
toilet *toilet* toy-let
tonight *vanaand* vi-naant
toothache *tandpyn* tant-payn
toothbrush *tandeborsel* tan-di-bawr-sil
toothpaste *tandepasta* tan-di-pas-ta
torch (flashlight) *flits* flits

tourist office *toeristekantoor* tu-ris-ti-kan-toor
towel *handdoek* han-duk
translate *vertaal* fir-taal
travel agency *reisagentskap* rays-a-khent-skap
travellers cheque *reisigerstjek* ray-si-khirs-chek
trousers *broek* bruk
twin beds *twee beddens* twey be-dins
tyre *band* bant

U

underwear *onderklere* on-dir-kley-ri
urgent *dringend* dring-int

V

vacant *leeg* leykh
vegetable n *groente* khrun-ti
vegetarian n *vegetariër* fe-khee-ta-ree-ir
visa *visa* vee-sa

W

waiter *kelner* kel-nir
walk v *loop* loop
wallet *beursie* beyr-see
warm a *warm* va-rim
wash (something) *was* vas
watch n *horlosie* oor-loo-see
water *water* va-tir
we *ons* awns
weekend *naweek* naa-veyk
west *wes* ves
wheelchair *rolstoel* rawl-stul
when *wanneer* va-nir
where *waar* vaar
who *wie* vee
why *waarom* vaar-awm
window *venster* fens-tir
wine *wyn* vayn
with *met* met
without *sonder* sawn-dir
woman *vrou* froh
write *skryf* skrayf

Y

you sg inf/pol *jy/u* yay/ew
you pl inf/pol *julle/u* yeu-li/ew

Amharic

pronunciation

Vowels		Consonants	
Symbol	**English sound**	**Symbol**	**English sound**
a	run	b	bed
ai	aisle	ch	cheat
e	bet	ch'	strong ch
ee	see	d	dog
i	hit	f	fun
o	pot	g	go
ow	now	h	hat
u	put	j	jar
uh	ago	k	kit
'	like the pause in 'uh-oh' (comes before a vowel)	k'	strong k
		l	lot
		m	man
		n	not
		ny	canyon
		p	pet
		p'	popping p
		r	run (trilled)
		s	sun
		s'	hissing s
		sh	shot
		t	top
		t'	spitting t
		v	very
		w	win
		y	yes
		z	zero
		zh	pleasure

In this chapter,
the Amharic pronunciation
is given in light blue after each phrase.

Each syllable is separated
by a dot. For example:

ይቅርታ   yi·k'ir·ta

Amharic's glottalised consonants,
simplified as ch', k', p', s' and t'
in our pronunciation guide,
are made by tightening and releasing
the space between the vocal cords
when you pronounce the sound,
a bit like combining it with
the ' sound listed above.

28

AMHARIC
አማርኛ

introduction

If you're a reggae fan, you already know at least one phrase from Amharic (አማርኛ a·mar·nya), courtesy of Bob Marley and the Wailers' anthem 'One Love/People Get Ready' – *Fiqir bandinet* fi·k'ir band·nuht (one love) expresses the idea of unity or oneness central to Rastafarianism. Bob Marley wasn't the first to use Amharic for artistic purposes, of course: it's been used to create works of art for centuries. In fact, the earliest known Amharic writings are poems in praise of an emperor dating back to the 14th century AD. A Semitic language belonging to the Afro-Asiatic family, Amharic began to spread in the 10th to 12th centuries, when power shifted to the present Amhara region after the decline of the Aksumite Empire. Most of the world's 27 million Amharic speakers live in Ethiopia, where it's the official language and the most widely used of the more than 80 indigenous Ethiopian languages. Learning just a few basic phrases will smooth your way through this fascinating country.

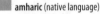 **amharic** (native language)    **amharic** (generally understood)

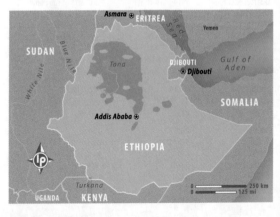

introduction – AMHARIC

29

language difficulties

Do you speak English?

እንግሊዘኛ ትችላለህ?   'in-glee-zuh-nya ti-chi-la-luh-hi m

እንግሊዘኛ ትችያለሽ?   'in-glee-zuh-nya ti-chia-luhsh f

Do you understand?

ገባህ/ገባሽ?   guh-bah/guh-bash m/f

I (don't) understand.

(አል)ገባኝ(ም)   ('al-)guh-bany(-mi)

Could you please ...?	እባክህ/እባክሽ ...?	'i-ba-kih/'i-ba-kish ... m/f
repeat that	ድገመው/	di-guh-muhw/
	ድገሚው	di-guh-meew m/f
speak more slowly	በዝግታ አውራ	buh-zi-gi-ta 'ow-ra m
	በዝግታ አውሪ	buh-zi-gi-ta 'ow-ree f
write it down	ጻፈው/ጻፊው	s'a-fuhw/s'a-feew m/f

time, dates & numbers

What time is it?	ስንት ሰአት ነው?	sint suh-'at nuhw
It's (two) o'clock.	(ስምንት) ሰአት ነው	(si-mint) suh-'at nuhw
Quarter past (one).	(ሰባት) ከሩብ ነው	(suh-bat) kuh-rub nuhw
Half past (one).	(ሰባት) ተኩል ነው	(suh-bat) tuh-kul nuhw
Quarter to (eight).	ለ(ሁለት) ሩብ ጉዳይ ነው	luh-(hu-luht) rub gu-dai nuhw
At what time ...?	በስንት ሰአት...?	buh-sint suh-'at ...
At ...	በ ...	buh ...
It's (15 December).	(ታህሳስ አስራ	(ta-hi-sas 'a-si-ra
	አምስት) ነው	'am-mist) nuhw

yesterday	ትላንትና	ti-lan-ti-na
today	ዛሬ	za-re
tomorrow	ነገ	nuh-guh

Monday	ሰኞ	suh-nyo
Tuesday	ማክሰኞ	mak-suh-nyo
Wednesday	ረብ	rob
Thursday	ሀሙስ	ha-mus
Friday	አርብ	'a-rib
Saturday	ቅዳሜ	k'i-da-me
Sunday	እሁድ	'i-hud

numbers

0	ዜሮ	ze·ro	16	አስራ ስድስት	a·si·ra si·dist
1	አንድ	and	17	አስራ ሰባት	a·si·ra suh·bat
2	ሁለት	hu·luht	18	አስራ ስምንት	a·si·ra si·mint
3	ሶስት	sost	19	አስራ ዘጠኝ	a·si·ra zuh·t'uhny
4	አራት	'ar·at	20	ሃያ	ha·ya
5	አምስት	'am·mist	21	ሃያ አንድ	ha·ya and
6	ስድስት	si·dist	22	ሃያ ሁለት	ha·ya hu·luht
7	ሰባት	suh·bat	30	ሰላሳ	suh·la·sa
8	ስምንት	si·mint	40	አርባ	'ar·ba
9	ዘጠኝ	zuh·t'uhny	50	ሃምሳ	ham·sa
10	አስር	a·sir	60	ስልሳ	sil·sa
11	አስራ አንድ	a·si·ra and	70	ሰባ	suh·ba
12	አስራ ሁለት	a·si·ra hu·luht	80	ሰማንያ	suh·ma·nia
13	አስራ ሶስት	a·si·ra sost	90	ዘጠና	zuh·t'uh·na
14	አስራ አራት	a·si·ra 'ar·at	100	መቶ	muh·to
15	አስራ አምስት	a·si·ra am·mist	1000	ሺ	shee

border crossing

I'm here ...	እዚህ ... ነኝ	'i·zeeh ... nuhny
in transit	በትራንዚዚ ላይ	buh·tran·zeet lai
on business	በስራ ጉዳይ ላይ	buh·si·ra gu·dai lai
on holiday	በእረፍት ላይ	buh·'i·ruhft lai

I'm here	እዚህ ያለሁት	'i·zeeh ya·luh·hut
for ...	ለ ... ነው	luh ... nuhw
(10) days	(አስር) ቀን	(a·sir) k'uhn
(three) weeks	(ሶስት) ሳምንት	(sost) sa·mint
(two) months	(ሁለት) ወር	(hu·luht) wuhr

I'm going to (Meta Abo).
(ሜታ አቦ) እንዳለሁ (me·ta 'a·bo) 'i·he·da·luh·hu

I'm staying at the (Hilton Hotel).
(ሂልተን ሆቴል) እኮያለሁ (heel·tuhn ho·tel) 'i·k'o·ya·luh·hu

tickets

A ... ticket (to Bahir Dar), please.	እንድ ... ትኬት (ወደባህር ዳር) እባክ/እባክሽ?	and ... ti·ket (wuh·duh ba·hir dar) 'i·ba·kih/'i·ba·kish m/f
one-way (going)	የእንድ ጉዞ (መሄጃ) ብቻ	yuh·and gu·zo (muh·he·ja) bi·cha
one-way (returning)	የእንድ ጉዞ (መመለሻ) ብቻ	yuh·and gu·zo (muh·muh·luh·sha) bi·cha
return	ደርሶ መልስ	duhr·so muh·lis

I'd like to ... my ticket, please.	... እፈልግ ነበር እባክህ ትኬቱን ስጠኝ ... እፈልግ ነበር እባክሽ ትኬቱን ስጪኝ	... 'i·fuh·lig nuh·buhr 'i·ba·kih ti·ke·ten si·t'uhny m ... 'i·fuh·lig nuh·buhr 'i·ba·kish ti·ke·ten si·ch'eeny f
cancel	መሰረዝ	muh·suh·ruhz
change	መቀየር	muh·k'uh·yuhr
collect	መውሰድ	muhw·suhd

I'd like a smoking/nonsmoking seat, please.

| መቀመጫ የሚጨስበት/ የማይጨስበት ቦታ ጋ እፈልጋለሁ | muh·k'uh·muh·ch'a yuh·mee·ch'uhs·buht/ yuh·mai·ch'uhs·buht bo·ta ga 'i·fuh·li·ga·luh·hu |

Is there a toilet?

| ሽንት ቤት አለው? | shint bet 'a·luhw |

Is there air conditioning?

| ኮንትለ·ተር አለው? | vent·le·tuhr 'a·luhw |

How long does the trip take?

| ጉዞው ምን ያህል ይፈጃል? | gu·zo·wi min ya·hil yi·fuh·jal |

Is it a direct route?

| ይሄ ዋናው መንገድ ነው? | yi·he wa·now muhn·guhd nuhw |

transport

Where does the flight (to Addis Ababa) arrive/depart?

| (የአዲስ አበባ) በረራ መቼ ይደርሳል/ይነሳል? | (yuh·'a·dees 'a·buh·ba) buh·ruh·ra muh·che yi·duhr·sal/yi·nuh·sal |

How long will it be delayed?

| ምን ያህል ይዘገያል? | min ya·hil yi·zuh·guh·yal |

Is this the ... to (Dire Dawa)?	ይህ ... ወደ (ድሬዳዋ) የሚሄደው ነው?	yih ... wuh-duh (di-re da-wa) yuh-mee-he-duhw nuhw
boat	ጀልባ	juhl-ba
bus	አውቶቢስ	'ow-to-bees
plane	አውሮፕላን	ow-rop-lan
train	ባቡር	ba-bur

I'd like to hire a ... (with air conditioning).	እባክህ/እባክሽ (ኤየር ኮንዲሽንር ያለው) ... መከራየት እፈልጋለሁ?	'i-ba-kih/'i-ba-kish ('e-yuhr kon-dee-shi-nuhr ya-luhw) ... muh-kuh-ra-yuht 'i-fuh-li-ga-luh-hu m/f
car	መኪና	muh-kee-na
4WD	ፎር ዊል ድራይቭ	for weel di-ra-yiv

How much is it to ...?

ወደ ... ለመሄድ ዋጋው ስንት ነው?
wuh-duh ... luh-muh-hed wa-gow sint nuhw

Please take me to (the museum).

እባክህ/እባክሽ ወደ (ሙዚየም) ውሰደኝ/ውሰጂኝ
'i-ba-kih/'i-ba-kish wuh-duh (mu-zee-yuhm) wi-suh-duhny/wi-suh-jeeny m/f

How much is it for (three) days/weeks?

ለ(ሶስት) ቀን/ሳምንት ዋጋው ስንት ነው?
luh-(sost) k'uhn/sa-mint wa-gow sint nuhw

directions

Where's the (nearest) ...?	(ቅርብ) ያለ ... የት ነው?	(k'irb) ya-luh ... yuht nuhw
internet café	ኢንተርኔት ካፌ	'een-tuhr-net ka-fe
market	ገበያ	guh-buh-ya

Is this the road to the museum?

ይህ መንገድ ወደ ሙዚየም ይወስዳል?
yih muhn-guhd wuh-duh mu-zee-yuhm yi-wuhs-dal

Can you show me (on the map)?

(ካርታ ላይ) ልታሳየኝ ትችላለህ/ትችያለሽ?
(kar-ta lai) li-ta-sa-yuhny ti-chi-la-luh/ti-chi-ya-luhsh m/f

What's the address?

አድራሻው የት ነው?
'ad-ra-show yuht nuhw

How far is it?
ምን ያህል ይርቃል?   min yahl yir·k'al

How do I get there?
እዚያ እንዴት መሄድ ይቻላል?   'i·zee·ya 'in·det muh·hed yi·cha·lal

Turn left/right.
ወደ ግራ/ቀኝ ታጠፍ   wuh·duh gi·ra/k'uhny ta·t'uhf

It's ...	... ነው	... nuhw
behind ...	... ከጀርባ	... kuh·juhr·ba
in front of ...	... ፊት ለፊት	... feet luh·feet
near ...	... አጠገብ	... 'a·t'uh·guhb
next to ...	... ቀጥሎ	... k'uh·t'i·lo
on the corner	መታጠፊያው ላይ	muh·ta·t'uh·fee·yow lai
opposite ...	... ትይዩ	... ti·yi·yu
straight ahead	ቀጥታ	k'uh·t'i·ta
there	እዚያ	'i·zee·ya

accommodation

Where's a ...?	... የት ነው?	... yuht nuhw
camping ground	የድንኩዋኑ ቦታ	yuh·din·ku·wa·nu bo·ta
guesthouse	የእንግዳ ማረፊያ	yuh·'in·gi·da ma·ruh·fee·ya
hotel	ሆቴሉ	ho·te·lu
youth hostel	ሆስቴሉ	hos·te·lu

Can you recommend somewhere (cheap/good)?
(ርካሽ/ጥሩ) ቦታ ልትጠቁመኝ   (ri·kash/t'i·ru) bo·ta li·ti·t'uh·k'u·muhny
ትችላለህ/ትችያለሽ?   ti·chi·la·luh·hi/ti·chi·ya·luhsh m/f

I'd like to book a room, please.
እባክህ/እባክሽ ክፍል ቡክ   'i·ba·kih/'i·ba·kish ki·fil buk
ማድረግ ፈልጌ ነበር?   mad·ruhg fuh·li·ge nuh·buhr m/f

I have a reservation.
ክፍል ቡክ አድርጌ ነበር   ki·fil buk 'ad·ri·ge nuh·buhr

Do you have a ... room?	... ክፍል አላችሁ?	... ki·fil 'a·la·chi·hu
single	አንድ	and
double	ሁለት	hu·luht
twin	ሁለት አል.ጋ ያለው	hu·luht 'al·ga ya·luhw

How much is it per night/person?
በቀን/በሰው ዋጋው ስንት ነው?   buh·k'uhn/buh·suhw wa·gow sint nuhw

I'd like to stay for (two) nights.

(ሁለት) ቀን መቆየት
እፈልጋለሁ

(hu·luht) k'uhn muh·k'o·yuht
'i·fuh·li·ga·luh·hu

What time is check-out?

ክፍል መልቀቂያው
ስንት ሰአት ነው?

ki·fil muhl·k'uh·k'ee·yow
sint suh·'at nuhw

Am I allowed to camp here?

እዚህ ግቢ ድንኩዋን
መትከል እችላለሁ?

'i·zeeh gi·bee din·ku·wan
muht·kuhl 'i·chi·la·luh·hu

banking & communications

I'd like to ...	እባክህ/እባክሽ ...	i·ba·kih/i·ba·kish ...
	እፈልጋለሁ	'i·fuh·li·ga·luh·hu m/f
arrange a transfer	ገንዘብ ማዘወር	guhn·zuhb ma·za·wuhr
cash a cheque	ቼክ መመንዘር	chek muh·muhn·zuhr
change a travellers cheque	ትራብሎርስ ቼክ መመንዘር	ti·rav·luhrs chek muh·muhn·zuhr
change money	ገንዘብ መመንዘር	guhn·zuhb muh·muhn·zuhr
withdraw money	ገንዘብ ማውጣት	guhn·zuhb mow·t'at

I want to ...	... እፈልጋለሁ	... 'i·fuh·li·ga·luh·hu
buy a phonecard	የስልክ ካርድ መግዛት	yuh·silk kard muhg·zat
call (Australia)	(አውስትራሊያ) መደወል	('owst·ra·lee·ya) muh·duh·wuhl
reverse the charges	በተዘዋዋሪ መደወል	buh·tuh·zuh·wa·wa·ree muh·duh·wuhl
use a printer	ፕሪንተር መጠቀም	pi·reen·tuhr muht·'uh·k'uhm
use the internet	ኢንተርኔት መጠቀም	'een·tuhr·net muh·t'uh·k'uhm

How much is it per hour?

በሰአት ስንት ነው?

buh·suh·'at sint nuhw

How much does a (three-minute) call cost?

የ(ሶስት ደቂቃ)
ጥሪ ዋጋው ስንት ነው?

yuh·(sost duh·k'ee·k'a)
t'i·ree wa·gow sint nuhw

(One birr) per minute/hour.

(አንድ ብር) በደቂቃ/በሰአት

(and bir) buh·duh·k'ee·k'a/buh·suh·'at

tours

When's the next ...?	የሚቀጥለው ... መቼ ነው?	yuh-mee-k'uh-t'i-luhw ... muh-che nuhw
day trip	ውሎ ገባ ጉዞ	wi-lo guh-ba gu-zo
tour	ሽርሽር	shi-ri-shir
Is ... included?	... ይጨምራል?	... yi-ch'uh-mi-ral
accommodation	መኝታን	muh-nyi-tan
the admission	የአገልግሎት	yuh-'a-guhl-gi-lot
charge	ዋጋን	wa-gan
food	ምግብን	mi-gib-n
transport	ትራንስፖርትን	ti-rans-por-tin

How long is the tour?
ሽርሽሩ ምን ያህል ጊዜ ይፈጃል? shi-ri-shi-ru min ya-hil gee-ze yi-fuh-jal

What time should we be back?
በስንት ሰአት እንመለሳለን? buh-sint suh-'at 'in-muh-luh-sa-luhn

shopping

I'm looking for ...
... እፈልጋለሁ ... 'i-fuh-li-ga-luh-hu

I need film for this camera.
ለዚህ ካሜራ የሚሆን ፊልም luh-zeeh ka-me-ra yuh-mee-hon feelm
እፈልጋለሁ 'i-fuh-li-ga-luh-hu

Can I listen to this?
ይህንን ማዳመጥ እችላለሁ? yi-hi-ni na-da-muht' 'i-chi-la-luh-hu

Can I have my ... repaired?
... ማስጠገን እችላለሁ? ... mas-t'uh-guhn 'i-chi-la-luh-hu

When will it be ready?
መቼ ይደርሳል? muh-che yi-duhr-sal

How much is it?
ዋጋው ስንት ነው? wa-gow sint nuhw

Can you write down the price?
ዋጋውን ልትጽፍልኝ ትችላለህ? wa-gown li-ti-s'if-liny ti-chi-la-luh

What's your lowest price?
መጨረሻዋን ስንት muh-ch'uh-ruh-sha-win sint
ትለዋለህ? ti-luh-wa-luh-hi

I'll give you (five) birr.
(አምስት) ብር እከፍላለሁ   ('am·mist) bir 'i·kuhf·la·luh·hu

There's a mistake in the bill.
ቢሉ ላይ ስሁተት አለ   bee·lu lai sih·tuht 'a·luh

It's faulty.
የተበላሻ ነው   yuh·tuh·buh·la·shuh nuhw

I'd like a receipt/refund, please.
እባክህ/እባክሽ ደረሰኝ/   i·ba·kih/'i·ba·kish duh·ruh·suhny/
ገንዘቤ እንዲመለስልኝ   guhn·zuh·be 'in·dee·muh·luhs·liny
እፈልጋለሁ   'i·fuh·li·ga·luh·hu m/f

Do you accept ...?	... ትቀበላላችሁ?	... ti·k'uh·buh·la·la·chi·hu
credit cards	ክሬዲት ካርድ	ki·re·deet kard
debit cards	ዴቢት ካርድ	de·beet kard
travellers cheques	ትራቭለርስ ቼክ	ti·rav·luhrs chek

Could you ...?	... ትችላለህ?	... ti·chi·la·luh
burn a CD from	ሲዲ ከይኤስ ቢ	see·dee kuh yu 'es bee
my memory card	ኮፒ	ko·pee
develop this film	ይህንን ፈልም	yi·hi·nin feelm
	ልታጥብልኝ	li·ta·t'ib·liny

making conversation

Hello.	ሰላም	suh·lam
Good night.	ደህና እደር/እደሪ	duh·na 'i·duhr/'i·duh·ree m/f
Goodbye.	ደህና ሁን/ ሁኚ	duh·na hun/hun·yee m/f

Mr	አቶ	'a·to
Mrs	ወይዘሮ	wuhy·zuh·ro
Ms/Miss	ወይዘሪት	wuhy·zuh·reet

How are you?
እንዴት ነህ/ነሽ?   'in·det nuh·hi/nuhsh m/f

Fine, and you?
ይመስጉነው አንተስ/አንቺስ?   yi·muhs·guh·nuhw 'an·tuhs/'an·chees m/f

What's your name?
ማን ትባላለህ?/ትባያለሽ?   man ti·ba·la·luh/ti·ba·ya·luhsh m/f

My name's ...
... ነኝ   ... nuhny

I'm pleased to meet you.

በመተዋወቃችን ደስ ብሎኛል   buh·muh·tuh·wa·wuh·k'a·chin duhs bi·lon·yal

This is my ...	እሱ ...·ዬ ነው	'i·su ...·ye nuhw
boyfriend	የወንድ ጉዋደኛ	yuh·wuhnd gu·wa·duhn·ya
brother	ወንድም	wuhn·dim
daughter	ሴት ልጅ	set lij
father	አባት	'a·bat
friend	ጉዋደኛ	gu·wa·duh·nya
girlfriend	የሴት ጉዋደኛ	yuh·set gu·wa·duh·nya
husband	ባል	bal
mother	እናት	'i·nat
partner	ባልንጀራ/ሽርካ	bal·ni·juh·ra/shi·ri·ka m/f
sister	እህት	'i·hit
son	ልጅ	lij
wife	ሚስት	mist

Here's my ...	... ይኸው	... yi·huh·wi
What's your ...?	... ልትሰጠኝ ትችላለህ?	... li·ti·suh·t'uhny ti·chi·la·luh
address	አድራሻህን	'ad·ra·sha·hin
email address	ኢ·ሜልህን	'ee·me·li·hin
phone number	ስልክ ቁጥርህን	silk k'u·t'ir·hin

| Where are you from? | ከየት ነህ? | kuh·yuht nuh·hi |

I'm from ...	እኔ ከ· ... ነኝ	'i·ne kuh·... nuhny
Australia	አውስትራሊያ	'owst·ra·lee·ya
New Zealand	ኒው ዝላንድ	neew zi·land
the UK	እንግሊ.ዝ	'in·gleez
the USA	አሜሪካ	'a·me·ree·ka

I'm married.	አግብቻለሁ	'ag·bi·cha·luh·hu
I'm not married.	አላገባሁም	'a·la·guh·ba·hum
Can I take a photo (of you)?	ፎቶ ላነሳ(ህ)/ላነሳ(ሽ) እችላለሁ?	fo·to la·nuh·sa(h)/la·nuh·sa(sh) 'i·chi·la·luh·hu m/f

eating out

Can you recommend a ...?	ጥሩ ... ልትጠቁመኝ ትችላለህ?	t'i·ru ... li·ti·t'uh·k'u·muhny ti·chi·la·luh
bar	ቡና ቤት	bu·na bet
dish	ምግብ	mi·gib
place to eat	ምግብ ቤት	mi·gib bet

I'd like ...,	እፈልጋለሁ/እፈልጋለሁ ...	'i·ba·kih/'i·ba·kish ...
please.	እፈልጋለሁ	'i·fuh·li·ga·luh·hu m/f
the bill	ቢል	beel
the menu	ሜኑ	me·nu
a table for	ጠረጴዛ	t'uh·ruh·p'e·za
(two)	(ለሁለት) ሰው	(luh·hu·luht) suhw
that dish	ያንን ምግብ	ya·nin mi·gib

Do you have	የጾም ምግብ	yuh·s'om mi·gib
vegetarian food?	አላችሁ?	'a·la·chi·hu

Could you	ምግብ ያለ	mi·gib ya·luh ...
prepare a meal	ልታዘጋጂልን ትችያለሽ?	li·ta·zuh·ga·jee·lin ti·chi·ya·luhsh f
without ...?	ምግብ ያለ ...	mi·gib ya·luh ...
	ልታዘጋጅልን ትችላለህ?	li·ta·zuh·gaj·lin ti·chi·la·luh·hi m
eggs	እንቁላል	'in·k'u·lal
meat stock	ስጋ	si·ga

(cup of) coffee ...	(አንድ ስኒ) ቡና ...	(and si·nee) bu·na ...
(cup of) tea ...	(አንድ ስኒ) ሻይ ...	(and si·nee) shai ...
with milk	በወተት	buh·wuh·tuht
without sugar	ያለ ስኩዋር	ya·luh si·ku·war

(boiled) water	(የፈላ) ውሃ	(yuh·fuh·la) wi·ha

emergencies

Help!	እርዳታ እርዳታ!	'ir·da·ta 'ir·da·ta
I'm lost.	ጠፋብኝ	t'uh·fa·biny

Call ...!	... ጥራልኝ/ጥሪልኝ	... t'i·ra·liny/t'i·ree·liny m/f
an ambulance	አምቡላንስ	'am·bu·lans
a doctor	ዶክተር	dok·tuhr
the police	ፖሊስ	po·lees

Could you help me, please?
ልትረዳኝ ትችላለህ? — lit·ruh·dany ti·chi·la·luh m
ልትረጂኝ ትችያለሽ? — lit·ruh·jeeny ti·chi·ya·luhsh f

Where are the toilets?
ሽንት ቤት የት ነው? — shint bet yuht nuhw

I want to report an offence.
ጥቃቱን ሪፖርት ማድረግ — t'i·k'a·tun ree·port mad·ruhg
እፈልጋለሁ — 'i·fuh·li·ga·luh·hu

I have insurance.		
ኢንሹራንስ አለኝ		'in·shu·rans 'a·luhny

I want to contact my consulate/embassy.		
ከቆንስላዬ/ከኤምባሲዬ ጋር		kuh·k'ons·la·ye/kuh·'em·ba·see·ye gar
መገናኘት እፈል ጋለሁ		muh·guh·na·nyuht 'i·fuh·li·ga·luh·hu

I've been ...	እኔ ...	'i·ne ...
assaulted	ተጠቃሁ	tuh·t'uh·k'a·hu
raped	ተደፈርኩ	tuh·duh·fuhr·ku
robbed	ተዘረፍኩ	tuh·zuh·ruhf·ku

I've lost my ...	... ጠፋብኝ	... t'uh·fa·biny
My ... was/were stolen.	የኔ ... ተሰረቀ	yuh·ne ... tuh·suh·ruh·k'uh
bags	ሻንጣ	shan·t'a
credit card	ክሬዲት ካርድ	ki·re·deet kard
handbag	የጅ ቦርሳ	yuhj bor·sa
jewellery	ጌጣጌጥ	ge·t'a·get'
money	ገንዘብ	guhn·zuhb
passport	ፓስፖርት	pas·port
travellers cheques	ትራቨለርስ ቼክ	ti·rav·luhrs chek
wallet	የኪስ ቦርሳ	yuh·kees bor·sa

medical needs

Where's the nearest ...?	በቅርብ ያለ ... የት ነው?	buh·k'irb ya·luh ... yuht nuhw
dentist	የጥርስ ሃኪም	yuh·t'irs ha·keem
doctor	ዶክተር	dok·tuhr
hospital	ሆስፒታል	hos·pee·tal
pharmacist	ፋርማሲስት	far·ma·seest

I need a doctor (who speaks English).		
(እንግሊዘኛ የሚናገር)		('in·glee·zuhn·ya yuh·mee·na·guhr)
ሃኪም እፈልጋለሁ		ha·keem 'i·fuh·li·ga·luh·hu

Could I see a female doctor?		
ሴት ዶክተር ልታዩኝ ትችላለች?		set dok·tuhr li·ta·yuhny ti·chi·la·luhch

It hurts here.		
እዚህ ጋ ያመኛል		'i·zeeh ga ya·muhn·yal

I'm allergic to (penicillin).		
ለ(ፔኒሲሊን) አለርጂ ነኝ		luh·(pe·nee·see·leen) 'a·luhr·jee nuhny

english–amharic dictionary

In this dictionary, words are marked as n (noun), a (adjective), v (verb), ⓜ (masculine), ⓕ (feminine), sg (singular), pl (plural), inf (informal) and pol (polite) where necessary.

A

accommodation ማደሪያ ma-duh-ree-ya
adaptor አዳፕተር a-dap-tuhr
after በኋላ buh-hu-wa-la
airport አይሮፕላን ማረፊያ ai-ror-plan ma-ruh-fee-ya
alcohol አልኮል al-kol
all ሁሉ hu-lu
allergy አለርጂ 'a-luhr-jee
and እና i-na
ankle ቁርጭምጭሚት k'ur-ch'im-ch'im-it
antibiotics አንቲባዮቲክ an-tee-ba-yo-teek
arm ክንድ kind
aspirin አስፒሪን asp-ree-in
asthma አስም as-m
ATM ኤ-ቲኤም ey-tee-em

B

baby ህጻን hi-s'an
back (body) ጀርባ juh-ri-ba
backpack ባክ ፓክ bak pak
bad መጥፎ muht'-fo
baggage claim ሻንጣ መጠየቂያ shan-t'a muh-t'uh-yuh-k'ee-ya
bathroom መታጠቢያ ቤት muh-ta-t'uh-bi-ya bet
battery ባትሪ ድንጋይ ba-tree din-gai
beautiful ቆንጆ k'on-jo
bed አል*ጋ al-ga
beer ቢራ bee-ra
bees ንብ nib
before በፊት buh-feet
bicycle ብስክለት bisk-let
big ትልቅ ti-lik'
blanket ብርድ ልብስ bird libs
blood group የደም አይነት yuh-duhm 'ai-nuht
bottle ጠርሙስ t'uhr-mus
bottle opener ጠርሙስ መክፈቻ t'uhr-mus muhk-fuh-cha
boy ልጅ lij
brakes (car) ፍሬን fi-ren

breakfast ቁርስ k'urs
bronchitis ብሮንካይተስ bi-ron-kaits

C

cancel መሰረዝ muh-suh-ruhz
can opener ጣሳ መክፈቻ t'a-sa muhk-fuh-cha
cash n ገንዘብ guhn-zuhb
cell phone ሞባይል mo-bail
centre n ማእከል ma-'i-kuhl
cheap ርካሽ ri-kash
check (bill) ቼክ chek
check-in ን ቼክ ኢ.ን chek een
chest ደረት duh-ruht
child ልጅ lij
cigarette ሲጋራ see-ga-ra
city ከተማ kuh-tuh-ma
clean a ንጹህ ni-s'uh
closed ዝግ zig
codeine ኮዴን ko-din
cold a ጉንፋን gun-fan
collect call በተከፋይ buh-tuh-zuh-wa-wa-ree
condom ኮንደም kon-duhm
constipation ድርቀት dir-k'uht
contact lenses የአይን መነጽር yuh-ain muh-nuh-s'ir
currency exchange የmeasurement ምንዛሬ yuh-wich' mi-ni-za-ree
customs (immigration) ጉምሩክ gum-ruk

D

dairy products የወተት ተዋጽኦ yuh-wuh-tuht tuh-wa-s'i-'o
dangerous አደገኛ 'a-duh-guhn-ya
date (time) ቀን k'uhn
day ቀን k'uhn
diaper ዳይፐር dai-puhr
diarrhoea ተቅማጥ tuh-k'i-mat'
dinner እራት i-rat
dirty ቆሻሻ k'o-sha-sha
disabled አካለ ስንኩል 'a-ka-luh sin-kul

double bed ሁለት አልጋ በአንድ ክፍል
  hu-luht al-ga buh-an-id ki-fil
drink n መጠጥ muh-t'uht'
drivers licence መንጃ ፈቃድ muhn-ja fuh-k'ad
drug (illicit) አደንዛዥ ዕጽ 'a-duhn-zazh 'is

E

ear ጆሮ jo-ro
east ምስራቅ mis-rak'
email ኢሜይል 'ee-me-yil
English (language) እንግሊዘኛ 'ing-lee-zuhn-ya
exchange rate የውጭ ምንዛሪ ዋጋ
  yuh-wich' min-za-ree wa-ga
exit n መውጫ muh-wi-ch'a
expensive ውድ wid
eye አይን 'ain

F

fast ፈጣን fuh-t'an
fever ትኩሳት ti-ku-sat
finger ጣት t'at
first class አንደኛ ማእረግ
  'an-duh-nya ma-'i-ruhg
fish n አሳ 'a-sa
food ምግብ mi-gib
foot እግር 'i-gir
fork ሹካ shu-ka
free (of charge) ነጻ nuh-s'a
fruit ፍራፍሬ fi-ra-fi-re
funny አስቂኝ 'as-k'eeny

G

game park ፓርክ park
gift ስጦታ si-t'o-ta
girl ልጃገረድ li-ja-guh-ruhd
glass (drinking) ብርጭቆ bir-ch'i-k'o
glasses መነጽር muh-nuh-'sir
gluten እንጉባራቴ 'an-s'uh-ba-ra-k'ee
good ጥሩ t'i-ru
guide n መሪ muh-ree

H

hand እጅ 'ij
happy ደስታ duh-si-ta
have አለሙ/አላት ⑩/① 'a-luhw/'a-lat

he እሱ 'i-su
head ራስ ras
headache ራስ ምታት ras mi-tat
heart ልብ lib
heart condition የልብ ሁኔታ yuh-lib hu-na-te
heat n ሙቀት mu-k'uht
here እዚህ 'i-zeeh
high ከፍ ያለ kuhf-ya-luh
highway የቀለበት መንገድ
  yuh-k'uh-luh-buht muhn-guhd
homosexual n&a ሆሞ ho-mo
hot ሙቅ muk'
hungry ረሃብ ruh-hab

I

I እኔ 'i-ne
identification (card) መታወቂያ muh-ta-wuh-k'ee-ya
ill ታመመ ta-muh-muh
important አስፈላጊ 'as-fuh-la-gee
internet ኢንተርኔት 'een-tuhr-net
interpreter አስተርጉዋሚ 'as-tuhr-gu-wa-mee

J

job ስራ si-ra

K

key ቁልፍ k'u-lif
kilogram ኪሎ ግራም kee-lo gi-ram
kitchen ማድ ቤት mad bet
knife ቢላዋ bee-la-wa

L

laundry (place) ላውንደሪ la-win-duh-ree
lawyer ጠበቃ t'uh-buh-k'a
left-luggage office እቃ መረከቢያ መጋዘን
  'i-k'a muh-ruh-kuh-bee-ya muh-ga-zuhn
leg እግር 'i-gir
lesbian n&a ሌዝቢያን lez-bee-yan
less ያነሰ ya-nuh-suh
letter (mail) ደብዳቤ duhb-da-be
like v ወደደ wuh-duh-duh
lost-property office ፖሊስ ጣቢያ
  po-lees t'a-bee-ya
love v አፈቀረ 'a-fuh-k'uh-ruh
lunch ምሳ mi-sa

M

man ሰው suhw
matches ክብሪት kib-reet
meat ስጋ si-ga
medicine መድሃኒት muhd-ha-neet
message መልእክት muhl-'ikt
month ወር wuhr
morning ጠዋት t'uh-wat
mouth አፍ 'af
movie ሲኒማ see-nee-ma
MSG ሜሴንጀር me-sen-juhr
museum ሙዚየም mu-zee-yuhm
music ሙዚቃ mu-zee-k'a

N

name n ስም sim
napkin ናፕኪን nap-keen
nappy ዳይፐር dai-puhr
national park ብሄራዊ ፓርክ bi-he-ra-wee park
nausea ማጥወልወል mat'-wuhl-wuhl
neck አንገት 'an-guht
new አዲስ 'a-dees
news ዜና ze-na
newspaper ጋዜጣ ga-ze-t'a
night ምሽት mi-shit
nightclub የምሽት ክበብ yuh-mi-shit ki-buhb
noisy የሚረብሽ yuh-mee-ruh-bish
nonsmoking የማይጨስበት yuh-mai-ch'uhs-buht
north ሰሜን suh-men
nose አፍንጫ 'a-fin-ch'a
now አሁን 'a-hun
number ቁጥር k'u-t'ir
nuts አቾሎኒ 'o-cho-lo-nee

O

oil (engine) የሞተር ዘይት yuh-mo-tuhr zuh-yit
OK እሺ 'i-shee
old አሮጌ 'a-ro-ge
open a ክፍት kift
outside ውጪ wi-ch'ee

P

package ፓኬጅ pa-kej
pain ህመም hi-muhm

paper ወረቀት wuh-ruh-k'uht
park (car) v ማቆም ma-k'om
passport ፓስፖርት pas-port
pay v ክፍል ki-fuhl
pen ብእር bi-'ir
petrol ቤንዚን ben-zeen
pharmacy ፋርማሲ far-ma-see
plate ሳህን sa-hin
postcard ፖስት ካርድ post kard
post office ፖስታ ቤት pos-ta bet
pregnant እርጉዝ 'ir-guz

Q

quiet ጸጥ ያለ s'uht' ya-luh

R

rain n ዝናብ zi-nab
razor ምላጭ mi-lach'
registered mail ሪኮማንዴ ree-ko-man-de
rent v ተከራየ ⓜ tuh-kuh-ra-yuh
repair v ጠገነ ⓜ tuh-guh-nuh
reservation መያዣ muh-yaz
restaurant ሪስቶራንት res-to-rant
return v መለሰ/መለሰች ⓜ/ⓕ
   muh-luh-suh/muh-luh-suhch
road መንገድ muhn-guhd
room ክፍል ki-fil

S

sad ሀዘን ha-zuhn
safe a ሰላም suh-lam
sanitary napkin ሞደስ mo-des
seafood የባህር ምግቦች yuh-ba-hir mi-gib-och
seat መቀመጫ muh-k'uh-muh-ch'a
send መላክ muh-lak
sex ጾታ s'o-ta
shampoo ሻምፑ sham-pu
share (a dorm, etc) ለሁለት መከራየት
   luh-hu-luht muh-kuh-ra-yuht
shaving cream የጺም መላጫ ሳሙና
   yuh-s'eem muh-la-ch'a sa-mu-na
she እስዋ 'i-su-wa
sheet (bed) አንሶላ 'an-so-la
shirt ሸሚዝ shuh-meez
shoes ጫማ ch'a-ma
shop n ሱቅ suk'

shower n ሻወር sha-wuhr
skin ቆዳ k'o-da
skirt ቀሚስ k'uh-mis
sleep ተኛ ⓜ tuh-nya
small ትንሽ ti-nish
smoke (cigarettes) v ማጨስ ma-ch'uhs
soap ሳሙና sa-mu-na
some ጥቂት t'i-k'eet
soon በቅርብ buh-k'irb
sore throat የቆሰለ ጉሮሮ yuh-k'o-suh-luh gu-ro-ro
south ደቡብ duh-bub
speak ተናገር tuh-na-guhr
spoon ማንኪያ man-kee-ya
stamp ቴምብር tem-bir
stand-by ticket የተጠባባቂ ትኬት yuh-tuh-t'uh-ba-ba-k'ee ti-ket
station (train) ጣቢያ t'a-bee-ya
stomach ሆድ hod
stop v ቆመ k'o-muh
stop (bus) n ፌርማታ fer-ma-ta
street መንገድ muhn-guhd
student ተማሪ tuh-ma-ree
sunscreen የጸሀይ መከላከያ yuh-s'uh-hai muh-kuh-la-kuh-ya
swim v ዋና wa-nyuh

T

tampons ጎዝ goz
teeth ጥርስ t'irs
telephone n ስልክ silk
television ቲቪ tee-vee
temperature (weather) ሙቀት mu-k'uht
tent ድንኳን din-ku-wan
that (one) ያ ya
they እነሱ 'i-nuh-su
thirsty መጠማት muh-t'uh-mat
this (one) ይህ yih
throat ጉሮሮ gu-ro-ro
ticket ትኬት ti-ket
time ጊዜ gee-ze
tired ደከመ duh-kuh-muh
tissues ሶፍት soft
today ዛሬ za-re
toilet ሽንት ቤት shint bet
tonight ዛሬ ማታ za-re ma-ta
toothache የጥርስ ህመም yuh-t'irs hi-muhm
toothbrush ጥርስ ብሩሽ yuh-t'irs bi-rush
toothpaste የጥርስ ሳሙና yuh-t'irs sa-mu-na
torch (flashlight) ባትሪ bat-ree

towel ፎጣ fo-t'a
translate መተርጎም muh-tuhr-gom
travel agency የጉዞ ወኪል yuh-gu-zo wuh-keel
trousers ሱሪ su-ree
twin beds ሁለት አልጋ hu-luht al-ga
tyre ጎማ go-ma

U

underwear ውታንታ bu-tan-ta
urgent አስቸኩዋይ as-chuh-ku-wai

V

vacant ክፍት ቦታ kift bo-ta
vegetable n አትክልት 'at-kilt
vegetarian a አትክልት ተመጋቢ 'at-kilt tuh-muh-ga-bee
visa ቪዛ vee-za

W

waiter አስተናጋጅ as-tuh-na-gaj
walk v በእግር መጉዋዝ buh-'i-gir muh-gu-waz
wallet የኪስ ቦርሳ yuh-kees bor-sa
warm a ሙቅ muk'
wash (something) ማጠብ ma-t'uhb
watch n ማየት ma-yuht
water ውሀ wi-ha
we እኛ 'i-nya
weekend የሳምንቱ መጨረሻ yuh-sa-min-tu muh-ch'uh-ruh-sha
west ምእራብ mi-'i-rab
wheelchair ዊል ቸር weel chuhr
when መቼ muh-che
where የት yuht
who ማን man
why ለምን luh-min
window መስኮት muhs-kot
wine ወይን wuh-yin
with ጋር gar
without ያለ ya-luh
woman ሴት set
write መጻፍ muh-s'af

Y

you sg inf አንተ/አንቺ ⓜ/ⓕ an-tuh/an-chee
you sg pol እርስዎ 'ir-si-wo
you pl inf&pol እናንተ 'in-an-tuh

Arabic

pronunciation

Vowels		Consonants	
Symbol	English sound	Symbol	English sound
a	act	b	bed
aa	father	d	dog
aw	paw	dh	that
ay	say	f	fun
e	bet	gh	a guttural sound, like the French 'r'
ee	see	h	hat
i	hit	j	jar
oo	zoo	k	kit
u	put	kh	as the 'ch' in the Scottish 'loch'
'	a pronounced with the throat constricted – like the pause in the middle of 'uh-oh'	l	lot
		m	man
		n	not
		r	run
		s	sun
		sh	shot
		t	top
		th	thin
		w	win
		y	yes
		z	zero

In this chapter, the Arabic pronunciation is given in green after each phrase.

Each syllable is separated by a dot, and the syllable stressed in each word is italicised.

For example:

نعم.   na·'am

العربية – pronunciation

introduction

It may have given us the terms 'algebra' and 'massacre', but we can also thank Arabic for the names of more pleasant things like 'alcohol', 'coffee' and 'jasmine'. Arabic (العربية al-'a-ra-bee-ya) belongs to the Semitic branch of the Afro-Asiatic language family, and is closely related to Hebrew and Aramaic. The language of the Quran (Koran), Arabic owes its wide spread to the advent of Islam and the subsequent rise of the Muslim Empire during the 7th and 8th centuries. It's the sixth-most spoken language in the world, with more than 200 million native speakers worldwide, it's the official language of the Arab nations that spread across the Middle East and North Africa (comprising 323 million people), and it's a national language of Mali, Senegal and Somalia. Though there are many groups of Arab dialects – which can be broadly divided into North African and Middle Eastern dialects – Modern Standard Arabic (MSA) is the form of Arabic used by the media and taught in schools in the Arab world. So if you're planning to visit an Arabic-speaking country, start getting your mind – and tongue – around some MSA phrases!

■ **arabic** (native language)   ■ **arabic** (generally understood)

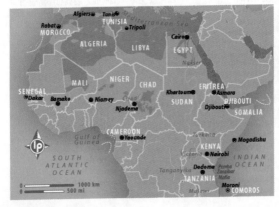

Do you speak English?

هل تتكلّم/تتكلّمينَ | hal ta·ta·*kal*·la·mu/ta·ta·kal·la·*mee*·na
الإنجليزية؟ | al-'inj·lee·*zee*·ya m/f

Do you understand?

هل تفهمُ/تفهمينَ؟ | hal *taf*·ha·mu/taf·ha·*mee*·na m/f

I (don't) understand.

أنا (لا) أفهم. | 'a·naa (laa) 'af·ham

Could you	لو سمحتَ	law sa·*mah*·ta
please ...?	يمكنكَ أن ...؟	yum·*ki*·nu·ka 'an ... m
repeat that	تكرّر ذلك	tu·*ka*·ri·ra *dhaa*·lik
speak more slowly	تتكلّم ببطء	ta·ta·*kal*·la·ma bi·*but'*
write it down	تكتبّه على الورقة	tak·*tu*·ba·hu 'a·laa al·*wa*·ra·ka

time, dates & numbers

What time is it?	كم الساعة الآن؟	kam as·*saa*·'a·tul 'aan
It's one o'clock.	الساعة الواحدة.	as·*saa*·'a·tul *waa*·hi·da
It's (two) o'clock.	الساعة (الثانية).	as·*saa*·'a·tu (ath·*thaa*·nee·ya)
Quarter past (two).	(الثانية) والربع.	(ath·thaa·*nee*·ya·tu) war·*rub*·'u
Half past (two).	(الثانية) والنصف.	(ath·thaa·*nee*·ya·tu) wan·*nus*·fu
Quarter to (two).	(الثانية) إلا الربع.	(ath·thaa·*nee*·ya·tu) 'il·la ar·*rub*·'u
At what time ...?	في أيّ ساعةٍ ...؟	fee 'ay·yee saa·'a·tin ...
At ...	في ...	fee ...
It's (15 December).	انّه (الخامس عشر من ديسمبر).	'in·na·hu (al·*khaa*·mis 'a·shar min dee·*sem*·bir)

yesterday	أمس	'am·si
today	اليوم	al·*yawm*
tomorrow	غداً	gha·dan

Monday	يوم الاثنين	yawm al·'ith·*nayn*
Tuesday	يوم الثلاثاء	yawm ath·thu·laa·*thaa'*
Wednesday	يوم الأربعاء	yawm al·'ar·bi·*'aa*
Thursday	يوم الخميس	yawm al·kha·*mees*
Friday	يوم الجمعة	yawm al·*jum*·'a
Saturday	يوم السبت	yawm as·*sabt*
Sunday	يوم الأحد	yawm al·'a·had

numbers

0	٠	صفر	sifr	16 ١٦	ستة عشر sit·ta·ta 'a·shar
1	١	واحد	waa·hid	17 ١٧	سبعة عشر sa·ba·ta 'a·shar
2	٢	اثنان	'ith·naan	18 ١٨	ثمانية عشر tha·maa·ni·ya·ta 'a·shar
3	٣	ثلاثة	tha·laa·tha	19 ١٩	تسعة عشر tis·'a·ta 'a·shar
4	٤	أربعة	'ar·ba·a	20 ٢٠	عشرون 'ish·roon
5	٥	خمسة	kham·sa	21 ٢١	واحد وعشرون waa·hid wa·'ish·roon
6	٦	ستة	sit·ta	22 ٢٢	اثنان وعشرون 'ith·naan wa·'ish·roon
7	٧	سبعة	sa·b'a	30 ٣٠	ثلاثون tha·laa·thoon
8	٨	ثمانية	tha·maa·ni·ya	40 ٤٠	أربعون 'ar·ba·oon
9	٩	تسعة	tis·'a	50 ٥٠	خمسون kham·soon
10	١٠	عشرة	'a·sha·ra	60 ٦٠	ستون sit·toon
11	١١	احد عشر	'a·ha·da 'a·shar	70 ٧٠	سبعون sab·oon
12	١٢	اثنا عشر	'ith·naa 'a·shar	80 ٨٠	ثمانون tha·maa·noon
13	١٣	ثلاثة عشر	tha·laa·tha·ta 'a·shar	90 ٩٠	تسعون tis·'oon
14	١٤	أربعة عشر	'ar·ba·'a·ta 'a·shar	100 ١٠٠	مائة mi·'a
15	١٥	خمسة عشر	kham·sa·ta 'a·shar	1000 ١٠٠٠	ألف 'alf

border crossing

I'm here ...	... غرض زيارتي هو	gha·ra·du zee·yaa·ra·tee hu·wa ...
in transit (to) ...	... العبور (إلى)	al-'u·boo·ru ('i·laa) ...
on business	التجارة	at·ti·jaa·ra
on holiday	السياحة	as·see·yaa·ha

I'm here for ...	... مدّة إقامتي هنا	mud·da·tu 'i·kaa·ma·tee hu·na ...
(10) days	(عشرة) أيّام	('a·sha·ra·tu) ay·yaam
(three) weeks	(ثلاثة) أسابيع	(tha·laa·tha·tu) 'a·saa·bee'
(four) months	(أربعة) أشهر	('ar·ba·'a·tu) 'ash·hur

I'm going to (Khartoum).

سأسافر إلى (الخرطوم).   sa·'u·saa·fi·ru 'i·laa (al·khar·toom)

I'm staying at the (Hilton).

سأقيم بـ(فندق الهلتون).   sa·'u·kee·mu bi-(fun·du·kil hil·toon)

tickets

A ... ticket (to Cairo), please.	... تذكرة (إلى القاهرة)، لوسمحتَ.	tadh·ka·ra·tu ... ('i-laa al-kaa-hi-ra) law sa·mah·ta
one-way	ذهاب فقط	dha·haa·bu fa·kat
return	ذهاب وإياب	dha·haa·bu wa-'ee·yaab
I'd like to ... my my ticket, please.	أريد أن ... تذكرتي، لوسمحتَ.	'u·ree·du 'an ... tadh·ki·ra·tee law sa·mah·ta
cancel	ألغي	'ul·ghi·ya
change	أغير	'u·ghay·yi·ra
collect	أجمع	'aj·ma·a
I'd like a ... seat, please.	أريد مقعداً ... لوسمحتَ.	'u·ree·du mak·'a·dan ... law sa·mah·ta
nonsmoking	في قسم غير المدخّنين	fee kis·mi ghay·ril mu·dakh·khi·neen
smoking	في قسم المدخّنين	fee kis·mil mu·dakh·khi·neen

Is there air conditioning?

هل يوجد مكيف الهواء؟   hal yoo·ja·du mu·kay·ya·ful ha·waa'

Is there a toilet?

هل يوجد دورات المياه   hal yoo·ja·du daw·raa·tul mee·yaah

How long does the trip take?

كم مدّة الرحلة   kam mud·da·ti ar·rih·la

Is it a direct route?

هل الطريق مباشر؟   hal at·ta·reek mu·baa·shir

transport

Where does flight (CL58) arrive/depart?

من أين تغادر / تصل رحلة (سي ال ٥٨)؟   min 'ay·na tu·ghaa·di·ru/ta·si·lu rih·la (see el tha·maa·ni·ya wa kham·soon)

How long will it be delayed?

كم ساعةٍ سيتأخّر؟   kam saa·'a·tin sa·ya·ta·'akh·khir

Is this the ...	... هل هذا الـ	hal *haa*-dhaa al ...
to (Alexandria)?	إلى (الاسكندرية)؟	*i*-laa (al-*is*-kan-da-*ree*-ya)
boat	سفينة	sa-*fee*-na
bus	باص	baas
plane	طائرة	taa-*i*-ra
train	قطار	ki-*taar*

How much is it to ...?

كم الأجرة إلى ...؟   kam al-*'uj*-ra-ti *i*-laa ...

Please take me to (this address).

أوصلني عند (هذا العنوان)   *'aw*-sal-nee 'ind (*haa*-dhaa al-'un-*waan*)
لو سمحتَ.   law sa-*mah*-ta

I'd like to hire a ...	... أريدُ أن أستأجرَ	*u*-*ree*-du an *as*-*ta*'-ji-ra ...
car	سيارة	say-*yaa*-ra
4WD	سيارة ذات الدفع	say-*yaa*-ra that ad-daf-'il
	الرباعي	ru-*baa*-'ee

| with air conditioning | ذات مكيف الهواء | thaat mu-*kay*-ya-ful ha-*waa*' |

How much is it for (three) days/weeks?

كم الأجرة لـ(ثلاثة)   kam al-*'uj*-ra li-(tha-*laa*-tha-ti)
أيّام/أسابيع؟   *'ay-yaam*/*'a-saa-bee*'

directions

Where's (the nearest) ...?	... أين (أقرب)؟	*'ay*-na ('*ak*-ra-bu) ...
internet café	مقهى الانترنت	*mak*-ha al-'in-*tir*-net
market	سوق	sook

Is this the road to (Asmara)?

هل هذا الشارع إلى   hal *haa*-dhaa ash-*shaa*-ri-'u *i*-laa
(اسمره)؟   (as-ma-ra)

Can you show me (on the map)?

هل يمكنك أن توضح لي   hal yum-*ki*-nu-ka 'an tu-*wad*-da-ha lee
(على الخريطة)؟ m   ('a-laa al-kha-*ree*-ta)

هل يمكنك أن توضحي لي   hal yum-*ki*-nu-ki 'an tu-*wad*-da-hee lee
(على الخريطة)؟ f   ('a-laa al-kha-*ree*-ta)

What's the address?

ما هو العنوان؟   maa *hu*-wa al-'un-*waan*

How far is it?

كم يبعد المكان من هنا؟

kam yab'u-du al-ma-kaa-nu min hu-naa

How do I get there?

كيف أصلُ إلى هناك؟

kay-fa 'a-si-lu 'i-laa hu-naak

Turn left/right.

اتجه إلى اليمين/اليسار .

'it-ta-jih 'i-laa al-ya-meen/al-ya-saar m

اتجهي إلى اليمين/اليسار.

'it-ta-ji-hee 'i-laa al-ya-meen/al-ya-saar f

It's ...	هو/هي ...	*hu-wa/hi-ya ...* m/f
behind ...	وراء ...	*wa-raa' ...*
in front of ...	أمامَ ...	*'a-maam ...*
near (to ...)	قريب (من ...)	*ka-reeb (min ...)*
next to ...	بجانب ...	*bi-jaa-ni-bi ...*
on the corner	عند الزاوية	*'an-da az-zaa-wi-ya*
opposite ...	بمقابل ...	*bi-mu-kaa-bil ...*
straight ahead	إلى الأمام	*'i-laa al-'a-maam*
there	هناك	*hu-naak*

accommodation

Where's a ...?	أين أجدُ ...؟	*'ay-na 'a-ji-du ...*
camping ground	مخيم	*mu-khay-yam*
guesthouse	بيت للضيوف	*bayt li-du-yoof*
hotel	فندق	*fun-duk*
youth hostel	فندق شباب	*fun-duk sha-baab*

Can you recommend somewhere cheap/good?

هل يمكنكَ أن توصيَ

hal yum-ki-nu-ka 'an too-see-ya

بمكان رخيص/جيّد؟

bi-ma-kaan ra-khees/jay-yid m

هل يمكنكِ أن توصي

hal yum-ki-nu-ki 'an too-see

بمكان رخيص/جيّد؟

bi-ma-kaan ra-khees/jay-yid f

I'd like to book a room, please.

أريد أن أحجزَ غرفة

'u-ree-du 'an 'ah-ji-za ghur-fa

لو سمحتَ.

law sa-mah-ta

I have a reservation.

عندي حجز.

'in-dee hajz

Do you have	هل عندكم	hal 'in-da-kum
a ... room?	غرفة ...؟	ghur-fa ...
single	بسرير منفرد	bi-sa-ree-rin mun-fa-rid
double	بسرير مزدوّج	bi-sa-ree-rin muz-daw-waj
twin	بسريرين منفردين	bi-sa-ree-ray-ni mun-fa-ri-day-ni

How much is	كم ثمنه	kam tha-ma-nu-hu
it per ...?	لـ ...؟	li ...
night	ليلةٍ واحدة	lay-la-tin waa-hid
person	شخصٍ واحد	shakh-sin waa-hid

I'd like to stay for (three) nights.

أريد الإقامة لمدّة (ثلاث) ليالي   'u-ree-du al-'i-kaa-ma li-mud-da-ti (tha-laa-thi) lay-yaa-lee

What time is check-out?

في أيّ ساعةٍ المغادرة؟   fee 'ay-yee saa-'a-tin al-mu-ghaa-da-ra

Am I allowed to camp here?

هل من الممكن أن أخيّم هنا؟   hal min al-mum-kin 'an 'u-khay-ya-ma hu-naa

banking & communications

I'd like to ...	أريدُ أن ...	'u-ree-du 'an ...
arrange a transfer	أقومَ بتحويل مالي	'a-koo-ma bi-tah-wee-li maa-lee
cash a cheque	أصرفَ شيك	'as-ru-fa sheek
change a travellers cheque	أحوّلَ شيكاً سياحي	'u-haw-wi-la shee-kan see-yaa-hee
change money	أحوّلَ النقود	'u-haw-wi-la an-nu-kood
withdraw money	أسحبّ نقود	'as-hu-ba nu-kood

I'd like to ...	أريد أن ...	'u-ree-du 'an ...
buy a phonecard	أشتريَ بطاقة تلفونية	'ash-ta-ree-ya bi-taa-ka ti-li-foo-nee-ya
call (Canada)	اتّصلَ بـ(كندا)	'at-ta-si-la bi-(ka-na-daa)
get internet access	أستخدمَ الانترنت	'as-takh-di-ma al-'in-tir-net
reverse the charges	أقومَ باتّصال والأجرة على الشخص المتلقي الاتّصال	'a-koo-ma bi-'it-ti-saa-li wal-'uj-ra 'a-laa ash-shakh-sil mut-la-kee al-'it-ti-saal
use a printer	أستخدمَ آلة الطباعة	'as-takh-di-ma 'aa-lat at-ta-baa-'a

How much is it per hour?

ما تكلفة الساعة الواحدة؟

maa tak-*li*-fa-tu as-*saa*-'a-til *waa*-hi-da

How much does a (three)-minute call cost?

كم تكلفة الاتصال لمدّة (ثلاث) دقائق؟

kam tak-*li*-fa-til 'it-ti-*saa*-li li-*mud*-da-ti (tha-*laa*-thi) da-*kaa*-'ik

(One pound) per minute/hour.

(جنيه واحدة) بدقيقة/بساعة.

(ju-*nay*-ha waa-hi-da) bi-da-*kee*-ka/ bi-*saa*-'a

tours

When's the	متى الـ ...	*ma*-taa al- ...
next ...?	القادم؟	al-*kaa*-dim
day trip	رحلة يومية	*rih*-la yaw-*mee*-ya
tour	دورة	*daw*-ra

Is ... included?	هل يتضمّنُ على ...؟	hal ya-ta-*dam*-ma-nu 'a-laa ...
accommodation	سكن	*sa*-kan
the admission charge	ثمن الدخول	*tha*-man ad-du-*khool*
food	الطعام	at-ta-*'aam*
transport	المواصلات	al-mu-waa-sa-*laat*

How long is the tour?

كم مدّة الدورة؟

kam *mud*-da-ti ad-*daw*-ra

What time should we be back?

في أيّ ساعةٍ يجب أن نرجعَ إلى هنا؟

fee 'ay-yee *saa*-'a-tin ya-ji-bu 'an *nar*-ja-'a 'i-laa hu-naa

shopping

I'm looking for ...

أبحثُ عن ...

'*ab*-ha-thu 'an ...

I need film for this camera.

حتاج إلى فيلماً لهذه الكاميرا.

'ah-*taa*-ju 'i-laa *feel*-man li-haa-dhi-hil kaa-*mee*-raa

Can I listen to this?

هل يمكنني أن أسمعَ إلى هذا؟

hal yum-*ki*-nu-nee 'an '*as*-ma-'a 'i-laa haa-dhaa

Can I have my ... repaired?

هل يمكنكَ أن تصلّحَ لي ...؟

hal yum-*ki*-nu-ka 'an *tus*-li-ha lee ...

When will it be ready?

متى يكون جاهز؟   ma·taa ya·koo·nu jaa·hiz

How much is it?

كم سعره؟   kam si'·ru·hu

Can you write down the price?

هل يمكنك أن تكتبّ لي السعر؟   hal yum·ki·nu·ka 'an tak·tu·ba lee as·si'r m

هل يمكنك أن تكتبي لي السعر؟   hal yum·ki·nu·ki 'an tak·tu·bee lee as·si'r f

What's your lowest price?

ما أحسنُ سعر لديكم؟   maa 'ah·sa·nu si'·ri la·day·kum

I'll give you (five pounds).

سأدفع (خمس جنيهات).   sa·ad·fa·'u bi (kham·su ju·nay·haat)

There's a mistake in the bill.

يوجد خطأ في الحساب.   yoo·jad kha·ta' feel hi·saab

It's faulty.

هذا لا يعمل.   haa·dhaa laa ya'·mal

I'd like a (receipt/refund).

أريد (وصل/استرداد مال).   'u·ree·du (wa·sil/'is·tir·daad maal)

Do you accept ...?	هل تقبلونَ ...؟	hal tak·ba·loo·na ...
credit cards	بطاقات الرصيد	bi·taa·kaat ar·ra·seed
debit cards	بطاقات الاقتراض	bi·taa·kaat al·'ik·ti·raad
travellers cheques	شيكات سياحية	shee·kaat see·yaa·hee·ya

Could you ...?	هل يمكنك ...؟	hal yum·ki·nu·ka ... m
	هل يمكنك ...؟	hal yum·ki·nu·ki ... f
burn a CD from my memory card	جهّز قرصاً مدمّج من بطاقتي الذاكرة	tu·jah·hi·za kur·san mu·dam·maj min bi·taa·ka·tee adh·dhaa·ki·ra
develop this film	حمّض هذا الفيلم	tu·ham·mi·da haa·dhaa al·feelm

making conversation

Hello.	السلام عليكم.	as·sa·laa·mu 'a·lay·kum
Good night.	تصبح على الخير.	tus·bi·hu 'a·laa al·khayr
Goodbye.	إلى اللقاء.	'i·laa al·li·kaa'
Mr	سيّد	say·yeed
Mrs/Miss	سيّدة	say·yee·da

How are you?

كيف حالك؟   kay·fa haa·lu·ka m
كيف حالك؟   kay·fa haa·lu·ki f

Fine, thanks. And you?

بخير شكراً. وأنتَ/أنتِ؟   bi-khay-rin shuk-ran wa-'an-ta/wa-'an-ti m/f

What's your name?

ما اسمكَ/اسمكِ   maa 'is-mu-ka/'is-mu-ki m/f

My name is ...

اسمي ...   'is-mee ...

I'm pleased to meet you.

أنا سعيدٌ/سعيدةٌ   'a-naa sa-'ee-dun/sa-'ee-da-tun
بالتعرّف عليك.   bit-ta-'ar-ruf 'a-layk m/f

This is my ...   هذا/هذه ...   haa-dhaa/haa-dhi-hi ... m/f
   brother   أخي   'a-khee
   daughter   ابنتي   'ib-na-tee
   father   أبي   'a-bee
   friend   صديقي/صديقتي   sa-dee-kee/sa-dee-ka-tee m/f
   husband   زوجي   zaw-jee
   mother   أمّي   'um-mee
   sister   أختي   'ukh-tee
   son   ابني   'ib-nee
   wife   زوجتي   zaw-ja-tee

Here's my ...   هذا ...   haa-dhaa ...
What's your ...?   ما ...؟   maa ...
   (email) address   عنوانكَ/عنوانكِ   un-waa-nu-ka/un-waa-nu-ki
   (البريد الالكتروني)   (al-ba-ree-deel 'i-lik-troo-nee) m/f
   phone number   رقم هاتفكَ/   rak-mu haa-ti-fu-ka/
   هاتفكِ   haa-ti-fu-ki m/f

Where are you from?   من أين أنتَ/أنتِ؟   min 'ay-na 'an-ta/'an-ti m/f

I'm from ...   أنا من ...   'a-naa min ...
   Australia   أستراليا   'us-traa-li-yaa
   Canada   كندا   ka-na-daa
   New Zealand   نيو زيلندا   nee-yoo zee-lan-daa
   the UK   بريطانيا   ba-ree-taa-ni-ya
   the USA   أمريكا   'am-ree-kaa

I'm (not) married.   أنا (لستُ)   'a-naa (las-tu)
   متزوّج/متزوّجة.   mu-ta-zaw-waj/mu-ta-zaw-wa-ja m/f
Can I take   يمكنني أن آخذ   yum-ki-nu-nee 'an 'aa-khu-dha
a photo of you?   صورتكَ/صورتكِ؟   soo-ra-tu-ka/soo-ra-tu-ki m/f

العربية – making conversation

eating out

Can you recommend a ...?	هل يمكنكَ أن توصيَ بـ ... ؟	hal yum·ki·nu·ka 'an too·see·ya ... m
	هل يمكنكِ أن توصي بـ ... ؟	hal yum·ki·nu·ki 'an too·see ... f
bar	بار	baar
dish	وجبة	waj·ba
place to eat	مكان نأكل فيه	ma·kaa·nun na'·ku·lu fee·hi

I'd like ..., please.	أريدُ ... ، لو سمحتَ.	'u·ree·du ... law sa·mah·ta
the bill	الحساب	al·hi·saab
the menu	قائمة الطعام	kaa·'i·ma·tu at·ta·'aam
a table for (four)	طاولة لـ (أربعة) أشخاص	taa·wi·la·tan li·('ar·ba·'a·ti) 'ash·khaas
that dish	تلك الوجبة	til·kal waj·ba

| Do you have vegetarian food? | هل لديكم طعامٌ نباتيّ؟ | hal la·day·ku·mu ta·'aa·mun na·baa·tee |

Could you prepare a meal without ...?	هل من الممكن أن تعدَّ وجبةً بدون ... ؟	hal min al·mum·kin 'an tu·'id·da waj·ba·tan bi·doo·ni ...
eggs	بيض	bayd
meat stock	مرق اللحم	ma·rak al·lah·mi

(cup of) coffee ...	(فنجانُ) قهوة ...	(fin·jaa·nu) kah·wa ...
(cup of) tea ...	(كأسُ) شاي ...	(ka'·su) shaa·ee ...
with milk	بحليب	bi·ha·leeb
without sugar	بدون سكّر	bi·doo·ni suk·kar

| (boiled) water | ماء (مغلي) | maa' (magh·lee) |

emergencies

Call ...!	اتصلْ /اتصلي بـ ... !	'it·ta·sil/'it·ta·si·lee bi· ... m/f
an ambulance	سيارة الإسعاف	say·yaa·ra·til 'is·'aaf
a doctor	طبيب	ta·beeb
the police	الشرطة	ash·shur·ta

Could you help me, please?

| | هل من الممكن أن تساعدني/تساعديني؟ | hal min al·mum·kin 'an tu·saa·'i·du·ne·nee/tu·saa·'i·dee·na·nee m/f |

I'm lost.

| | أنا ضائع/ضائعة. | 'a·naa daa·'i'/daa·'i·'a m/f |

Where are the toilets?

أينَ دورات المياه؟   'ay·na daw·raa·tul mee·yaah

I want to report an offence.

أريد أن أُبلِغ عن جريمة.   'u·ree·du 'an 'u·bal·li·gha 'an ja·ree·ma

I have insurance.

عندي تأمين.   'in·dee al·ta'·meen

I want to contact my consulate/embassy.

أريد أن اتصل   'u·ree·du 'an 'at·ta·si·la
بقنصليتي/بسفارتي.   bi·kun·su·li·ya·tee/bi·sa·faa·ra·tee

I've been assaulted.	اعتدى عليّ شخص.	i·'ta·daa 'a·la·yee shakhs
I've been raped.	اغتصبني شخص.	'igh·ta·sa·ba·nee shakhs
I've been robbed.	سرقني شخص.	sa·ra·ka·nee shakhs
My ... was/were	... كان مسروق.	... kaa·na mas·rook m
stolen.	... كانت مسروقة.	... kaa·nat mas·roo·ka f
bag	حقيبتي	ha·kee·ba·tee
money	نقودي	nu·koo·dee
passport	جواز سفري	ja·waa·zu sa·fa·ree
wallet	محفظتي	mah·fa·dha·tee

medical needs

Where's the nearest ...?	أين أقربُ ...؟	'ay·na 'ak·ra·bu ...
dentist	طبيب الأسنان	ta·bee·bul 'as·naan
doctor	طبيب/طبيبة	ta·beeb/ta·bee·ba m/f
hospital	مستشفى	mus·tash·faa
pharmacist	صيدلية	say·da·lee·ya

I need a doctor (who speaks English).

أحتاج إلى طبيب   'ah·taa·ju 'i·laa ta·bee·bin
(يتكلم الانجليزية).   (ya·ta·kal·la·mu al·'inj·lee·zee·ya)

Could I see a female doctor?

هل من الممكن أن أقابِلا طبيبة؟   hal min al·mum·kin 'an 'u·kaa·bi·la ta·bee·ba

It hurts here.

يؤلمني هنا.   yu'·li·mu·nee hu·naa

I've run out of my medication.

لقد نفذتُ جميع أدويتي.   la·kad na·fadh·tu ja·mee·'u 'ad·wi·ya·tee

I'm allergic to (penicillin).

عندي حساسيّة من   'an·dee has·saa·see·ya min
(البنسلين).   (al·bi·ni·si·leen)

english–arabic dictionary

Words in this dictionary are marked with n (noun), a (adjective), v (verb), sg (singular) and pl (plural), ⓜ masculine and ⓕ feminine where necessary. Where both the masculine and the feminine forms of a word are given, they're marked with ⓜ/ⓕ. Verbs are given in the third-person singular, in the present tense.

A

accommodation سكن sa-kan ⓜ
adaptor الموصل al-mu-was-sil ⓜ
after بعد ba'-da
airport مطار ma-taar ⓜ
alcohol الكحول al-ku-hool ⓜ
all كلّ kul-lū
allergy حساسية has-saa-si-ya ⓕ
and و wa
ankle كاحل kaa-hil ⓜ
antibiotics مضاد حيوي mu-daa-dun ha-ya-wee ⓜ
arm ذراع dhi-raa' ⓜ
asthma الربو ar-rabw ⓜ
ATM جهاز الصرافة ji-haaz as-sar-raa-fa ⓜ

B

baby طفلٌ صغير/طفلةٌ صغيرة tif-lun sa-gheer/tif-la-tun sa-ghee-ra ⓜ/ⓕ
back شنطة shan-ta ⓕ
backpack شنطة ظهر shan-ta-tu dhahr ⓕ
bad سيء/سيئة say-yi'/say-yi'-a ⓜ/ⓕ
baggage claim مكان لجمع الأمتعة ma-kaa-nun li-jam'-il 'am-ti-'a ⓜ
bank بنك bank ⓜ
bathroom غرفة الحمام ghur-fa-tul ham-maam ⓕ
battery بطارية ba-taa-ri-ya ⓕ
beautiful جميل/جميلة ja-meel/ja-mee-la ⓜ/ⓕ
bed سرير sa-reer ⓜ
beer بيرة bee-ra ⓕ
before قبل kab-la
bicycle درّاجة dar-raa-ja ⓕ
big كبير/كبيرة ka-beer/ka-bee-ra ⓜ/ⓕ
blanket بطانية ba-taa-ni-ya ⓕ
bottle زجاجة zu-jaa-ja ⓕ
bottle opener فاتح الزجاجات faa-ti-hu az-zu-jaa-jaat ⓜ
boy ولد wa-lad ⓜ
breakfast فطور fu-toor ⓜ
bronchitis التهاب الشُّعب il-ti-haab ash-shu-'ab ⓜ

C

café مقهى mak-han ⓜ
cancel يلغي/تلغي yul-ghee/tul-ghee ⓜ/ⓕ
can opener فاتح العلبة faa-ti-hu at-tan-ka ⓜ
cash n نقد nukd ⓜ
cell phone هاتف محمول haa-ti-fu mah-mool ⓜ
centre n مركز mar-kaz ⓜ
cheap رخيص/رخيصة ra-khees/ra-khee-sa ⓜ/ⓕ
check (bill) الحساب al-hi-saab ⓜ
check-in مكتب التسجيل mak-ta-bu at-tas-jeel ⓜ
chest صدر sadr ⓜ
child طفل/طفلة tif-la/tif-la ⓜ/ⓕ
cigarette سجارة si-jaa-ra ⓕ
city مدينة ma-dee-na ⓕ
clean a نظيف/نظيفة na-dheef/na-dhee-fa ⓜ/ⓕ
closed مغلق/مغلقة mugh-lak/mugh-la-ka ⓜ/ⓕ
cold a بارد/باردة baa-rid/baa-ri-da ⓜ/ⓕ
collect call
اتصال والأجرة على الشخص المتلقي الاتصال
it-ti-saal wal-'uj-ra-'a-laa al-shakh-sil mut-la-kee al-'it-ti-saal ⓜ
condom الواقي al-waa-kee ⓜ
contact lenses عدسة لاصقة a-da-sa-tun laa-si-ka ⓕ
cough n سعال su-'aal ⓜ
currency exchange صرافة sa-raa-fa ⓕ
customs (immigration) جمارك ja-maa-rik ⓕ

D

dairy products الألبان al-'al-baan ⓕ
dangerous خطر/خطرة khatr/khat-ra ⓜ/ⓕ
date (time) تاريخ taa-reekh ⓜ
day يوم yawm ⓜ
diaper حفاظة طفل ha-faa-dha-tu tifl ⓜ
diarrhoea الاسهال is-haal ⓜ
dinner عشاء 'a-shaa' ⓜ
dirty وسخ/وسخة wakh/was-kha ⓜ/ⓕ
disabled معاق/معاقة mu-'aak/mu-'aa-ka ⓜ/ⓕ
double bed سرير مزدوج sa-ree-run muz-daw-waj ⓜ
drink n مشروب mash-roob ⓜ
drivers licence رخصة القيادة rukh-sa-tul kee-yaa-da ⓕ
(drug) illicit مخدّر mu-khad-dir ⓜ

E

ear أذن 'u-dhun ①
east شرق shark ⓜ
economy class الدرجة العادية ad-da-ra-ja-tul 'aa-diy-ya ①
elevator مصعد mas-'ad ⓜ
email البريد الالكتروني al-ba-ree-dul 'i-lik-troo-nee ①
English (language) الإنجليزية al-'inj-lee-zee-ya ①
exchange rate سعر التحويل si'-ru at-tah-weel ⓜ
exit n مخرج makh-raj
expensive غال/غالية ghaa-lin/ghaa-lee-ya ⓜ/①
eye عين 'ayn ⓜ

F

fast سريع/سريعة sa-ree-'/sa-ree-'a ⓜ/①
fever حمى hum-maa ①
finger إصبع 'is-ba'
first-aid kit صندوق للإسعاف الأولي sun-doo-kun lil-'is-'a-fil 'aw-wa-lee ⓜ
first class الدرجة الأولى ad-da-ra-ja-tul 'oo-la ①
fish n سمك sa-mak ⓜ
food طعام ta-'aam ⓜ
foot قدم qa-dam ⓜ
fork شوكة shaw-ka ①
free (of charge) مجاناً ma-jaa-nan
fruit فاكهة faa-ki-ha ①
funny مضحك/مضحكة mud-hik/mud-hi-ka ⓜ/①

G

game park مدينة ملاه متنقلة ma-dee-na-tu ma-laa'hin mu-ta-nak-ka-la ①
gift هدية ha-dee-ya ①
girl بنت bint ①
glass (drinking) كأس ka's ⓜ
glasses نظارات na-dhaa-raat ①
gluten الغلوتين al-ghloo-teen ⓜ
good جيّد/جيّدة jay-yid/jay-yi-da ⓜ/①
gram غرام ghraam ⓜ

H

hand يد yad ①
happy سعيد/سعيدة sa-'eed/sa-'ee-da ⓜ/①
have عند 'ind
he هو hu-wa ⓜ
head رأس ra's ⓜ
headache صداع su-daa' ⓜ
heart قلب kalb ⓜ
heart condition مشكلة القلب mush-ki-la-tul kalb ①

heat n حرارة ha-raa-ra ①
here هنا hu-naa
high عال/عالية 'aa-lin/'aa-li-ya ⓜ/①
highway طريق عام ta-ree-ku 'aam ⓜ
homosexual لوطي/سحاقية loo-tee/su-haa-kee-ya ⓜ/①
hot حار/حارة haar/haa-ra ⓜ/①
hungry جائع/جائعة jaa-'i'/jaa-'i-'a ⓜ/①

I

identification (card) شخصية shakh-see-ya ①
ill مريض/مريضة ma-reed/ma-ree-da ⓜ/①
important مهم/مهمة mu-him/mu-him-ma ⓜ/①
internet الإنترنت 'in-tir-net
interpreter مترجم فوري/مترجمة فورية mu-tar-jim faw-ree/mu-tar-ji-ma faw-ree-ya ⓜ/①

J

job عمل 'a-mal ⓜ

K

key مفتاح mif-taah ⓜ
kilogram كيلوغرام kee-loo-ghraam ⓜ
kitchen مطبخ mat-bakh ⓜ
knife سكين sik-keen ⓜ

L

laundry (place) مغسل magh-sal ⓜ
lawyer محام/محامية mu-haa-min/mu-haa-mee-ya ⓜ/①
left-luggage office مكتب للاحتفاظ بالأمتعة mak-ta-bu li-li-'ih-ti-faa-dhi bil-'am-ti-'a ⓜ
leg رجل rijl ⓜ
lesbian سحاقية su-haa-kee-ya ①
less أقل 'a-kal-lu
letter (mail) رسالة ri-saa-la ①
like V يحب/تحب yu-hib-bu/tu-hib-bu ⓜ/①
lost-property office مكتب للأغراض الضائعة mak-ta-bu lil-'agh-raa-di ad-daa-'i-'a ⓜ
love V يحب / تحب yu-hib-bu/tu-hib-bu ⓜ/①
lunch غداء gha-daa' ⓜ

M

man رجُل ra-jul ⓜ
matches كبريت kib-reet ⓜ
meat لحم lahm ⓜ
medicine دواء da-waa' ⓜ

message رسالة ri-*saa*-la ⓕ
mobile phone هاتف محمول
haa-ti-fun mah-*mool*
month شهر shahr ⓜ
morning صباح sa-*baah*
motorcycle دراجة نارية dar-*raa*-ja-tun naa-*ree*-ya ⓕ
mouth فم famm ⓜ
movie فيلم feelm ⓜ
MSG أحدى الصوديوم الغلوتينات
'a-ha-dee as-soo-de-*oom* al-ghloo-tee-*naat* ⓜ
museum المتحف al-*mat*-haf ⓜ
music الموسيقى al-*moo*-see-kaa ⓕ

N

name اسم ism ⓜ
napkin محرمة *mah*-ra-ma ⓕ
nappy حفاظة طفل ha-*faa*-dha-tu tifl ⓜ
national park حديقة وطنية
ha-*dee*-ka-tun wa-ta-*nee*-ya ⓕ
nausea غثيان gha-*ta*-yaan ⓜ
neck رقبة *ra*-ka-ba ⓕ
new جديد/جديدة ja-*deed*/ja-*dee*-da ⓜ/ⓕ
news الأخبار al-'akh-*baar* ⓜ
newspaper جريدة ja-*ree*-da ⓕ
night ليل layl ⓜ
nightclub ملهى ليلى *mil*-han *lay*-lee ⓜ
noisy ضجيجة/ضجيج *da*-jeej/*da*-jee-ja ⓜ/ⓕ
nonsmoking غير المدخنين
ghay-ri al-mu-dakh-khi-*neen*
north شمال sha-*maal* ⓜ
nose أنف 'anf ⓜ
now الآن al-*'aan*
number رقم rakm ⓜ
nuts مكسرات mu-ka-si-*raat*

O

oil (engine) نفط naft ⓜ
OK تمام ta-*maam*
old قديم/قديمة ka-*deem*/ka-*dee*-ma ⓜ/ⓕ
open a مفتوح/مفتوحة maf-*tooh*/maf-*too*-ha ⓜ/ⓕ
outside خارج / خارجة *khaa*-rij/*khaa*-ri-ja ⓜ/ⓕ

P

package طرد tard ⓜ
pain ألم *'a*-lam ⓜ
palace قصر kasr ⓜ
paper ورقة *wa*-ra-ka ⓕ
park (car) v يوقف / توقف *yoo*-ki-fu/*too*-ki-fu ⓜ/ⓕ
passport جواز سفر ja-*waaz*-zu sa-*far* ⓜ
pay v يدفع / تدفع *yad*-fa-'u/*tad*-fa-'u ⓜ/ⓕ
pen قلم *ka*-lam ⓜ

petrol نفط naft ⓜ
pharmacy صيدلية say-da-*lee*-ya ⓕ
plate صحن sahn ⓜ
postcard بطاقة المعايبة bi-*taa*-ka-tul mu-*'aa*-ya-da ⓕ
post office مكتب البريد *mak*-ta-bul ba-*reed*
pregnant حامل *haa*-mil ⓕ

Q

quiet هادئ/هادئة *haa*-din/*haa*-di-ya ⓜ/ⓕ

R

rain n مطر *ma*-tar ⓜ
razor موسى *moo*-saa ⓜ
registered mail بريد مسجّل
ba-*reed* mu-*saj*-jal
rent v يستأجر/تستأجر
yas-ta'-ji-ru/*tas*-ta'-ji-ru ⓜ/ⓕ
repair v يصلح / تصلح *yus*-li-hu/*tus*-li-hu ⓜ/ⓕ
reservation حجز hajz ⓜ
restaurant مطعم *mat*-'am ⓜ
return v يرجع/ترجع *yar*-ja-'u/*tar*-ja-'u ⓜ/ⓕ
road شارع *shaa*-ri' ⓜ
room غرفة *ghur*-fa ⓕ

S

sad حزين/حزينة ha-*zeen*/ha-*zee*-na ⓜ/ⓕ
safe a آمن/آمنة *'aa*-min/*'aa*-mi-na ⓜ/ⓕ
sanitary napkin منديل نسائي
min-*dee*-lun ni-*saa*-'ee ⓜ
seafood الطعام البحري at-ta-*'aa*-mul ba-ha-*ree*
seat مقعد *mak*-'ad ⓜ
send يبعث/تبعث *yab*-'a-thu/*tab*-'a-thu ⓜ/ⓕ
sex جنس jins ⓜ
shampoo الشامبو ash-*shaam*-boo ⓜ
share (a dorm, etc) يشارك/ تشارك
yu-*shaa*-ri-ku/tu-*shaa*-ri-ku ⓜ/ⓕ
shaving cream معجون الحلاقة
ma-*'joo*-nul hal-*laa*-ka ⓜ
she هي *hi*-ya ⓕ
sheet (bed) شرشف *shar*-shaf ⓜ
shirt قميص ka-*mees* ⓜ
shoes حذاء hi-*dhaa'*
shop n دكان duk-*kaan* ⓜ
shower n دوش doosh ⓜ
skin جلد jild ⓜ
skirt تنورة tan-*noo*-ra ⓕ
sleep v ينام / تنام ya-*naa*-mu/ta-*naa*-mu ⓜ/ⓕ
small صغير/صغيرة sa-*gheer*/sa-*ghee*-ra ⓜ/ⓕ
smoke (cigarettes) v يدخن / تدخن
yu-*dakh*-khi-nu/tu-*dakh*-khi-nu ⓜ/ⓕ
soap صابون *saa*-boon ⓜ

some بعض ba'-du
soon قريب ka-ree-ban
sore throat ألم في حلقي 'a-la-mu fee hal-kee ⓜ
south جنوب ja-noob
souvenir shop دكان التذكارات
duk-kaa-nu at-tidh-kaa-raat ⓜ
speak v نتكلّم / يتكلّم
ya-ta-kal-la-mu/ta-ta-kal-la-mu ⓜ/ⓕ
spoon ملعقة mal-'a-ka ⓕ
stamp طابع taa-bi' ⓜ
stand-by ticket تذكرة بديلة
tadh-ki-ra-tun ba-dee-la ⓕ
station (train) محطّة mu-hat-ta-tu ⓕ
stomach معدة ma'-i-da ⓕ
stop v يقف / تقف ya-ki-fu/ta-ki-fu ⓜ/ⓕ
stop (bus) موقف maw-ki-fu ⓜ
street شارع shaa-ri'
student طالب/طالبة taa-lib/taa-li-ba ⓜ/ⓕ
sunscreen معجون واقي من الشمس
ma'-joo-nun waa-kee min ash-shams
swim v يسبح / تسبح yas-ba-hu/tas-bu-hu ⓜ/ⓕ

T

tampons الصمام النسائيّ
as-si-maa-mu an-ni-saa-'ee ⓜ
teeth أسنان as-naan
telephone n هاتف haa-tif ⓜ
television التلفزيون ti-li-fi-si-yoon ⓜ
temperature (weather) درجة الحرارة
da-ra-ja-tul ha-raa-ra ⓕ
tent خيمة khay-ma ⓕ
that (one) ذلك/تلك dhaa-li-ka/til-ka ⓜ/ⓕ
they هم/هنّ hum/hun-na ⓜ/ⓕ
thirsty عطشان/عطشانة
'at-shaan/'at-shaa-na ⓜ/ⓕ
this (one) هذا/هذه haa-dhaa/haa-dhi-hi ⓜ/ⓕ
throat حلق khalk ⓜ
ticket تذكرة tadh-ki-ra ⓕ
time وقت wakt ⓜ
tired تعبان/تعبانة ta'-baan/ta'-baa-na ⓜ/ⓕ
tissues محارم ma-haa-ram ⓕ
today اليوم al-yawm ⓜ
toilet دورات المياه daw-raa-tul mi-yaah ⓕ
tonight ليلة اليوم lay-la-tul yawm ⓕ
toothache ألم في الأسنان 'a-la-mu fee l 'as-naan ⓜ
toothbrush فرشاة الأسنان far-shaa-tul 'as-naan ⓕ
toothpaste معجون الأسنان ma'-joo-nul 'as-naan ⓜ
torch(flashlight) مشعل كهربائي
mish-'a-lun kah-ra-baa-'ee ⓜ
tourist office مكتب السياحة
mak-ta-bu as-si-yaa-ha ⓜ
towel منشفة man-sha-fa ⓕ
translate يترجم / تترجم
yu-tar-ji-mu/tu-tar-ji-mu ⓜ/ⓕ

travel agency وكالة سفر wa-kaa-la-tu sa-far ⓕ
travellers cheque شيك سياحي
shee-kun si-yaa-hee ⓜ
trousers بنطلون ban-ta-loon ⓜ
twin beds سريرين منفردين
sa-ree-ray-ni mun-fa-ri-dayn ⓜ
tyre إطار السيّارة 'i-taa-ru as-say-yaa-ra ⓕ

U

underwear ملابس داخلية
ma-laa-bi-sun daa-khi-lee-ya ⓕ
urgent مستعجل/مستعجلة
mus-ta'-jal/mus-ta'-ja-la ⓜ/ⓕ

V

vacant شاغر/شاغرة shaa-ghir/shaa-ghi-ra ⓜ/ⓕ
vegetable n خضراوات khud-raa-waat ⓕ
vegetarian a نباتي/نباتية
na-baa-tee/na-baa-tee-ya ⓜ/ⓕ
visa تأشيرة ta'-shee-ra ⓕ

W

waiter نادل/نادلة naa-dil/naa-di-la ⓜ/ⓕ
walk v يمشي/تمشي yam-shee/tam-shee ⓜ/ⓕ
wallet محفظة mah-fa-dha ⓕ
warm دافئ/دافئة daa-fi'/daa-fi-'a ⓜ/ⓕ
wash (something) يغسل / تغسل
yagh-si-lu/tagh-si-lu ⓜ/ⓕ
watch n ساعة اليد saa-'a-tul yad ⓕ
water ماء maa' ⓜ
we نحن nah-nu
weekend نهاية الأسبوع ni-haa-ya-tul 'us-boo' ⓕ
west غرب gharb ⓜ
wheelchair كرسي المقعدين kur-see al-muk-'a-deen ⓜ
when متى ma-taa
where أين 'ay-na
who من man
why لماذا li-maa-dhaa
window شبّاك shub-baak ⓜ
wine نبيذ na-beedh ⓜ
with مع ma-'a
without بدون bi-doo-ni
woman امرأة 'im-ra-'a ⓕ
write يكتب / تكتب yak-tu-bu/tak-tu-bu ⓜ/ⓕ

Y

you sg أنت/أنت 'an-ta/'an-ti ⓜ/ⓕ
you pl أنتم/أنتنّ 'an-tum/'an-tun-na ⓜ/ⓕ

French

pronunciation

Vowels		Consonants	
Symbol	**English sound**	**Symbol**	**English sound**
a	run	b	bed
ai	aisle	d	dog
air	fair	f	fun
e	bet	g	go
ee	see	k	kit
eu	nurse	l	lot
ew	ee with rounded lips	m	man
ey	as in 'bet', but longer	n	not
o	pot	ny	canyon
oo	zoo	ng	ring
om/on/ong	as in 'pot', but nasal	p	pet
um/un/ung	as in 'act', but nasal	r	run (throaty)
		s	sun
In this chapter, the French pronunciation is given in green after each phrase.		sh	shot
		t	top
Each syllable is separated by a dot. For example:		v	very
Bonjour. bon-zhoor		w	win
		y	yes
French's nasal vowels, simplified as om/on/ong and um/un/ung above, are pronounced as if you're trying to force the sound out of your nose.		z	zero
		zh	pleasure

FRENCH
français

language difficulties

Do you speak English?	*Parlez-vous anglais?*	par-ley-voo ong-gley
Do you understand?	*Comprenez-vous?*	kom-pre-ney-voo
I understand.	*Je comprends.*	zhe kom-pron
I don't understand.	*Je ne comprends pas.*	zhe ne kom-pron pa
Could you please	*Pourriez-vous ...,*	poo-ree-yey voo ...
please ...?	*s'il vous plaît?*	seel voo pley
repeat that	*répéter*	rey-pey-tey
speak more slowly	*parler plus lentement*	par-ley plew lon-te-mon
write it down	*l'écrire*	ley-kreer

time, dates & numbers

What time is it?	*Quelle heure est-il?*	kel eur ey-teel
It's one o'clock.	*Il est une heure.*	ee-ley ewn eu
It's (ten) o'clock.	*Il est (dix) heures.*	ee-ley (deez) eu
Quarter past (one).	*Il est (une) heure et quart.*	ee-ley (ewn) eu ey kar
Half past (one).	*Il est (une) heure et demie.*	ee-ley (ewn) eu ey de-mee
Quarter to (one).	*Il est (une) heure moins le quart.*	ee-ley (ewn) eu mwun le kar
At what time ...?	*À quelle heure ...?*	a kel eu ...
At ...	*À ...*	a ...
It's (18 October).	*C'est le (dix-huit octobre).*	sey le (dee-zwee tok-to-bre)
Monday	*lundi*	lun-dee
Tuesday	*mardi*	mar-dee
Wednesday	*mercredi*	mair-kre-dee
Thursday	*jeudi*	zheu-dee
Friday	*vendredi*	von-dre-dee
Saturday	*samedi*	sam-dee
Sunday	*dimanche*	dee-monsh

language difficulties – FRENCH

65

yesterday	*hier*	ee-yair
today	*aujourd'hui*	o-zhoor-dwee
tomorrow	*demain*	de-mun

numbers

0	*zéro*	zey-ro	16	*seize*	sez	
1	*un*	un	17	*dix-sept*	dee-set	
2	*deux*	deu	18	*dix-huit*	dee-zweet	
3	*trois*	trwa	19	*dix-neuf*	deez-neuf	
4	*quatre*	ka-tre	20	*vingt*	vung	
5	*cinq*	sungk	21	*vingt et un*	vung tey un	
6	*six*	sees	22	*vingt-deux*	vung-deu	
7	*sept*	set	30	*trente*	tront	
8	*huit*	weet	40	*quarante*	ka-ront	
9	*neuf*	neuf	50	*cinquante*	sung-kont	
10	*dix*	dees	60	*soixante*	swa-sont	
11	*onze*	onz	70	*soixante-dix*	swa-son-dees	
12	*douze*	dooz	80	*quatre-vingts*	ka-tre-vung	
13	*treize*	trez	90	*quatre-vingt-dix*	ka-tre-vung-dees	
14	*quatorze*	ka-torz	100	*cent*	son	
15	*quinze*	kunz	1000	*mille*	meel	

border crossing

I'm here ...	*Je suis ici ...*	zhe swee zee-see ...
in transit	*de passage*	de pa-sazh
on business	*pour le travail*	poor le tra-vai
on holiday	*pour les vacances*	poor ley va-kons

I'm here for ...	*Je suis ici pour ...*	zhe swee zee-see poor ...
(10) days	*(dix) jours*	(dees) zhoor
(three) weeks	*(trois) semaines*	(trwa) se-men
(two) months	*(deux) mois*	(deu) mwa

I'm going to (Yaoundé).
Je vais à (Yaoundé).   zhe vey a (ya-oon-dey)

I'm staying at the (Mercure Hotel).
Je loge au (Mercure).   zhe lozh o (mer-kewr)

tickets

One ... ticket (to Douala), please.	Un billet ... (pour Douala), s'il vous plaît.	um bee·yey ... (poor dwa·la) seel voo pley
one-way	simple	sum·ple
return	aller et retour	a·ley ey re·toor
Is there ...?	Est-qu'il y a ...?	es·keel ya ...
air conditioning	la climatisation	la klee·ma·tee·za·syon
a toilet	des toilettes	dey twa·let
I'd like a ... seat, please.	Je voudrais une place ..., s'il vous plaît.	zhe voo·drey ewn plas ... seel voo pley
nonsmoking	non-fumeur	non·few·mer
smoking	fumeur	few·mer

transport

Is this the ... to (Libreville)?	Est-ce le ... pour (Libreville)?	es le ... poor (lee·brer·veel)
boat	bateau	ba·to
bus	bus	bews
train	train	trun

How much is it to ...?
C'est combien pour aller à ...? — sey kom·byun poor a·ley a ...

Please take me to (this address).
Conduisez-moi à (cette adresse), s'il vous plaît. — kon·dwee·zey mwa a (set a·dres) seel voo pley

I'd like to hire a ...	Je voudrais louer ...	zhe voo·drey loo·wey ...
car (with air conditioning)	une voiture (avec climatisation)	ewn vwa·tewr (a·vek klee·ma·tee·za·syon)
4WD	un quatre-quatre	un ka·tre ka·tre

directions

Where's the nearest ...?	Où est-ce qu'il y a ... le plus proche?	oo es·keel ya ... le plew prosh
internet café	le cybercafé	le see·bair·ka·fey
market	le marché	le mar·shey
It's ...	C'est ...	sey ...
behind ...	derrière ...	dair·yair ...
in front of ...	devant ...	de·von ...
near (to ...)	près (de ...)	prey (de ...)
next to ...	à côté de ...	a ko·tey de ...
on the corner	au coin	o kwun
opposite ...	en face de ...	on fas de ...
straight ahead	tout droit	too drwa
there	là	la

accommodation

I'd like to book a room, please.
Je voudrais réserver   zhe voo·drey rey·zair·vey
une chambre, s'il vous plaît.   ewn shom·bre seel voo pley

I'd like to stay for (two) nights.
Je voudrais rester pour (deux) nuits.   zhe voo·drey res·tey poor (deu) nwee

Do you have a ... room?	Avez-vous une chambre ...?	a·vey·voo ewn shom·bre ...
single	à un lit	a un lee
double	avec un grand lit	a·vek ung gron lee
twin	avec des lits jumeaux	a·vek dey lee zhew·mo
How much is it per ...?	Quel est le prix par ...?	kel ey le pree par ...
night	nuit	nwee
person	personne	pair·son

banking & communications

I'd like to ...	*Je voudrais ...*	zhe voo·drey ...
change a travellers cheque	*changer des chèques de voyage*	shon·zhey dey shek de vwa·yazh
change money	*changer de l'argent*	shon·zhey de lar·zhon
get internet access	*me connecter à l'internet*	me ko·nek·tey a lun·tair·net
withdraw money	*retirer de l'argent*	re·tee·rey de lar·zhon

shopping

I'm looking for ...
Je cherche ...   zhe shairsh ...

How much is it?
C'est combien?   sey kom·byun

Can you write down the price?
Pouvez-vous écrire le prix?   poo·vey·voo ey·kreer le pree

Do you accept ...?	*Est-ce que je peux payer avec ...?*	es·ke zhe pe pey·yey a·vek ...
credit cards	*une carte de crédit*	ewn kart de krey·dee
travellers cheques	*des chèques de voyages*	dey shek de vwa·yazh

making conversation

Hello.	*Bonjour.*	bon·zhoor
Good night.	*Bonsoir.*	bon·swar
Goodbye.	*Au revoir.*	o re·vwar

Mr	*Monsieur*	me·syeu
Mrs	*Madame*	ma·dam
Miss	*Mademoiselle*	mad·mwa·zel

How are you?	*Comment allez-vous?*	ko·mon ta·ley·voo
Fine, thanks. And you?	*Bien, merci. Et vous?*	byun mair·see ey voo

What's your name?	*Comment vous appelez-vous?*	ko·mon voo za·pley·voo
My name's ...	*Je m'appelle ...*	zhe ma·pel ...
I'm pleased to meet you.	*Enchanté(e).* m/f	on·shon·tey
This is my ...	*Voici mon/ma ...* m/f	vwa·see mon/ma ...
boyfriend	*petit ami*	pe·tee ta·mee
daughter	*fille*	fee·ye
friend	*ami/amie* m/f	a·mee
girlfriend	*petite amie*	pe·tee ta·mee
husband	*mari*	ma·ree
son	*fils*	fees
wife	*femme*	fam
I'm ...	*Je suis ...*	zhe swee ...
married	*marié/mariée* m/f	mar·yey
single	*célibataire* m&f	sey·lee·ba·tair
Here's my ...	*Voici mon ...*	vwa·see mon ...
What's your ...?	*Quel est votre ...?* pol	kel ey vo·tre ...
	Quel est ton ...? inf	kel ey ton ...
address	*adresse*	a·dres
email address	*e-mail*	ey·mel
phone number	*numéro de téléphone*	new·mey·ro de tey·ley·fon
Where are you from?	*Vous venez d'où?* pol	voo ve·ney doo
	Tu viens d'où? inf	tew vyun doo
I'm from ...	*Je viens ...*	zhe vyun ...
Australia	*d'Australie*	dos·tra·lee
Canada	*du Canada*	dew ka·na·da
New Zealand	*de la Nouvelle-Zélande*	de la noo·vel·zey·lond
the UK	*du Royaume-Uni*	dew rwa·om ew·nee
the USA	*des Etats Unis*	dey ey·tas ew·nee
Can I take a photo?	*Est-ce que je peux prendre une photo?*	es·ke zhe peu pron·dre ewn fo·to

eating out

I'd like ..., please.	Je voudrais ...,	zhe voo·drey ...
	s'il vous plaît.	seel voo pley
the bill	l'addition	la·dee·syon
the menu	la carte	la kart
a table for (two)	une table pour	ewn ta·ble poor
	(deux) personnes	(deu) pair·son
that dish	ce plat	se pla

| Do you have | Vous faites les repas | voo fet ley re·pa |
| vegetarian food? | végétariens? | vey·zhey·ta·ryun |

Could you prepare	Pouvez-vous préparer	poo·vey·voo prey·pa·rey
a meal without ...?	un repas sans ...?	un re·pa son ...
eggs	œufs	eu
meat stock	bouillon gras	boo·yon gra

emergencies

| Help! | Au secours! | o skoor |

Call ...!	Appelez ...!	a·pley ...
an ambulance	une ambulance	ewn om·bew·lons
the police	la police	la po·lees

Could you help me, please?
Est-ce que vous pourriez   es·ke voo poo·ryey
m'aider, s'il vous plaît?   mey·dey seel voo pley

Could I use the telephone?
Est-ce que je pourrais utiliser   es·ke zhe poo·rey ew·tee·lee·zey
le téléphone?   le tey·ley·fon

I'm lost.
Je suis perdu/perdue. m/f   zhe swee pair·dew

Where are the toilets?
Où sont les toilettes?   oo son ley twa·let

I've been assaulted.
J'ai été violenté/violentée. m/f   zhey ey·tey vyo·lon·tey

I've been raped.
J'ai été violé/violée. m/f   zhey ey·tey vyo·ley

I've lost my ...	J'ai perdu ...	zhey pair-dew ...
My ... was/were stolen.	On m'a volé ...	on ma vo-ley ...
bags	mes valises	mey va-leez
credit card	ma carte de crédit	ma kart de krey-dee
handbag	mon sac à main	mon sak a mun
jewellery	mes bijoux	mey bee-zhoo
money	mon argent	mon ar-zhon
passport	mon passeport	mom pas-por
travellers cheques	mes chèques de voyage	mey shek de vwa-yazh
wallet	mon portefeuille	mom por-te-feu-ye
I want to contact my ...	Je veux contacter mon ...	zher veu kon-tak-tey mon ...
consulate	consulat	kon-sew-la
embassy	ambassade	om-ba-sad

medical needs

Where's the nearest ...?	Où y a t-il ... par ici?	oo ee a teel ... par ee-see
dentist	un dentiste	un don-teest
doctor	un médecin	un meyd-sun
hospital	un hôpital	u-no-pee-tal
pharmacist	une pharmacie	ewn far-ma-see

I need a doctor (who speaks English).
J'ai besoin d'un médecin (qui parle anglais).
zhey be-zwun dun meyd-sun (kee parl ong-gley)

It hurts here.
J'ai une douleur ici.
zhey ewn doo-leur ee-see

I'm allergic to (penicillin).
Je suis allergique à (la pénicilline).
zhe swee za-lair-zheek a (la pey-nee-see-leen)

english–french dictionary

French nouns and adjectives in this dictionary have their gender indicated by ⓜ (masculine) or ⓕ (feminine). If it's a plural noun, you'll also see pl. Words are also marked as n (noun), a (adjective), v (verb), sg (singular), pl (plural), inf (informal) and pol (polite) where necessary.

A

accommodation *logement* ⓜ lozh-mon
adaptor *adaptateur* ⓜ a-dap-ta-teur
after *après* a-prey
airport *aéroport* ⓜ a-ey-ro-por
alcohol *alcool* ⓜ al-kol
all a *tout/toute* ⓜ/ⓕ too/toot
allergy *allergie* ⓕ a-lair-zhee
and *et* ey
ankle *cheville* ⓕ she-vee-ye
antibiotics *antibiotiques* ⓜ pl on-tee-byo-teek
anti-inflammatories *anti-inflammatoires* ⓜ pl un-tee-un-fla-ma-twar
arm *bras* ⓜ bra
aspirin *aspirine* ⓕ as-pee-reen
asthma *asthme* ⓜ as-meu
ATM *guichet automatique de banque* ⓜ gee-shey o-to-ma-teek de bonk

B

baby *bébé* ⓜ bey-bey
back (body) *dos* ⓜ do
backpack *sac à dos* ⓜ sak a do
bad *mauvais/mauvaise* ⓜ/ⓕ mo-vey/mo-veyz
baggage claim *retrait des bagages* ⓜ re-trey dey ba-gazh
bank *banque* ⓕ bonk
bathroom *salle de bain* ⓕ sal de bun
battery (car) *batterie* ⓕ bat-ree
battery (general) *pile* ⓕ peel
beautiful *beau/belle* ⓜ/ⓕ bo/bel
bed *lit* ⓜ lee
bee *abeille* ⓕ a-bey
beer *bière* ⓕ byair
before *avant* a-von
bicycle *vélo* ⓜ vey-lo
big *grand/grande* ⓜ/ⓕ gron/grond
blanket *couverture* ⓕ koo-vair-tewr
blood group *groupe sanguin* ⓜ groop song-gun

bottle *bouteille* ⓕ boo-tey
bottle opener *ouvre-bouteille* ⓜ oo-vre-boo-tey
boy *garçon* ⓜ gar-son
brakes (car) *freins* ⓜ frun
breakfast *petit déjeuner* ⓜ pe-tee dey-zheu-ney
bronchitis *bronchite* ⓕ bron-sheet

C

café *café* ⓜ ka-fey
cancel *annuler* a-new-ley
can opener *ouvre-boite* ⓜ oo-vre-bwat
cash *argent* ⓜ ar-zhon
cell phone *téléphone portable* ⓜ tey-ley-fon por-ta-ble
centre *centre* ⓜ son-tre
cheap *bon marché* ⓜ bon mar-shey
check (bill) *addition* ⓕ la-dee-syon
check-in *enregistrement* ⓜ on-re-zhee-stre-mon
chest *poitrine* ⓕ pwa-treen
child *enfant* ⓜ&ⓕ on-fon
cigarette *cigarette* ⓕ see-ga-ret
city *ville* ⓕ veel
clean a *propre* ⓜ&ⓕ pro-pre
closed *fermé/fermée* ⓜ/ⓕ fair-mey
codeine *codéine* ⓕ ko-dey-een
cold a *froid/froide* ⓜ/ⓕ frwa/frwad
collect call *appel en PCV* ⓜ a-pel on pey-sey-vey
condom *préservatif* ⓜ prey-zair-va-teef
constipation *constipation* ⓕ kon-stee-pa-syon
contact lenses *verres de contact* ⓜ pl vair de kon-takt
cough *toux* ⓕ too
currency exchange *taux de change* ⓜ to de shonzh
customs (immigration) *douane* ⓕ dwan

D

dairy products *produits laitiers* ⓜ pl pro-dwee ley-tyey
dangerous *dangereux/dangereuse* ⓜ/ⓕ don-zhreu/don-zhreuz
day *date de naissance* ⓕ dat de ney-sons
diaper *couche* ⓕ koosh

diarrhoea *diarrhée* ① dya-rey
dinner *dîner* ⑩ dee-ney
dirty *sale* ⑩&① sal
disabled *handicapé/handicapée* ⑩/① on-dee-ka-pey
double bed *grand lit* ⑩ gron lee
drink *boisson* ① bwa-son
drivers licence *permis de conduire* ⑩
   pair-mee de kon-dweer
drug (illicit) *drogue* ① drog

E

ear *oreille* ① o-rey
east *est* ⑩ est
economy class *classe touriste* ① klas too-reest
elevator *ascenseur* ⑩ a-son-seur
email *e-mail* ⑩ ey-mel
English (language) *anglais* ⑩ ong-gley
exchange rate *taux de change* ⑩ to de shonzh
exit *sortie* ① sor-tee
expensive *cher/chère* ⑩/① shair
eye *œil* ⑩ eu-ye

F

fast *rapide* ⑩&① ra-peed
fever *fièvre* ① fyev-re
finger *doigt* ⑩ dwa
first-aid kit *trousse à pharmacie* ① troos a far-ma-see
first class *première classe* ① pre-myair klas
fish *poisson* ⑩ pwa-son
food *nourriture* ① noo-ree-tewr
foot *pied* ⑩ pyey
fork *fourchette* ① foor-shet
free (of charge) *gratuit/gratuite* ⑩/①
   gra-twee/gra-tweet
fruit *fruit* ⑩ frwee
funny *drôle* ⑩&① drol

G

gift *cadeau* ⑩ ka-do
girl *fille* ① fee-ye
glasses *lunettes* ① pl lew-net
gluten *gluten* ⑩ glew-ten
good *bon/bonne* ⑩/① bon
gram *gramme* ⑩ gram
guide *guide* ⑩ geed

H

hand *main* ① mun
happy *heureux/heureuse* ⑩/① eu-reu/eu-reuz
have *avoir* a-vwar
he *il* eel
head *tête* ① tet
headache *mal à la tête* ⑩ mal a la tet
heart *cœur* ⑩ keur
heart condition *maladie de cœur* ① ma-la-dee de keur
heat *chaleur* ① sha-leur
here *ici* ee-see
high *haut/haute* ⑩/① o/ot
highway *autoroute* ① o-to-root
homosexual n *homosexuel/homosexuelle* ⑩/①
   o-mo-sek-swel
hot *chaud/chaude* ⑩/① sho/shod
(be) hungry *avoir faim* a-vwar fum

I

I *je* zhe
identification (card) *carte d'identité* ①
   kart dee-don-tee-tey
ill *malade* ⑩&① ma-lad
important *important/importante* ⑩/①
   um-por-ton/um-por-tont
internet *Internet* ⑩ un-tair-net
interpreter *interprète* ⑩&① un-tair-pret

K

key *clé* ① kley
kilogram *kilogramme* ⑩ kee-lo-gram
kitchen *cuisine* ① kwee-zeen
knife *couteau* ⑩ koo-to

L

laundry (place) *blanchisserie* ① blon-shees-ree
lawyer *avocat/avocate* ⑩/① a-vo-ka/a-vo-kat
left-luggage office *consigne* ① kon-see-nye
leg *jambe* ① zhomb
lesbian n *lesbienne* ① les-byen
less *moins* mwun
letter (mail) *lettre* ① le-trer
like v *aimer* ey-mey
lost-property office *bureau des objets trouvés* ⑩
   bew-ro dey zob-zhey troo-vey

love v *aimer* ey-mey
lunch *déjeuner* ⓜ dey-zheu-ney

M

man *homme* ⓜ om
matches *allumettes* ⓕ pl a-lew-met
meat *viande* ⓕ vyond
medicine *médecine* ⓕ med-seen
message *message* ⓜ mey-sazh
mobile phone *téléphone portable* ⓜ tey-ley-fon por-ta-ble
month *mois* ⓜ mwa
morning *matin* ⓜ ma-tun
motorcycle *moto* ⓕ mo-to
mouth *bouche* ⓕ boosh
movie *film* ⓜ feelm
MSG *glutamate de sodium* ⓜ glew-ta-mat de so-dyom
museum *musée* ⓜ mew-zey
music *musique* ⓕ mew-zeek

N

name *nom* ⓜ nom
napkin *serviette* ⓕ sair-vyet
nappy *couche* ⓕ koosh
national park *parc national* ⓜ park na-syo-nal
nausea *nausée* ⓕ no-zey
neck *cou* ⓜ koo
new *nouveau/nouvelle* ⓜ/ⓕ noo-vo/noo-vel
news ⓕ pl *les nouvelles* ley noo-vel
newspaper *journal* ⓜ zhoor-nal
night *nuit* ⓕ nwee
nightclub *boîte* ⓕ bwat
noisy *bruyant/bruyante* ⓜ/ⓕ brew-yon/brew-yont
nonsmoking *non-fumeur* non-few-meur
north *nord* ⓜ nor
nose *nez* ⓜ ney
now *maintenant* mun-te-non
number *numéro* ⓜ new-mey-ro

O

oil *huile* ⓕ weel
OK *bien* byun
old *vieux/vieille* ⓜ/ⓕ vyeu/vyey
open a *ouvert/ouverte* ⓜ/ⓕ oo-vair/oo-vairt
outside *dehors* de-or

P

package *paquet* ⓜ pa-key
pain *douleur* ⓕ doo-leur
paper *papier* ⓜ pa-pyey
park (car) v *garer (une voiture)* ga-rey (ewn vwa-tewr)
passport *passeport* ⓜ pas-por
pay *payer* pey-yey
pen *stylo* ⓜ stee-lo
petrol *essence* ⓕ ey-sons
pharmacy *pharmacie* ⓕ far-ma-see
plate *assiette* ⓕ a-syet
postcard *carte postale* ⓕ kart pos-tal
post office *bureau de poste* ⓜ bew-ro de post
pregnant *enceinte* on-sunt

R

rain n *pluie* ⓕ plwee
razor *rasoir* ⓜ ra-zwar
registered mail *en recommandé* on re-ko-mon-dey
rent v *louer* loo-ey
repair v *réparer* rey-pa-rey
reservation *réservation* ⓕ rey-zair-va-syon
restaurant *restaurant* ⓜ res-to-ron
return v *revenir* rev-neer
road *route* ⓕ root
room *chambre* ⓕ shom-bre

S

sad *triste* treest
safe a *sans danger* ⓜ&ⓕ son don-zhey
sanitary napkin *serviette hygiénique* ⓕ sair-vyet ee-zhyey-neek
seafood *fruits de mer* ⓜ frwee de mair
seat *place* ⓕ plas
send *envoyer* on-vwa-yey
sex *sexe* ⓜ seks
shampoo *shampooing* ⓜ shom-pwung
share (a dorm) *partager* par-ta-zhey
shaving cream *mousse à raser* ⓕ moos a ra-zey
she *elle* el
sheet (bed) *drap* ⓜ dra
shirt *chemise* ⓕ she-meez
shoes *chaussures* ⓕ pl sho-sewr
shop *magasin* ⓜ ma-ga-zun
shower *douche* ⓕ doosh
skin *peau* ⓕ po

skirt *jupe* ① zhewp
sleep V *dormir* dor·meer
small *petit/petite* ⓜ/① pe·tee/pe·teet
smoke (cigarettes) V *fumer* few·mey
soap *savon* ⓜ sa·von
some *quelques* kel·ke
soon *bientôt* byun·to
sore throat *mal à la gorge* ⓜ mal a la gorzh
south *sud* ⓜ sewd
souvenir shop *magasin de souvenirs* ⓜ
  ma·ga·zun de soov·neer
speak *parler* par·ley
spoon *cuillère* ① kwee·yair
stamp *timbre* ⓜ tum·bre
stand-by ticket *billet stand-by* ⓜ bee·yey stond·bai
station (train) *gare* ① gar
stomach *estomac* ⓜ es·to·ma
stop V *arrêter* a·rey·tey
stop (bus) *arrêt* ⓜ a·rey
street *rue* ① rew
student *étudiant/étudiante* ⓜ/①
  ey·tew·dyon/ey·tew·dyont
sunscreen *écran solaire* ⓜ ey·kron so·lair
swim V *nager* na·zhey

T

tampons *tampons* ⓜ pl tom·pon
teeth *dents* ① don
telephone n *téléphone* tey·ley·fon
television *télé(vision)* ① tey·ley(vee·zyon)
temperature (weather) *température* ① tom·pey·ra·tewr
that (one) *cela* se·la
they *ils/elles* ⓜ/① eel/el
(be) thirsty *avoir soif* a·vwar swaf
this (one) *ceci* se·see
throat *gorge* ① gorzh
ticket *billet* ⓜ bee·yey
time *temps* ⓜ tom
tired *fatigué/fatiguée* ⓜ/① fa·tee·gey
tissues *mouchoirs en papier* ⓜ pl moo·shwar om pa·pyey
today *aujourd'hui* o·zhoor·dwee
toilet *toilettes* ① pl twa·let
tonight *ce soir* se swar
toothache *mal aux dents* ⓜ mal o don
toothbrush *brosse à dents* ① bros a don

toothpaste *dentifrice* ⓜ don·tee·frees
torch (flashlight) *lampe de poche* ① lomp de posh
tourist office *office de tourisme* ⓜ o·fees·de too·rees·me
towel *serviette* ① sair·vyet
travel agency *agence de voyage* ① a·zhons de vwa·yazh
travellers cheque *chèque de voyage* ⓜ shek de vwa·yazh
trousers *pantalon* ⓜ pon·ta·lon
twin beds *lits jumeaux* ⓜ pl dey lee zhew·mo
tyre *pneu* ⓜ pneu

V

vacant *libre* ⓜ & ① lee·bre
vegetable *légume* ⓜ ley·gewm
vegetarian a *végétarien/végétarienne* ⓜ/①
  vey·zhey·ta·ryun/vey·zhey·ta·ryen
visa *visa* ⓜ vee·za

W

waiter *serveur/serveuse* ⓜ/① sair·veur/sair·veurz
walk V *marcher* mar·shey
wallet *portefeuille* ⓜ por·te·feu·ye
warm a *chaud/chaude* ⓜ/① sho/shod
wash (something) *laver* la·vey
watch *montre* ① mon·tre
water *eau* ① o
we *nous* noo
west *ouest* ⓜ west
wheelchair *fauteuil roulant* ⓜ fo·teu·ye roo·lon
when *quand* kon
where *où* oo
who *qui* kee
why *pourquoi* poor·kwa
window *fenêtre* ① fe·ney·tre
wine *vin* ⓜ vun
with *avec* a·vek
without *sans* son
woman *femme* ① fam
write *écrire* ey·kreer

Y

you sg inf *tu* tew
you sg pol *vous* voo
you pl *vous* voo

Hausa

pronunciation

Vowels		Consonants	
Symbol	English sound	Symbol	English sound
a	run	b	bed
aa	father	b'	strong b with air sucked inward
ai	aisle	ch	cheat
aw	law	d	dog
ay	say	d'	strong d with air sucked inward
e	bet	g	go
ey	as in 'bet', but longer	h	hat
ee	see	j	jar
i	hit	k	kit
o	pot	k'	strong k
oo	zoo	l	lot
ow	now	m	man
u	put	n	not
'	like the pause in 'uh-oh' (comes before a vowel)	p	pet
		r	run
		s	sun
		sh	shot
		t	top
		ts'	as in 'lets', but spat out
		w	win
		y	yes
		y'	spat out y
		z	zero

In this chapter, the Hausa pronunciation is given in purple after each phrase. Each syllable is separated by a dot. For example:

Na gode.   naa gaw·dey

Hausa's glottalised consonants, simplified here as b', d', k', ts' and y', are made by tightening and releasing the space between the vocal cords when you pronounce the sound. The b' and d' sounds have an extra twist – instead of breathing out, you breathe in.

introduction

According to some scholars, the name 'Hausa' is derived from a phrase meaning 'to climb/ride the bull'. As one of the lingua francas of West Africa, Hausa (*Hausa* how·sa) is spoken by around 40 million people. For over half of these, Hausa is their first language. Most native speakers live in northern Nigeria and southern Niger, where Hausa is one of the national languages. There's a small community of native speakers in the Blue Nile area of Sudan, and it's also spoken in parts of Benin, Cameroon, and Ghana. Hausa is one of the Chadic languages (in the Afro-Asiatic language family), which came from the southern shores of Lake Chad in present-day northeastern Nigeria and northern Cameroon, and gradually migrated westward over the centuries. In the past, Hausa was written in *ajami*, a modified form of Arabic script, but since the early 19th century it has also been written in many areas with a slightly modified Roman alphabet. This alphabet, called *boko*, is now the official written form.

 **hausa** (native language)    **hausa** (generally understood)

language difficulties

Do you speak English?	Kana/Kina jin turanci? m/f	ka·naa/ki·naa jin too·ran·chee
Do you understand?	Ka/Kin gane? m/f	kaa/kin gaa·ney
I understand.	Na gane.	naa gaa·ney
I don't understand.	Ban gane ba.	ban gaa·ney ba
Could you please ...?	Za ka/ki iya ...? m/f	zaa ka/ki i·ya ...
repeat that	maimaita wannan	mai·mai·ta wan·nan
speak more slowly	yi magana sannu-sannu	yi ma·ga·naa san·nu·san·nu
write it down	rubuta wannan	ru·boo·ta wan·nan

time, dates & numbers

What time is it?	K'arfe nawa ne?	k'ar·fey na·wa ney
It's one o'clock.	K'arfe d'aya ne.	k'ar·fey d'a·ya ney
It's (two) o'clock.	K'arfe (biyu) ne.	k'ar·fey (bi·yu) ney
Quarter past (one).	K'arfe (d'aya) da kwata.	k'ar·fey (d'a·ya) da kwa·taa
Half past (one).	K'arfe (d'aya) da rabi.	k'ar·fey (d'a·ya) da ra·bee
Quarter to (eight).	(K'arfe takwas) ba kwata.	(k'ar·fey tak·was) baa kwa·taa
At what time ...?	K'arfe nawa ...?	k'ar·fey na·wa ...
At ...	A ...	a ...
It's (15 December).	Yau (sha biyar ga watan Disamba).	yow (shaa bi·yar ga wa·tan di·sam·ba)

yesterday	jiya	ji·ya
today	yau	yow
tomorrow	gobe	gaw·be

Monday	Littinin	lit·ti·nin
Tuesday	Talata	ta·laa·taa
Wednesday	Laraba	laa·ra·baa
Thursday	Alhamis	al·ha·mis
Friday	Juma'a	ju·ma·'aa
Saturday	Asabar	a·sa·bar
Sunday	Lahadi	la·ha·di

numbers

0	sifiri	si·fi·ree	15	(goma) sha biyar	(gaw·ma) shaa bi·yar
1	d'aya	d'a·ya	16	(goma) sha shida	(gaw·ma) shaa shi·da
2	biyu	bi·yu	17	(goma)	(gaw·ma)
3	uku	u·ku		sha bakwai	shaa bak·wai
4	hud'u	hu·d'u	18	(goma)	(gaw·ma)
5	biyar	bi·yar		sha takwas	shaa tak·was
6	shida	shi·da	19	(goma) sha tara	(gaw·ma) shaa ta·ra
7	bakwai	bak·wai	20	ashirin	a·shi·rin
8	takwas	tak·was	21	ashirin da d'aya	a·shi·rin da d'a·ya
9	tara	ta·ra	22	ashirin da biyu	a·shi·rin da bi·yu
10	goma	gaw·ma	30	talatin	ta·laa·tin
11	(goma)	(gaw·ma)	40	arba'in	ar·ba·'in
	sha d'aya	shaa d'a·ya	50	hamsin	ham·sin
12	(goma)	(gaw·ma)	60	sittin	sit·tin
	sha biyu	shaa bi·yu	70	saba'in	sa·ba·'in
13	(goma)	(gaw·ma)	80	tamanin	ta·maa·nin
	sha uku	shaa u·ku	90	tasa'in	ta·sa·'in
14	(goma)	(gaw·ma)	100	d'ari	d'a·ree
	sha hud'u	shaa hu·d'u	1000	dubu	du·boo

border crossing

I'm here ...	Na zo nan ...	naa zaw nan ...
in transit	don ya	don yaa
	da zango	da zan·goo
on business	don yin kasuwanci	don yin ka·su·wan·chee
on holiday	don yi hutu	don yi hoo·too
I'm here for ...	Zan yi ... a nan.	zan yi ... a nan
(10) days	kwana (goma)	kwaa·naa (gaw·ma)
(three) weeks	mako (uku)	maa·kaw (u·ku)
(two) months	wata (biyu)	waa·taa (bi·yu)

I'm going to (Zaria).
Za ni (Zazzau). zaa ni (zaz·zow)

I'm staying at the (Daula Hotel).
Ina zaune a (Daula Hotel). i·naa zow·ne a (dow·la haw·tel)

tickets

One ... ticket (to Zinder), please.	*Tikitin ... guda d'aya (zuwa Zandar), don Allah.*	ti·ki·tin ... gu·daa d'a·ya (zu·waa zan·dar) don al·laa
one-way	*zuwa*	zu·waa
return	*zuwa da dawowa*	zu·waa da daa·waw·waa

I'd like to ... my ticket, please.	*Ina son in ... tikitina, don Allah.*	i·naa son in ... ti·ki·ti·naa don al·laa
cancel	*soke*	saw·kye
change	*canja*	chan·ja
collect	*karb'i*	kar·b'i

I'd like a smoking/nonsmoking seat, please.
Ina son abin zama ga masu/   i·naa son a·bin za·maa ga maa·su/
marasa shan taba, don Allah.   ma·ra·saa shan taa·baa don al·laa

Is there a toilet?
Akwai ban d'aki?   a·kwai ban d'aa·kee

Is there air conditioning?
Akwai na'urar sanyaya d'aki?   a·kwai naa·'oo·rar san·ya·ya d'aa·kee

How long does the trip take?
Tafiyar za ta dad'e?   ta·fi·yar zaa ta da·d'ee

Is it a direct route?
Wannan ce hanya kai tsaye?   wan·nan chey han·yaa kai ts'a·ye

transport

Where does flight (BA527) arrive/depart?
A ina jirgin sama (BA 527)   a i·naa jir·gin sa·ma (bi ei faiv too se·ven)
zai sauka/tashi?   zai sow·kaa/taa·shi

How long will it be delayed?
Minti nawa zai makara?   min·tee na·wa zai ma·ka·ra

Is this the ... (to Maiduguri)? m/f	*Wannan ... (zuwa Maiduguri) ne/ce? m/f*	wan·nan ... (zu·waa mai·du·gu·ri) ney/chey
boat	*jirgin ruwa* m	jir·gin ru·waa
bus	*mota* f	maw·taa
plane	*jirgin sama* m	jir·gin sa·ma
train	*jirgin k'asa* m	jir·gin k'a·saa

How much is it to ...?
Nawa ne kud'in zuwa ...?
na·wa ney ku·d'in zu·waa ...

Please take me to (this address).
Ka/Ki d'auke ni zuwa (wurin mai lambar wannan adireshi), don Allah. m/f
ka/ki d'ow·key ni zu·waa (wu·ree mai lam·bar wan·nan a·di·rey·shee) don al·laa

I'd like to hire a ... (with air conditioning).
Ina son in yi hayar ... (tare da AC).
i·naa son in yi ha·yar ... (taa·re da ai·si)

   car   *mota*   maw·taa
   4WD   *mota mai juyawa da k'afa hud'u*   maw·taa mai joo·yaa·waa da k'a·faa hu·d'u

How much is it for (three) days/weeks?
Nawa ne kud'in na kwana/mako (uku)?
na·wa ney ku·d'in na kwaa·naa/maa·kaw (u·ku)

directions

Where's the (nearest) ...?
Ina ... (mafi kusa)?
i·naa ... (ma·fee ku·sa)

   internet café   *internet cafe*   in·tey·net ka·fey
   market   *kasuwa*   kaa·su·waa

Is this the road to (Lagos)?
Wannan hanya zuwa (Ikko) ce?
wan·nan han·ya zu·waa (ik·ko) chey

Can you show me (on the map)?
Za ka/ki iya nuna mini (a taswira)? m/f
za ka/ki i·ya noo·naa mi·ni (a tas·wi·raa)

What's the address?
Mene ne adireshin?
mey·ney ney a·di·rey·shin

How far is it?
Mil nawa ne?
mil na·wa ney

How do I get there?
Ina ne hanyar zuwa can?
i·naa ney han·yar zu·waa chan

Turn left/right.
Yi hagu/dama.
yi ha·gu/daa·ma

directions – HAUSA

83

It's ...	Ga shi/ta ... m/f	ga shi/ta ...
behind ...	bayan ...	baa·yan ...
in front of ...	gaban ...	ga·ban ...
near (to ...)	kusa (da ...)	ku·sa (da ...)
next to ...	daf da ...	daf da ...
on the corner	a kwana	a kwa·na
opposite ...	daura da ...	dow·ra da ...
straight ahead	mik'e sosai	mee·k'yey so·sai
there	can	chan

accommodation

Where's a ...?	Ina ... yake?	i·naa ... yak·yey
camping ground	wurin da aka kafa tanti-tanti	wu·rin da a·ka ka·fa tan·ti·tan·ti
guesthouse	gidan saukar bak'i	gi·dan sow·kar baa·k'ee
hotel	hotal	haw·tal
youth hostel	makwancin matasa	ma·kwan·chin ma·taa·saa

Can you recommend somewhere (cheap/good)?
Za ka/ki iya gaya mini ina za a
sami wani wuri (mai araha/kyau)? m/f

zaa ka/ki i·ya gaa·yaa mi·ni i·naa za a
saa·mi wa·ni wu·ree (mai a·ra·haa/kyow)

I'd like to book a room, please.
Ina son a kama mini d'aki,
don Allah.

i·naa son a kaa·maa mi·ni d'aa·kee
don al·laa

I have a reservation.
An kama mini d'aki a nan.

an kaa·maa mi·ni d'aa·kee a nan

Do you have a ... room?	Kana/Kina da d'aki ...? m/f	ka·naa/ki·naa da d'aa·kee ...
single	ga mutum d'aya	ga mu·tum d'a·ya
double	ga mutane biyu	ga mu·taa·ney bi·yu
twin	biyu wad'anda aka had'a su	bi·yu wa·d'an·da a·ka ha·d'a su

How much is it per ...?	Nawa ne kud'in ... d'aya?	na·wa ney ku·d'in ... d'a·ya
night	kwana	kwaa·naa
person	mutum	mu·tum

I'd like to stay for (two) nights.
Ina son in yi kwana (biyu) a nan. i·naa son in yi kwaa·naa (bi·yu) a nan

What time is check-out?
Yaushe zan fita daga d'aki? yow·she zan fi·ta da·ga d'aa·kee

Am I allowed to camp here?
Za a bar ni in d'an zauna a nan? zaa a bar ni in d'an zow·naa a nan

banking & communications

Note that in Nigeria, unless you have a Nigerian bank account, it will be difficult to do any of the following things, except for changing money.

I'd like to ...	*Ina son in ...*	i·naa son in ...
arrange a transfer	*aika da kud'i*	ai·kaa da ku·d'ee
cash a cheque	*chanja cek na banki*	chan·ja chek na ban·kee
	zuwa kud'i	zu·waa ku·d'ee
change a travellers cheque	*canja cek*	chan·ja chek
	zuwa kud'i	zu·waa ku·d'ee
change money	*canja kud'i*	chan·ja ku·d'ee
withdraw money	*karb'i kud'i*	kar·b'i ku·d'ee

I want to ...	*Ina son ...*	i·naa son ...
to call (Singapore)	*buga waya zuwa (Singapur)*	bu·ga wa·yaa zu·waa (sin·ga·pur)
reverse the charges	*mutumin da zan buga masa waya ya biya kud'in waya*	mu·tu·min da zan bu·ga ma·sa wa·yaa ya bi·ya ku·d'in wa·yaa
use a printer	*yin amfani da printer*	yin am·faa·nee da prin·ter
use the internet	*yin amfani da internet*	yin am·faa·nee da in·tey·net

How much is it per hour?
Nawa ne kud'in wannan don tsawon awa d'aya? na·wa ney ku·d'in wan·nan don ts'aa·won a·waa d'a·ya

How much does a (three-minute) call cost?
Nawa ne kud'in buga waya (wanda ya yi minti uku)? na·wa ney ku·d'in bu·ga wa·yaa (wan·da ya yi min·tee u·ku)

(30 naira) per minute/hour.
(Naira talatin) don tsawon minti/awa d'aya. (nai·ra ta·laa·tin) don ts'aa·won min·tee/a·waa d'a·ya

tours

When's the next ...?	Yaushe za a yi ...?	yow·she zaa a yi ...
day trip	tafiya ta kwana d'aya	ta·fi·yaa ta kwaa·naa d'a·ya
tour	zagaye	zaa·ga yey
Is ... included?	Akwai ... a kud'in nan?	ak·wai ... a ku·d'in nan
accommodation	masauki	ma·sow·kee
the admission charge	tikitocin shiga	ti·ki·taw·chin shi·ga
food	wasu wurare	wa·su wu·raa·rey
	abinci	a·bin·chi
transport	sufuri	su·fu·ree

How long is the tour?
Awa nawa za a yi zagayen?
a·wa na·wa zaa a yi zaa·ga·yen

What time should we be back?
K'arfe nawa za a koma?
k'ar·fey na·wa zaa a kaw·maa

shopping

I'm looking for ...
Ina neman ...
i·naa ne·man ...

I need film for this camera.
Ina son fim na wannan kyamara.
i·naa son fim na wan·nan kya·ma·ra

Can I listen to this?
Zan iya sauraron wannan?
zan i·ya sow·raa·ron wan·nan

Can I have my ... repaired?
Za ka/ki iya gyara mini ...? m/f
zaa ka/ki i·ya gya·raa mi·ni ...

When will it be ready?
Yaushe zan samu?
yow·she zan saa·moo

How much is it?
Kud'insa nawa ne?
ku·d'in·sa na·wa ney

Can you write down the price?
Za ka/ki iya rubuta mini nawa ne kud'insa? m/f
zaa ka/ki i·ya ru·boo·taa mi·ni na·wa ney ku·d'in·sa

What's your lowest price?
Mene ne kud'i na gaskiya?
mey·ney ney ku·d'ee na gas·ki·yaa

86

HAUSA – tours

I'll give you (five) naira.
Zan ba ka/ki Naira (biyar). m/f zan baa ka/ki nai·raa (bi·yar)

There's a mistake in the bill.
Akwai kuskure a bil. a·kwai kus·ku·rey a bil

It's faulty.
An yi kuskure. an yi kus·ku·rey

I'd like a refund, please.
Ina son a dawo mini da i·naa son a daa·waw mi·ni da
kud'ina, don Allah. ku·d'ee·naa don al·laa

I'd like a receipt, please.
Ba ni rasid'i, don Allah. baa ni raa·si·d'ee don al·laa

Could you ...? *Kana/Kina iya ...?* m/f ka·naa/ki·naa i·ya ...
  burn a CD from *sa abubuwa daga* sa a·boo·bu·waa da·ga
    my memory card *katin nan zuwa faifai* kaa·tin nan zu·waa fai·fai
  develop this *wanke wannan* wan·kye wa·nan
    film *fim* fim

making conversation

Hello. *Sannu.* san·nu
Good night. *Sai da safe.* say da saa·fe
Goodbye. *Sai wani lokaci.* say wa·ni law·ka·chee

Mr *Malam* maa·lam
Mrs/Ms/Miss *Malama* maa·la·maa

How are you?
Kana/Kina lafiya? m/f ka·naa/ki·naa laa·fi·yaa

Fine, and you?
Lafiya lau, kai/ke fa? m/f laa·fi·yaa low kai/kye fa

What's your name?
Ina sunanka/sunanki? m/f i·naa soo·nan·ka/soo·nan·ki

My name's ...
Sunana ... soo·naa·naa ...

I'm pleased to meet you.
Na ji murnar saduwa da kai/ke. m/f na ji mur·nar saa·du·waa da kai/kye

This is my ...	Wannan ... nawa/tawa. m/f	wan·nan ... naa·wa/taa·wa
boyfriend	saurayi	sow·ra·yee
daughter	y'a	y'aa
father	mahaifi	ma·hai·fee
friend	aboki m	a·baw·kee
girlfriend	budurwa	bu·dur·waa
husband	miji	mi·jee
mother	mahaifiya	ma·hai·fi·yaa
son	d'a	d'aa
wife	mata	maa·taa

Here's my ...	Ga ... nawa/tawa. m/f	gaa ... naa·wa/taa·wa
What's your ...?	Mene ne ...	mey·ney ney ...
address	adireshi(-nka/-nki m/f) m	a·di·rey·shi(·nka/·nki)
email address	adireshi(-nka/-nki m/f)	a·di·rey·shi(·nka/·nki)
	na i-mel m	na i·mel
phone number	lambar waya(-rka/-rki m/f) m	lam·bar wa·ya(·rka/·rki)

Where are you from?	Daga ina ka/kika fito? m/f	da·ga i·naa ka/·ki·ka fi·taw
I'm from ...	Na fito daga ...	naa fi·taw da·ga ...
Australia	Ostareliya	os·ta·rey·li·ya
Canada	Kyanada	kya·na·da
New Zealand	New Zeland	nyu zi·lan
the UK	Ingila	in·gi·la
the USA	Amirka	a·mir·ka

I'm married.	Ina da miji/mata. m/f	i·naa da mi·jee/maa·taa
I'm not married.	Ba ni da miji/mata. m/f	baa ni da mi·jee/maa·taa
Can I take a photo (of you)?	Zan iya d'aukar hoto(-nka/-nki)? m/f	zan i·ya d'ow·kar haw·taw(·nka/·nki)

eating out

Can you recommend a ...?	Za ka/ki iya gaya mini ... mai kyau? m/f	zaa ka/ki i·ya ga·yaa mi·ni ... mai kyow
bar	wurin shan giya	wu·rin shan gi·yaa
place to eat	wurin cin abinci	wu·rin chin a·bin·chi
dish	abinci	a·bin·chi

I'd like ..., please.	Ina son ..., don Allah.	i·naa son ... don al·laa
the bill	bil	bil
the menu	takardar bayyanin abinci	ta·kar·dar bay·ya·nin a·bin·chi
a table for (two)	tebur ga mutane (biyu)	tey·bur ga mu·taa·ney (bi·yu)
that dish	wannan abinci	wan·nan a·bin·chi

Do you have vegetarian food?	Kana/Kina da abinci maras nama? m/f	ka·naa/ki·naa da a·bin·chi maa·ras naa·maa

Could you prepare a meal without ...?	Kana/Kina iya yin abinci ba tare da ... ba? m/f	ka·naa/ki·naa i·ya yin a·bin·chi baa taa·re da ... ba
eggs	k'wai	k'wai
meat stock	nama	naa·maa

(cup of) coffee ...	kofi (guda d'aya) ...	kaw·fee (gu·daa d'a·ya) ...
(cup of) tea ...	shayi (guda d'aya) ...	shaa·yi (gu·daa d'a·ya) ...
with milk	da madara	da ma·da·raa
without sugar	ba sukari	baa su·ka·ree

(boiled) water	ruwa(-n da aka tafasa)	ru·wa(·n da a·ka ta·fa·saa)

emergencies

Help!	Taimake ni!	tai·ma·kyey ni

Call ...!	Kirawo ...!	ki·raa·waw ...
an ambulance	motar d'aukar maras lafiya	moo·tar d'ow·kar maa·ras laa·fi·yaa
a doctor	likita	li·ki·taa
the police	'yan sanda	'yan san·daa

Could you help me, please?
Kana iya ka taimake ni, don Alla. m   ka·naa i·ya ka tai·ma·kyey ni don al·laa
Kina iya ki taimake ni, don Alla. f   ki·naa i·ya ki tai·ma·kyey ni don al·laa

I'm lost.
Na manta hanya.   naa man·ta han·yaa

Where are the toilets?
Ina ban d'aki yake?   i·naa ban d'aa·kee yak·yey

I want to report an offence.
Ina son in sanar da ku wani laifi.   i·na son in sa·nar da koo wa·ni lai·fee

I have insurance.
Ina da inshora.
i·naa da in·shaw·raa

I want to contact my consulate/embassy.
Ina son in buga waya zuwa
ofishin jakadanci kasarmu.
i·naa son in bu·ga wa·yaa zu·waa
aw·fi·shin ja·kaa·dan·chee ka·sar·mu

I've been ...	An yi mini ...	an yi mi·ni ...
assaulted	farmaki	far·ma·kee
raped	fyad'e	fyaa·d'ey
robbed	sata	saa·taa

My ... was/were stolen.	An sace mini ...	an saa·chey mi·ni ...
bags	kaya	kaa·yaa
credit card	katin adashin banki	kaa·tin a·daa·shin ban·kee
jewellery	kayan ado	kaa·yan a·daw
money	kud'i	ku·d'ee
passport	fasfo	fas·faw
travellers cheques	cek	chek
wallet	alabe	a·la·bey

medical needs

Where's the nearest ...?	Ina ne/ce ... mafi kusa? m/f	i·naa ney/chey ... ma·fee ku·sa
dentist	likitan hak'ori m	li·ki·tan ha·k'aw·ree
doctor	likita m	li·ki·ta
hospital	asibiti f	a·si·bi·ti
pharmacist	kantin magani m	kan·tin maa·ga·nee

I need a doctor (who speaks English).
Ina bukatar likita
(wanda yake jin Turanci).
i·naa bu·kaa·tar li·ki·ta
(wan·da yak·yey jin too·ran·chee)

Could I see a female doctor?
Zan iya ganin likita mace?
zan i·ya ga·nin li·ki·ta ma·che

It hurts here.
Na ji ciwo a nan.
naa ji chee·waw a nan

I'm allergic to (penicillin).
An hana ni yin amfani
da (penisilin).
an ha·naa ni yin am·faa·nee
da (pe·ni·si·lin)

english–hausa dictionary

Hausa nouns in this dictionary have their gender marked with ⓜ (masculine) or ⓕ (feminine). If it's a plural noun, you'll also see pl. Note that some adjectives have only one form for both genders. Words are also marked as n (noun), a (adjective), v (verb), sg (singular) and pl (plural) where necessary.

A

accommodation *masauki* ⓜ ma-sow-kee
adaptor *macanjin wuta* ⓜ ma-chan-jin wu-taa
after *bayan* baa-yan
airport *filin jirgin sama* ⓕ fee-lin jir-gin sa-ma
alcohol *barasa* ⓕ baa-raa-saa
all *duk* duk
and *da* da
ankle *idon k'afa* ⓜ i-don k'a-fa
arm *hannu* ⓜ han-noo
asthma *ciwon asma* ⓜ chi-won as-maa

B

baby *jariri* ⓜ jaa-ree-ree
back (body) *baya* ⓜ baa-yaa
backpack *jakar baya* ⓕ ja-kar baa-yaa
bad *maras kyau* ma-ras kyow
bank *banki* ⓜ ban-kee
bathroom *ban d'aki* ⓜ ban d'aa-kee
battery *batir* ⓜ baa-tir
beautiful *mai kyau* mai kyow
bed *gado* ⓜ ga-daw
beer *giya* ⓕ gi-yaa
bees *zuma* ⓜ zu-maa
before *kafin* kaa-fin
bicycle *keke* ⓜ kyey-kyey
big *babba/manya* ⓜ/ⓕ bab-ba/man-yaa
blanket *bargo* ⓜ bar-gaw
blood group *irin jini* ⓜ i-rin ji-nee
bottle *kwalaba* ⓕ kwa-la-baa
bottle opener *mabud'in kwalaba* ⓜ
   ma-boo-d'in kwa-la-baa
boy *yaro* ⓜ yaa-raw
brakes (car) *birki* ⓜ bir-kee
breakfast *karin kumallo* ⓜ ka-rin ku-mal-law
bronchitis *mashak'o* ⓜ maa-shaa-k'aw

C

cancel *soke* saw-key
can opener *mabud'in gwangwani* ⓜ
   ma-boo-d'in gwan-gwa-nee
cash *kud'i* ⓜ ku-d'ee
cell phone *salula* ⓕ sa-loo-laa
centre *tsakiya* ⓕ ts'a-ki-yaa
cheap *mai araha* mai a-ra-haa
check (bill) *lissafi* ⓜ lis-saa-fee
chest *k'irji* ⓜ k'ir-jee
child *yaro* ⓜ yaa-raw
cigarette *taba* ⓕ taa-baa
city *birni* ⓜ bir-nee
clean a *mai tsabta* mai ts'ab-taa
closed a *rufe* a ru-fe
cold a *mai sanyi* mai san-yee
condom *roba* ⓜ raw-baa
constipation *kumburin ciki* ⓜ kum-bu-rin chi-kee
cough *tari* ⓜ taa-ree
currency exchange *canjin kud'i* ⓜ chan-jin ku-d'ee
customs (immigration) *kwastan* ⓜ kwas-tan

D

dangerous *mai had'ari* mai ha-d'a-ree
date (time) *kwanan wata* ⓜ kwaa-nan wa-taa
day (24 hours) *kwana* ⓜ kwaa-naa
daytime *rana* ⓕ raa-naa
diaper *banten jinjiri* ⓜ ban-ten jin-ji-ree
diarrhoea *gudawa* ⓕ gu-daa-waa
dinner *abincin dare* ⓜ a-bin-chin da-re
dirty *mai daud'a* mai dow-d'aa
disabled *nak'asasshe* na-k'a-sash-shey
double bed *gado ga mutane biyu* ⓜ
   ga-daw ga mu-taa-ney bi-yu
drink *abin sha* ⓜ a-bin sha
drivers licence *lasin tuk'i* ⓜ laa-sin too-k'ee
drug (illicit) *mugun k'waya* ⓜ moo-gun k'waa-yaa

E

ear *kunne* ⓜ kun-ney
east *gabas* ⓜ ga-bas
economy class *sikinkila* ⒻＦ si-kin-ki-la
elevator *lifta* ⒻＦ lif-taa
email *wasik'ar i-mel* ⒻＦ wa-see-k'ar ee-mel
English (language) *Turanci* ⓜ too-ran-chee
exchange rate *k'arfin kud'i* ⓜ k'ar-fin ku-d'ee
exit *mafita* ⒻＦ ma-fi-taa
expensive *mai tsada* mai ts'aa-daa
eye *ido* ⓜ i-daw

F

fast *mai sauri* mai sow-ree
fever *zazzab'i* ⓜ zaz-za-b'ee
finger *yatsa* ⒻＦ yaa-ts'aa
first class *faskila* fas-ki-la
fish *kifi* ⓜ kee-fee
food *abinci* ⓜ a-bin-chi
foot *k'afa* ⒻＦ k'a-faa
fork *cokali mai yatsu* ⓜ chaw-ka-lee mai yaa-ts'oo
free (of charge) *a kyauta* a kyow-taa
fruit *'ya'yan itace* pl y'a-y'an i-taa-chey
funny *mai ban dariya* mai ban daa-ri-yaa

G

game park *wurin shak'atawa* ⓜ wu-rin shaa-k'a-ta-waa
gift *kyauta* ⒻＦ kyow-taa
girl *yarinya* ⒻＦ yaa-rin-yaa
glass *kofi* ⓜ kaw-fee
glasses *tabarau* ⓜ ta-baa-row
good *mai kyau* mai kyow
guide n *ja-gora* ⓜ jaa-gaw-ra

H

hand *hannu* ⓜ han-noo
happy *mai farin ciki* mai fa-rin chi-kee
he *shi* shee
head *kai* ⓜ kai
headache *ciwon kai* ⓜ chee-won kai
heart *zuciya* ⒻＦ zoo-chi-yaa
heart condition *halin zuciya* ⓜ haa-lin zoo-chi-yaa
heat *zafi* ⓜ zaa-fee
here *nan* nan

high *dogo/doguwa* ⓜ/ⒻＦ daw-gaw/daw-gu-waa
highway *babbar hanya* ⒻＦ bab-bar han-yaa
homosexual n *d'an daudu* ⓜ d'an dow-du
hot *mai zafi* mai zaa-fee
hungry *mai jin yunwa* mai jin yun-waa

I

I *ni* nee
identification (card) *katin shaida* ⒻＦ kaa-tin shai-daa
ill *maras lafiya* ma-ras laa-fi-yaa
important *muhimmi/muhimmiya* ⓜ/ⒻＦ mu-him-mee/mu-him-mi-yaa
interpreter *mai fassara* ⓜ mai fas-sa-raa

K

key *makulli* ⓜ ma-kul-lee
kilogram *kilo* ⓜ ki-law
kitchen (modern) *kicin* ⓜ ki-chin
kitchen (traditional) *madafa* ⒻＦ ma-da-faa
knife *wuk'a* ⒻＦ wu-k'aa

L

laundry (place) *mawanka* ⒻＦ ma-wan-kaa
lawyer *lauya* ⓜ low-yaa
leg *k'afa* ⒻＦ k'a-faa
lesbian n *y'ar mad'igo* ⒻＦ y'ar maa-d'i-gaw
less (do less) v *rage* rag-yey
letter (mail) *wasik'a* ⒻＦ wa-see-k'aa
like v *so* so
love v *so* so
lunch *abincin rana* ⓜ a-bin-chin raa-naa

M

man *mutum* ⓜ mu-tum
matches *ashana* ⒻＦ a-shaa-naa
meat *nama* ⓜ naa-maa
medicine *magani* ⓜ maa-ga-nee
message *sak'o* ⓜ saa-k'aw
mobile phone *salula* ⒻＦ sa-loo-laa
month *wata* ⓜ waa-taa
morning *safiya* saa-fi-yaa
(in the) morning *safe* saa-fe
motorcycle *babur* ⓜ baa-bur
motorcycle taxi *acaba* ⒻＦ a-cha-baa

mouth *baki* ⓜ baa-kee
movie *fim* ⓜ fim
museum *gidan kayan tarihi* ⓜ
gi-dan kaa-yan taa-ree-hee
music *kad'e-kad'e* pl ka-d'ey-k'a-dey

N

name *suna* ⓜ soo-naa
napkin *takardar goge hannu* ⓕ ta-kar-dar gaw-ge
han-noo
nappy *banten jinjiri* ban-ten jin-ji-ree
national park *gandun daji* ⓜ gan-dun daa-jee
nausea *tashin zuciya* ⓕ taa-shin zoo-chi-yaa
neck *wuya* ⓕ wu-yaa
new *sabo/sabuwa* ⓜ/ⓕ saa-baw/saa-bu-waa
news *labari* ⓜ laa-baa-ree
newspaper *jarida* ⓕ ja-ree-daa
night *dare* da-rey
nightclub *kulob* ku-lob
noisy *mai k'ara* mai k'aa-raa
nonsmoking *ga marasa shan taba*
ga ma-ra-saa shan taa-baa
north *arewa* ⓕ a-rey-wa
nose *hanci* ⓜ han-chee
now *yanzu* yan-zu
number *lamba* ⓕ lam-baa
nuts *gyad'a* ⓕ gya-d'aa

O

oil (engine) *man inji* ⓜ man in-jee
OK *shi ke nan* shee kyey nan
old *tsoho/tsohuwa* ⓜ/ⓕ tsaw-haw/tsaw-hu-waa
open a *a bude* a boo-de
outside *waje* wa-je

P

package *k'unshi* ⓜ k'un-shee
pain *ciwo* ⓜ chee-waw
palace *fad'a* ⓕ faa-d'a
paper *takarda* ⓕ ta-kar-daa
park (car) v *ajiye* a-ji-ye
passport *fasfo* ⓜ fas-fo
pay v *biya* bi-yaa
pen *biro* ⓜ bee-raw
petrol *man fetur* ⓜ man fey-tur

pharmacy *kantin magani* ⓜ kan-tin maa-ga-nee
plate *faranti* ⓕ fa-ran-tee
postcard *katin gaisuwa* ⓕ kaa-tin gai-su-waa
post office *gidan waya* ⓜ gi-dan wa-yaa
pregnant *mai juna biyu* mai joo-naa bi-yu

Q

quiet *mai shiru* mai shi-roo

R

rain *ruwan sama* ⓜ ru-wan sa-ma
razor (modern) *reza* ⓕ rey-zaa
razor (traditional) *aska* ⓕ as-kaa
registered mail *wasik'a ta rajista* ⓕ
wa-see-k'aa ta ra-jis-taa
rent v *yi hayar* yi ha-yar
repair v *gyara* gyaa-raa
reservation (room) *kama d'aki* kaa-ma d'aa-kee
restaurant *gidan cin abinci* ⓜ gi-dan chin a-bin-chi
return v *koma* kaw-maa
road *hanya* ⓕ han-yaa
room *d'aki* ⓜ d'aa-kee

S

sad *mai bak'in ciki* mai ba-k'in chi-kee
safe (not dangerous) a *mai lafiya* mai laa-fi-yaa
safe (reliable) a *mai aminci* mai a-min-chee
seafood *abinci daga teku* a-bin-chi da-ga tey-ku
seat *abin zama* ⓜ a-bin za-maa
send *aika da* ai-kaa da
sex (gender) *jinsi* ⓜ jin-see
sex (intercourse) *jima'i* ⓜ ji-maa-'ee
shampoo *shamfu* ⓜ sham-fu
shaving cream *sabulu na aski* saa-bu-lu na as-kee
she *ita* i-ta
sheet (bed) *zanen gado* ⓜ za-nen ga-daw
shirt (modern) *taguwa* ⓕ ta-gu-waa
shirt (long traditional) *riga* ⓕ ree-gaa
shoes *takalma* taa-kal-maa
shop *kanti* ⓜ kan-tee
shower *shawa* ⓕ shaa-waa
skin *fata* ⓕ faa-taa
skirt (modern) *siket* si-ket
skirt (traditional) *zane* ⓜ za-ney
sleep v *yi barci* yi bar-chee

small *k'arami/k'arama* ⓜ/ⓕ k'a-ra-mee/k'a-ra-maa
soap *sabulu* ⓜ saa-bu-loo
some *kad'an* ka-d'an
soon *an jima* an ji-maa
sore throat *miki* ⓜ mee-kee
south *kudu* ⓜ ku-du
speak *yi magana* yi ma-ga-naa
spoon *cokali* chaw-ka-lee
stamp *kan sarki* ⓜ kan sar-kee
station (train) *tasha(-r jirgin k'asa)* ⓕ ta-sha(-r jir-gin k'a-saa)
stomach *ciki* ⓜ chi-kee
stop v *tsaya* ts'a-yaa
stop (bus) *tasha(-r mota)* ⓕ ta-sha(-r mo-taa)
street (in general) *hanya* ⓕ han-yaa
street (paved only) *titi* ⓕ tee-tee
student *d'alibi/d'aliba* ⓜ/ⓕ d'a-li-bee/d'aa-li-baa
swim v *yi iyo* yi i-yaw

T

teeth *hak'ora* pl ha-k'aw-raa
telephone *waya* ⓕ wa-yaa
television *talabijin* ⓕ ta-la-bi-jin
temperature (weather) *yanayi* ya-na-yee
tent *tanti* ⓜ tan-tee
that (one) *wancan/waccan* ⓜ/ⓕ wan-chan/wach-chan
they *su* soo
thirsty *mai jin k'ishirwa* mai jin k'i-shir-waa
this (one) *wannan* ⓜ&ⓕ wan-nan
throat *mak'ogwaro* ⓜ ma-k'aw-gwa-raw
ticket *tikiti* ti-ki-ti
time *lokaci* law-ka-chee
tired *mai gajiya* mai ga-ji-yaa
tissues *takardun share majina* pl ta-kar-dun shaa-re maa-ji-naa
today *yau* yow
toilet *ban d'aki* ⓜ ban d'aa-kee
tonight *yau da dare* yow da da-re
toothache *ciwon hak'ora* chi-won ha-k'aw-raa
toothbrush *buroshin goge baki* ⓜ bu-raw-shin gaw-gye baa-kee
toothpaste *man goge hak'ora* ⓜ man gaw-ge ha-k'aw-raa

torch (flashlight) *tocilan* ⓕ taw-chi-lan
towel *tawul* ⓕ taa-wul
translate *fassara* fas-sa-raa
travellers cheque *cek* ⓜ chek
trousers *wando* ⓜ wan-daw
tyre *taya* ⓕ taa-yaa

U

underwear (underpants) *kamfai* ⓜ kam-fai
urgent *na/ta gaggawa* ⓜ/ⓕ na/ta gag-gag-waa

V

vacant *wanda ba kome a wurin* wan-da baa kaw-mey a wu-rin
vegetarian a *ga wanda ba ya cin nama* ga wan-da ba baa yaa chin naa-maa

W

waiter *sabis* ⓜ&ⓕ saa-bis
walk v *yi yawo* yi yaa-waw
wallet *alabe* ⓜ a-la-bey
warm a *mai d'umi* mai d'u-mee
wash (something) *wanke* wan-kyey
watch *kallo* ⓜ kal-law
water *ruwa* ⓜ ru-waa
we *mu* moo
west *yamma* ⓕ yam-ma
wheelchair *keken gurgu* ⓜ key-ken gur-goo
when *yaushe* yow-shey
where *ina* i-naa
who *wane ne* waa-ney ney
why *saboda me* sa-baw-da mey
window *taga* ⓕ taa-gaa
wine *giya* ⓕ gi-yaa
wine (palm) *bammi* ⓜ bam-mee
with *tare da* taa-re da
without *ba tare da . . . ba* baa taa-re da . . . ba
woman *mace* ⓕ ma-che
write *rubuta* ru-boo-taa

Y

you sg *kai/ke* ⓜ/ⓕ kai/kyey
you pl *ku* koo

Malagasy

pronunciation

Vowels		Consonants	
Symbol	English sound	Symbol	English sound
aa	father	b	bed
ai	aisle	d	dog
e	bet	dz	adze
i	hit	f	fun
o	pot	g	go
ow	now	h	hat
u	put	k	kit
		l	lot
		m	man
		n	not
		ng	ring
		p	pet
		r	run
		s	sun
		t	top
		v	very
		w	win
		y	yes
		z	zero

In this chapter, the Malagasy pronunciation is given in pink after each phrase.

The pronunciation of Malagasy words is not always obvious from their written form. Unstressed syllables can be elided (dropped) and words may be pronounced in different ways depending on where they fall in a sentence. If you follow the pink pronunciation guides you can't go wrong, however.

Each syllable is separated by a dot, and the syllable stressed in each word is italicised.

For example:

Misaotra.   mi-*sotr*

introduction

As the official language of Madagascar, Malagasy (*malagasy* maa-*laa*-gaas) has around 18 million speakers. Malagasy belongs to the Malayo-Polynesian branch of the Austronesian language family and is unrelated to its neighbouring African languages. Its closest relative is the little-known Ma'anyan, a language from southern Borneo, with which it shares over 90 per cent of its vocabulary. This close relationship exists because Madagascar was first settled by Indonesians from southern Borneo. Over the centuries, the language has also been influenced by English and French – first in the 19th century by British and French missionaries, and later as a result of colonisation by the French in the first half of the 20th century. With proverbs like 'If a tree is good to be used for making a boat, it is because it grew on good soil' (*Ny hazo no vanon-ko lakana, dia ny tany naniriany no tsara* ni *haa*-zu nu va-nun-*ku laa*-kaa-naa de ni *taa*-ni naa-ni-*ri*-ni nu tsaar), Madagascar's language is just as colourful and fascinating as its wildlife, landscapes and people.

■ **malagasy** (native language)

language difficulties

Do you speak English?	Miteny anglisy ve ianao?	mi·ten aan·gi·lis ve i·aa·now
Do you understand?	Azonao ve?	aa·zu·now ve
I (don't) understand.	(Tsy) Azoko.	(tsi) aa·zuk
Could you please ...?	Mba afaka ... azafady?	mbaa aa·faak ... aa·zaa·faad
repeat that	averinao ve izany	aa·ve·ri·now ve i·zaan
speak more slowly	miteny miadana kokoa ve ianao	mi·ten mi·aa·daan ku·ku ve i·aa·now
write it down	soratanao ve izany	su·raa·taa·now ve i·zaan

time, dates & numbers

What time is it?	Amin'ny firy izao?	aa·min·ni·fi ri·zow
It's one o'clock.	Amin'ny iray ora izao.	aa·min·ni rai ur i·zow
It's (two) o'clock.	Amin'ny (roa) izao.	aa·min·ni (ru) i·zow
Quarter past (one).	(Iray) sy fahefany.	(rai) si faa·he·faan
Half past (one).	(Iray) sy sasany.	(rai) si saa·saan
Quarter to (eight).	(Valo) latsaka fahefany.	(vaal) laat·saa·kaa faa·he·faan
At what time ...?	Amin'ny firy ...?	aa·min·ni fir ...
At ...	Amin'ny ...	aa·min·ni ...
It's (15 December).	(Dimy ambinifolo Desambra) androany.	(dim aam·bin·ful de·saam·braa) aan·dru·aan

yesterday	omaly	u·maal
today	androany	aan·dru·aan
tomorrow	rahampitso	raa·haam·pits

Monday	Alatsinainy	aa·laat·si·nain
Tuesday	Talata	taa·laat
Wednesday	Alarobia	aa·laa·ru·bi
Thursday	Alakamisy	aa·laa·kaa·mis
Friday	Zomà	zu·maa
Saturday	Asabotsy	aa·saa·buts
Sunday	Alahady	aa·laa·haad

0	aotra	ow·traa	16	enina	e·ni·
1	isa/iray	i·saa/i·rai		ambinifolo	naam·bin·ful
2	roa	ru	17	fito	fi·tu·
3	telo	tel		ambinifolo	aam·bin·ful
4	efatra	e·faatr	18	valo	vaa·lu·
5	dimy	dim		ambinifolo	aam·bin·ful
6	enina	e·nin	19	sivy ambinifolo	si·vi·aam·bin·ful
7	fito	fit	20	roapolo	ru·aa·pul
8	valo	vaal	21	iraika	i·rai·
9	sivy	siv		ambiroampolo	kaam·bi·ro·pu
10	folo	ful	22	roa	ru
11	iraika	i·rai·		ambiroampolo	aam·bi·ro·pul
	ambinifolo	kaam·bin·ful	30	telopolo	te·lu·pul
12	roa	ru	40	efapolo	e·faa·pul
	ambinifolo	aam·bin·ful	50	dimampolo	di·maam·pul
13	telo	tel	60	enimpolo	e·ni·pul
	ambinifolo	aam·bin·ful	70	fitopolo	fi·tu·pul
14	efatra	e·faa·traam·	80	valopolo	vaa·lu·pul
	ambinifolo	bin·ful	90	sivifolo	si·vi·ful
15	dmy	dim	100	zato	zaat
	iambinifolo	aam·bin·ful	1000	arivo	aa·riv

border crossing

I'm here ...	... aho no eto.	... ow nu et
in transit	Mandalo fotsiny	maan·da·lu fut·sin
on business	Manao raharaha	maa·now raa·haa·raa
on holiday	Miala sasatra	mi·aa·laa saa·saatr

I'm here for ...	... aho no eto.	... ow nu et
(10) days	(Folo) andro	(ful) aandr
(three) weeks	(Telo) herinandro	(tel) he·ri·naandr
(two) months	(Roa) volana	(ru) vu·laan

I'm going to (Mahajanga).
Ho any (Mahajanga) aho.   ho aan (maa·haa·dzaang) ow

I'm staying at (the Zahamotel).
Mipetraka ao amin'ny (Zahamotel) aho. mi·pe·traa·kow aa·min·ni (zaa·mo·tel) ow

tickets

A ... ticket (to Toliary), please.	Tapakila ... iray (mankany Toliary), azafady.	taa-paa-*kil* ... *i*-rai (*maa*-kaan tu-*li*-iaar) aa-zaa-*faad*
one-way	mandroso	*maan*-drus
return	miverina	mi-*ve*-rin

I'd like to ... my ticket, please.	Mba te ... ny tapakilako aho, azafady.	mbaa te ... ni taa-paa-*ki*-laa-ku ow aa-zaa-*faad*
cancel	hanafoana	haa-naa-*fo*-naa
change	hanolo	*haa*-nul
collect	haka	*haa*-kaa

I'd like a ... seat, please.	Toerana ho an'ny ... no mba tiako, azafady.	tu-*e*-raa-naa u *aan*-ni ... nu mbaa *ti*-ku aa-zaa-*faad*
nonsmoking	tsy mifoka sigara	tsi mi-*fuk* si-gaar
smoking	mifoka	mi-*fuk*

Is there a toilet/air conditioning?
Misy efitra fidiovan/kilimatizera ve?   *mi*-si e-fi-traa fi-di-*u*-vaan/kli-*maa*-ti-zer ve

How long does the trip take?
Hafiriana ny dia?   haa-fi-*ri*-naa ni di

Is it a direct route?
Tsy mijanojanona ve?   tsi mi-dzaa-nu-*dzaa*-nu-naa ve

transport

Where does the (Air Madagascar) flight arrive/depart?
Aiza ny sidina (Air Madagascar) no tonga/miainga?   *ai*-zaa ni si-di-naa (air maa-daa-*gaa*-si-kaar) nu *tun*-gaa/mi-*ain*-gaa

How long will it be delayed?
Hafiriana ny fahatarany?   haa-fi-*ri*-naa ni faa-haa-*taa*-raan

Is this the ... to (Toamasina)?	Ity ve ny ... mankany (Toamasina)?	i-*ti* ve ni ... maa-*kaan* (to-*maa*-sin)
boat	sambo	saamb
bus	aotobisy	o-*to*-bis
plane	roaplanina	ro-plaan
train	lamasinina	laa-*maa*-sin

How much is it to …?
Ohatrinona ny …? o·*trin*·naa ni …

Please take me to (this address).
Mba ento any amin' mbaa *en*·tu aa·ni *aa*·min
(ityadiresy ity) aho azafady. (tiaa·di·*res* ti) ow aa·zaa·*faad*

I'd like to hire a car/4WD (with air conditioning).
Mba te hanarama fiara/4x4 mbaa te haa·naa·*raa*·maa fi·aar/kaat·*kaat*·raa
(misy kilimatizera) aho azafady. (mis kli·*maa*·ti·zer) ow aa·zaa·*faad*

How much is it for (three) days/weeks?
Ohatrinona ny (telo) o·*trin*·naa ni (*te*·lu)
andro/herinandro? *aan*·dru/he·ri·*naan*·dru

directions

Where's the (nearest) …?	*Aiza ny … (akaiky indrindra)?*	*ai*·zaa ni … (aa·*kaik* in·*drin*·draa)
internet café	*sibera*	*si*·ber
market	*tsena*	tsen

Is this the road to (Antsirabe)?
Ity ve ny lalana mankany (Antsirabe)? i·*ti* ve ni *laa*·laan maa·*kaan* (aan·tsi·raa·*be*)

Can you show me (on the map)?
Afaka asehonao ahy *aa*·faak aa·se·u·*now* waa
(eoamin'ny sarintany) ve? (e·uaa·min·*ni* saa·rin·*taan*) ve

What's the address?
Inona ny adiresy? *i*·nu·naa ni aa·di·*res*

How far is it?
Hafiriana avy eto? haa·fi·*ri*·naa *aa*·vi et

How do I get there?
Ahoana no lalako mankany? ow·*o*·naa nu *laa*·laa·ku *maa*·kaan

Turn left/right.
Mivilia ankavia/ankavanana. mi·vi·*li* aan·kaa·*vi*/aan·kaa·*vaa*·naan

It's ...	... ilay izy.	... i·lai iz
behind ...	Ao ambadiky ny ...	ow aam·baa·di·ki ni ...
in front of ...	Manoloana ny ...	maa·nu·lo·naa ni ...
near (to ...)	Akaiky ny	aa·kai·ki ni
next to ...	Manaraka ny	maa·naa·raa·kaa ni
on the corner	Eo an-jorony	e·waan·dzu·run
opposite ...	Mifanatrika ...	mi·faa·naa·trik ...
straight ahead	Mandeha mahitsy	maan·de maa·hits
there	Eo	e·u

accommodation

Where's a ...?	Aiza no misy ...?	ai·zaa nu mis ...
camping ground	toerana filasiana	tu·e·raan fi·laa·si·naa
guesthouse	tranom-bahiny	traa·num·baa·hin
hotel	hôtely	o·tel
youth hostel	fandraisana Tanora	faan·drai·saa·naa taa·nur

Can you recommend somewhere cheap/good?
Afaka manoro ahy toerana · aa·faa·kaa maa·nur waa tu·e·raa·naa
mora/tsara ve ianao? · mu·raa/tsaa·raa ve i·aa·now

I'd like to book a room, please.
Mba te hamandrika efitra · mbaa te haa·maan·dri·kaa e·fi·traa
iray aho, azafady. · rai ow aa·zaa·faad

I have a reservation.
Manana famandrihana iray aho. · maa·naa·naa faa·maan·dri·haa·naa rai ow

Do you have	Misy ... ve ato aminao	mis ... ve aat·waa·mi·now
a ... room?	efitra iray ...?	e·fi·traa i·rai ...
single	ho an'olon-tokana	waa·nu·lun·dru
double	misy fandriana lehibe	mis faan·dri·naa le·hi·be
twin	misy fandriana kely	mis faan·dri·naa kel

How much is it per night/person?
Ohatrinona isan' alina/olona? · o·trin i·saan aa·lin/u·lun

I'd like to stay for (two) nights.
Mba saika hipetraka (roa) alina aho. · mbaa sai·kaa i·pe·traa·kaa (ru) aa·li·now

What time is check-out?
Amin'ny firy no   aa·min·*ni* fir nu
fara-famerenana lakile?   faa·raa·faa·me·*re*·na·naa laa·ki·*le*

Am I allowed to camp here?
Mahazo milasy eto ve aho?   maa·*haa*·zu mi·*laas* e·tu ve *ow*

banking & communications

I'd like to ...	*Mba te ... aho azafady.*	mbaa te ... ow aa·zaa·*faad*
arrange a transfer	*hikarakara*	hi·kaa·*raa*·kaar
	famindram-bola	faa·min·*draam*·bul
cash a cheque	*hanakalo seky*	haa·naa·*kaa*·lu *se*·ki
change a travellers	*hanakalo seky de*	haa·naa·*kaa*·lu *se*·ki de
cheque	*voiazy*	vo·*yaa*·zi
change money	*hanakalo vola*	haa·naa·*kaa*·lu *vu*·laa
withdraw money	*hisintona vola*	hi·*sin*·tu·naa *vu*·laa

I want to ...	*Te ... aho.*	te ... ow
buy a phonecard	*hividy karatra*	*hi*·vid kaa·raa·traa
	telefaonina	te·le·*fon*
call (Singapore)	*hiantso an'l*	hi·*aan*·tsu aa·ni
	(Singapore)	(sin·gaa·*pur*)
reverse the	*hanafaona ny*	haa·naa·*fo*·naa ni
charges	*sarany*	*saa*·raa·ni
use the intenet	*hampiasa emprimanty*	haam·pi·*aas* em·pri·*maan*·ti
use a printer	*hijery enterinety*	hi·*dze*·ri en·*ter*·net

How much is it per hour?
Ohatrinona ny adiny iray?   o·*trin*·naa ni *aa*·din rai

How much does a (three-minute) call cost?
Ohatrinona ny miantso (telo minitra)?   o·*trin*·naa ni mi·*aant*·su (tel *mi·ni·*traa)

(One ariary) per minute.
(Ariary) ny iray minitra.   (aa·*ri*·aar) ni *i*·rai mi·*ni*·traa

tours

When's the	*Rahoviana ny*	row·*vi*·naa ni
next ...?	*... manaraka?*	... maa·*naa*·raa·kaa
day trip	*dia atoandro*	di aa·*tu*·aan·dru
tour	*toro*	tur

Is ... included?	*Ao antiny ve ...?*	ow aa·*naa*·ti·ni ve ...
accommodation	*ny toerana ipetrahana*	ni tu·e·raa·ni·*pe*·traa·haan
the admission charge	*ny vidim-pidirana*	ni vi·dim·pi·*di*·raan
food	*sakafo*	*saa*·kaaf
transport	*fitaterana*	fi·taa·*te*·raan

How long is the tour?
Hafiriana ny toro? — haa·fi·*ri*·naa ni tur

What time should we be back?
Amin'ny firy isika no
tokony ho tafaverina? — aa·min·ni fi·ri·si·kaa nu
tu·kun nu taa·faa·*ve*·rin

shopping

I'm looking for ...
Mitady ... aho. — mi·*taa*·di ... ow

I need film for this camera.
Mila pelikiola ho an'ity
fakantsary ity aho. — *mi*·laa pe·*li*·ki·ul waa·ni·*ti*
faa·*kaan*·tsaa·ri·*ti* ow

Can I listen to this?
Azoko henoina ve ity? — aa·zuk we·*nu*·naa ve i·*ti*

Can I have my ... repaired?
Afaka amboarina ve ny ... -ko? — aa·faa·kaamb·*waa*·rin ve ni ... ·ku

When will it be ready?
Rahoviana no vita? — row·*vi*·naa nu *vi*·taa

How much is it?
Ohatrinona? — o·*trin*

Can you write down the price?
Mba afaka soratanao ve ny vidiny? — mbaa *aa*·faa·kaa su·raa·*taa*·now ve ni *vi*·din

What's your lowest price?
Ohatrinona ny vidiny farany? — o·*trin*·naa ni *vi*·din *faa*·raan

I'll give you (five) ariary.
Omeko Ariary (dimy) ianao. — u·*me*·ku aa·ri·aa·ri (*di*·mi) *aa*·now

There's a mistake in the bill.
Miso diso ny fakitiora.　　　mis *di*·su ni faak·*tu*·raa

It's faulty.
Tsy marina io.　　　tsi maa·ri·*ni*·u

I'd like a receipt, please.
Mba mila resiò aho, azafady.　　　mbaa *mi*·laa re·si·*u* ow aa·zaa·*faad*

Do you accept …?	*Mandray … ve ianao?*	maan·*drai* … ve *i*·aa·now
credit cards	*karatra kiredy*	kaa·raa·traa kre·*di*
travellers cheques	*seky de voiazy*	se·ki de vo·*yaa*·zi

Could you …?	*Mba afaka … ve*	mbaa·*aa*·faak … ve
	ianao azafady?	*i*·aa·now aa·zaa·*faad*
burn a CD from	*mameno CD avy*	maa·*me*·nu se·*de aa*·vi
my memory card	*amin'ny*	aa·*min*·ni
	oridinaterako	o·ri·di·naa·*te*·raa·ku
develop this	*manasa ity*	maa·*naa*·saa i·*ti*
film	*pelikiola ity*	pe·*li*·ki·ul i·*ti*

making conversation

Hello.	*Manao ahoana.*	maa·*now* aa·hon
Good night.	*Tafandria mandry.*	taa·faan·*dri* maan·dri
Goodbye.	*Veloma.*	ve·*lum*

Mr	*Ingahy*	in·*gaa*
Mrs	*Ramatoa*	raa·maa·*tu*
Ms/Miss	*Ramatoakely*	raa·maa·*tu*·kel

How are you?
Manao ahoana ianao?　　　maa·*now* aa·ho·*ni*·aa·now

Fine, and you?
Tsara, ary ianao?　　　tsaar aa·ri·*aa*·now

What's your name?
Iza no anaranao?　　　*i*·zaa nu aa·*naa*·raa·now

My name's …
… no anarako.　　　… nu aa·*naa*·raa·ku

I'm pleased to meet you.
Faly mahafantatra anao.　　　*faa*·li *maa*·faan·taa·traa now

This is my ...	Izy no ... ko.	i-zi nu ... ku
boyfriend	sakaiza-	saa-kai-zaa-
brother (man/	rahalahi-/	raa-laa-hi-/
woman saying)	anadahi-	aa-naa-daa-hi-
daughter	zanaka vavi-	zaa-naa-kaa vaa-vi-
father	rai-	rai-
friend	nama-	naa-maa-
girlfriend	sakaiza-	saa-kai-zaa-
husband	vadi-	vaa-di-
mother	reni-	re-ni-
sister (man/	anabavi-/	aa-naa-baa-vi-/
woman saying)	rahavavi-	raa-vaa-vi-
son	zanaka lahi-	zaa-naa-kaa laa-hi-
wife	vadi-	vaa-di-

Here's my ...	Ity ny ... ko.	i-ti ni ... ku
What's your ...?	Inona ny ... nao?	i-nu-naa ni ... now
address	adiresi-	aa-di-re-si-
email address	adiresy maila-	aa-di-res mai-laa-
phone number	numerao telefaoni-	nu-me-row te-le-fon-

Where are you from?	Avy aiza ianao?	aa-vi ai-zaa i-aa-now

I'm from ...	Avy any ... aho.	aa-vi aa-ni ... ow
Australia	Aositralia	os-traa-li
Canada	Kanadà	kaa-naa-daa
New Zealand	Niò Zelandy	ni-u ze-laan-di
the UK	Angiletera	aan-gle-ter
the USA	Amerika	aa-me-rik

I'm (not) married.	(Tsy) Manam-bady aho.	(tsi) maa-naam-baa-di ow
Can I take a photo	Afaka maka sary	aa-faa-kaa maa-kaa saa-ri
(of you)?	(anao) ve aho?	(aa-now) ve ow

eating out

Can you	Afaka manoro ahy	aa-faa-kaa maa-nur waa
recommend a ...?	... tsara ve ianao?	... tsaar ve i-aa-now
bar	bara	baa-raa
dish	sakafo	saa-kaaf
place to eat	toerana	tu-e-raan
	hisakafoanana	i-saa-kaa-fu-aa-naan

I'd like …, please.	Mba mila …, azafady.	mbaa mi·laa … aa·zaa·faad
the bill	ny fakitiora	ni faak·ti·ur
the menu	ny lisitra sakafo	ni lis·traa saa·kaaf
a table for (two)	latabatra ho an' (olon·droa)	laa·taa·baa·traa waan (u·lun·dru)
that dish	iny sakafo iny	in saa·kaa·fu in

| Do you have vegetarian food? | Manana sakafo tsy misy hena ve ianareo? | maa·naa·naa saa·kaaf tsi mis he·naa ve i·aa·naa·re·u |

Could you prepare a meal without …?	Mba afaka manao sakafo tsy misy … ve ianareo?	mbaa aa·faak maa·now saa·kaaf tsi mis … ve i·aa·naa·re·u
eggs	atody	aa·tud
meat stock	hena	he·naa

(cup of) coffee …	kafe (iray kaopy) …	kaa·fe (i·rai kop) …
(cup of) tea …	dite (iray kaopy) …	di·te (i·rai kop) …
with milk	misy ronono	mis ru·nun
without sugar	tsy misy siramamy	tsi mis si·raa·maam

| (boiled) water | rano (mangotraka) | raa·nu (maan·gu·traak) |

emergencies

| Help! | Vonjeo! | vun·dze·u |
| I'm lost. | Very aho. | ve·ri ow |

Call …!	Antsoy ny…!	aant·su·i ni…
an ambulance	ambilansy	aam·bi·laans
a doctor	dokotera	duk·ter
the police	polisy	po·lis

Could you help me, please?
Mba ampio kely aho, azafady? mbaa aam·pi·u kel ow aa·zaa·faad

Where are the toilets?
Aiza ny trano fivoahana? ai·zaa ni traa·nu fi·vu·aa·haan

I want to report an offence.
Mba te hitatitra heloka iray aho. mbaa te hi·taa·ti·traa he·lu·ki rai ow

I have insurance.
Manana fiantohana aho. maa·naa·naa fi·aan·tu·haa·now

I want to contact my consulate/embassy.

Te hanatona ny masoivohonay aho. te haa-*naa*-tu-naa ni maa-su-i-*vu*-aa-nai ow

I've been ...	*Nisy ... aho.*	nis ... ow
assaulted	*nanafika*	naa-*naa*-fik
raped	*nanolana*	naa-*nu*-laan
robbed	*nangalatra*	naan-*gaa*-laa-traa

I've lost my ...	*Very ny ... ko.*	ve-ri ni ... ku
My ... was/were stolen.	*Nisy nangalatra ny ... ko.*	nis naan-*gaa*-laa-traa ni ... ku
bags	*haro-*	haa-ru-
handbag	*paoketra-*	po-*ke*-traa-
jewellery	*firava-*	fi-*raa*-vaa-
money	*vola-*	vu-laa-
passport	*pasipaoro-*	paa-si-*por*-
travellers cheques	*seki-*	se-ki-
wallet	*paoketra keli-*	po-*ke*-traa *kel*-

medical needs

Where's the nearest ...?	*Aiza ny ... akaiky indrindra?*	ai-zaa ni ... aa-*kaik* in-*drin*-draa
dentist	*mpanao nify*	paa-*now* nif
doctor	*dokotera*	duk-*ter*
hospital	*hôpitaly*	ho-pi-*taal*
pharmacist	*fivarotam-panafody*	fi-vaa-*ru*-taam-paa-naa-fud

I need a doctor (who speaks English).

Mba mila dokotera (miteny Angilisy) aho. mbaa *mi*-laa duk-te-*raa* (*mi*-ten aan-gi-*lis*) ow

Could I see a female doctor?

Mba afaka manatona dokotera vavy ve aho azafady? mbaa *aa*-faa-kaa maa-*naa*-tu-naa duk-te-*raa* vaav ve ow aa-zaa-*faad*

It hurts here.

Marary eto. maa-*raa*-ri et

I'm allergic to (penicillin).

Tsy mahazaka (penisilina) aho. tsi maa-haa-*zaa*-kaa (pe-*ni*-si-lin) ow

english–malagasy dictionary

In this dictionary, words are marked as n (noun), a (adjective), v (verb), ⓜ (masculine), ⓕ (feminine), sg (singular) and pl (plural) where necessary.

A

accommodation *toerana ipetrahana* tu-re-raa-ni-*pe*-traa-haan
adaptor *adapitera* aa-*da*-pi-ter
after *aoriana* ow-ri-*naa*
airport *tobi-piaramanidina* tu-bi-pi-aa-raa-maa-*ni*-din
alcohol *alikaola* aa-li-*ko*-laa
all *rehetra* re-*he*-traa
allergy *tsy fahazakana* tsi faa-haa-*zaa*-kaan
and *ary* aa-ri
ankle *kitrokely* ki-*tru*-kel
antibiotics *antibiôtika* aa-n-ti-bi-o-ti-kaa
anti-inflammatories *tsy mampivonto* tsi maam-pi-*vun*-tu
arm *sandry* saan-dri
aspirin *asipirinina* aa-si-*pi*-rin
asthma *asima* aas-maa

B

baby *zazakely* zaa-zaa-*ke*-li
back (body) *lamosina* laa-*mu*-si-naa
backpack *kitapo fibaby* ki-*taa*-pu fi-baab
bad *ratsy* raats
baggage claim *fijerena entana* fi-dze-re-naa *en*-taan
bank *banky* baan-ki
bathroom *efitra fandroana* e-fi-traa faan-*dru*-aan
battery *pila* pil
beautiful *tsara tarehy* tsaa-raa *taa*-re
bed *fandriana* faan-*drin*
beer *labiera* laa-*bi*-er
bees *tantely* taan-tel
before *mialoha* mi-aa-*lu*
bicycle *bisikileta* bis-ki-*le*-taa
big *ngeza* nge-zaa
blanket *firakotra* fi-*raa*-ku-traa
blood group *sokajin-drà* so-kaad-zin-*draa*
bottle *tavoahangy* taa-vu-*haan*-gi
bottle opener *famohana tavoahangy* faa-mu-*haa*-naa taa-vu-*haan*-gi
boy *lahy* laa
brakes (car) *fire* fre
breakfast *sakafo maraina* saa-kaaf maa-*rai*-naa
bronchitis *koha-davareny* ku-haa-daa-*vaa*-ren

C

café *kafe* kaa-fe
cancel *foanana* fu-*aa*-naa-naa
can opener *famohana kapoaka* faa-mu-*haa*-naa kaa-*pok*
cash n *lelavola* le-laa-vu-laa
cell phone *paoritabila* por-*taa*-bi-laa
centre n *ivo* i-vu
cheap *moravidy* mu-*raa*-vid
check (bill) *seky* se-ki
check-in n *tomboka fidirana* tum-bu-kaa fi-*di*-raan
chest *tratra* traa-traa
child *ankizy* aan-*kiz*
cigarette *sigara* si-*gaa*-raa
city *tanàn-dehibe* taa-*naan*-de-hi-be
clean a *madio* maa-di-u
closed *mihidy* mi-*hid*
codeine *kaodehinina* ko-de-in
cold a *mangatsiaka* maan-gaa-*tsik*
condom *kapoty* kaa-*po*-ti
constipation *fitohanana* fi-to-*haa*-naa-naa
contact lenses *solomaso* su-lu-*maa*-su
cough n *kohaka* ku-haak
currency exchange *fanakalozana devizy* faa-naa-kaa-*lu*-zaa-naa de-*viz*
customs (immigration) *ladoany* laa-*du*-aan

D

dairy products *ronono* ru-*nun*
dangerous *mampidi-doza* maam-*pi*-di-duz
date (time) n *daty* daa-ti
day *andro* aan-dru
diaper *tatin-jaza* taa-tind-zaa-zaa
diarrhoea *mivalana* mi-*vaa*-laan
dinner *sakafo hariva* saa-*kaa*-fu aa-*ri*-vaa
dirty *maloto* maa-lut
disabled *kilemaina* ki-le-*mai*-naa
double bed *fandriana lehibe* faan-*dri*-naa *le*-hi-be
drink v *andro* aan-dru *mi-su*-tru
drivers licence *perimia* per-*mi*
drug (illicit) *zava-mahadomelina* zaa-vaa-maa-*du*-mel

E

ear *sofina* su-fi-naa
east *atsinanana* aat-si-*naa*-naan
economy class *kilasy faharoa* ki-*laa*-si faa-haa-*ru*
elevator *asansera* aa-*saan*-ser
email n *mailaka* *mai*-laak
English (language) *angilisy* aan-gi-*lis*
exchange rate *vidy takalo* vi-di taa-*kaa*-lu
exit n *fivoahana* fi-vu-*aa*-haan
expensive *lafo* laa-fu
eye *maso* *maa*-su

F

fast a *haingana* hain-gaa-naa
fever *tazo* *taa*-zu
finger *rantsan-tanana* raant-saan-*taa*-naan
first-aid kit *fanafody vonjy taitra* faa-naa-fu-di vund-zi-*tai*-traa
first class *kilasy voalohany* ki-*laa*-si vu-aa-*lu*-haan
fish n *trondro* trun-dru
food *sakafo* saa-*kaaf*
foot *tongotra* tun-*gu*-traa
fork *forisety* fu-ri-*se*-ti
free (of charge) *maimaimpoana* mai-mai-*po*-naa
fruit *voankazo* vu-aan-*kaaz*
funny *mampiomehy* maam-pi-u-*me*

G

game park *kianjan-dalao* ki-aand-zaa-*daa*-low
gift *fanomezana* faa-nu-*me*-zaan
girl *vehivavy* ve-hi-vaav
glass (drinking) *vera* ve-raa
glasses *solomaso* su-lu-maas
gluten *gilotenina* glu-*ten*
good *tsara* tsaa-raa
gram *girama* *graa*-maa
guide n *mpitarika* pi-*taa*-ri-kaa

H

hand *tanana* *taa*-naa-naa
happy *faly* faa-li
have *manana* maa-naa-naa
he *izy* iz
head *loha* lu

headache *aretina an-doha* aa-re-tin-aan-*du*
heart *fo* fu
heart condition *toe-po* tu-e-*pu*
heat n *hafanana* haa-*faa*-naan
here *eto* e-tu
high *avo* aa-vu
highway *lalambe* laa-*laam*-be
homosexual n&a *sarindahy/sarimbavy* ⑩/① saa-rin-*daa*/saa-rim-*baa*-vi
hot *mahamay* maa-*mai*
hungry *noana* no-naa

I

I *aho* ow
identification (card) *kara-panondro* kaa-raa-*paa*-nun-dru
ill *marary* maa-*raa*-ri
important *zava-dehibe* zaa-vaa-de-hi-*be*
internet *enterinety* en-*ter*-net
interpreter *mpandika teny* paan-*di*-kaa *te*-ni

J

job *asa* aa-saa

K

key *lakile* laa-ki-le
kilogram *kilao* ki-*low*
kitchen *lakozia* laa-ku-zi
knife *antsy* aant-si

L

laundry (place) *fanasan-damba* faa-naa-saan-*daam*-baa
lawyer *mpisolo vava* mpi-su-lu va-*vaa*
left-luggage office *birao mpitahiry entana* bi-row pi-taa-hi-ri en-taa-naa
leg *ranjo* raand-zu
lesbian n&a *sarindahy* saa-rin-*daa*
less *kely kokoa* ke-li ku-*ku*
letter (mail) *taratasy* taa-*raa*-taas
like v *tia* ti
lost-property office *biraon' entana very* bi-row-ni-en-taa-naa-ve-ri
love v *tia* ti
lunch *sakafo atoandro* saa-*kaaf* waa-tu-*aan*-dru

M

man *lehilahy* le-hi-*laa*
matches *afokasoka* aa-fu-*kaa*-su-kaa
meat *hena* he-naa
medicine *fanafody* faa-naa-*fu*-di
message *hafatra* haa-faa-traa
mobile phone *paoritabila* por-*taa*-bi-laa
month *volana* vu-*laa*-naa
morning *maraina* maa-rai-naa
motorcycle *môtô* mo-*to*
mouth *vava* vaa-vaa
movie *sarimihetsika* saa-ri-mi-*het*-si-kaa
MSG *MSG* em-es-dze
museum *trano firaketana* traan fi-raa-*ke*-taan
music *mozika* mu-*zik*

N

name n *anarana* aa-*naa*-raan
napkin *serivietan-databatra*
  se-ri-vi-e-taan-daa-*taa*-baa-traa
nappy *te hatory* te haa-*tu*-ri
national park *parika nasiônaly* paar-kaa naa-si-o-*naa*-li
nausea *malohilohy* maa-*lo*-hi-lo-hi
neck *hatoka* haa-*tu*-kaa
new *vaovao* vow-*vow*
news *vaovao* vow-*vow*
newspaper *gazety* gaa-ze-ti
night *alina* aa-li-naa
nightclub *toeram-pandihizana* tu-e-raam-paan-di-*hi*-zaan
noisy *mitabataba* mi-taa-baa-*taa*-baa
nonsmoking *tsy mifoka sigara* tsi mi-*fu*-kaa si-*gaa*-raa
north *avaratra* aa-*vaa*-raa-traa
nose *orona* u-ru-naa
now *izao* i-*zow*
number *isa* i-*saa*
nuts *voanjo* vu-*aan*-dzu

O

oil (engine) *menaka* me-naa-kaa
OK *mety* me-ti
old *antitra* aan-ti-traa
open a *mivoha* mi-*vu*
outside *ivelany* i-ve-laa-ni

P

package *entana* en-*taa*-naa
pain *fanaintainana* faa-nain-*tai*-naa-naa

palace *rova* ru-vaa
paper *taratasy* taa-raa-taas
park (car) v *fijanonana* fid-zaa-*nu*-naan
passport *pasipaoro* paa-si-*po*-ru
pay v *karama* kaa-*raa*-maa
pen *penina* pen
petrol *lasantsy* laa-*saant*-si
pharmacy *farimasia* faa-ri-*maa*-si
plate *lovia* lu-*vi*
postcard *karatra paositaly* kaa-raa-traa pos-*taa*-li
post office *paositra* po-si-traa
pregnant *bevohoka* be-vu-kaa

Q

quiet *mangiangiana* maan-gin-*gi*-naa

R

rain n *orana* u-raan
razor *hareza* haa-rez
registered mail *taratasy rekômande*
  taa-raa-*taas* re-ko-maan-*de*
rent v *hofany* hu-faan
repair v *mamboatra* maam-*bo*-traa
reservation *famandrihana* faa-maan-*dri*-haan
restaurant *hôtely fisakafoana* o-te-li fi-saa-kaa-*fu*-aa-naa
return v *miverina* mi-*ve*-ri-naa
road *lalana* laa-laa-naa
room *efitra* e-fi-traa

S

sad *malahelo* maa-laa-*he*-lu
safe a *milamina* mi-*laa*-mi-naa
sanitary napkin *serivieta fidiovana*
  se-ri-vi-*e*-taa fi-di-*u*-vaa-naa
seafood *hazan-drano* haa-zaan-*draa*-nu
seat *fitoerana* fi-tu-e-raan
send *mandefa* maan-*def*
sex *vavy na lahy* vaa-vi na *laa*
shampoo *fanasam-bolo* faa-naa-saam-*bu*-lu
share (a dorm, etc) *mizara* mi-*zaa*-raa
shaving cream *kirema fiharatana* krem fi-haa-*raa*-taan
she *izy* iz
sheet (bed) *lambam-pandriana* laam-baam-paan-*dri*-naa
shirt *lobaka* lu-*baa*-kaa
shoes *kiraro* ki-*raa*-ru

shop n *fivarotana* fi-vaa-*ru*-taan
shower n *fandroana* faan-*dru*-naa
skin *hoditra* hu-di-traa
skirt *zipo* zi-po
sleep v *matory* maa-*tu*-ri
small *kely* ke-li
smoke (cigarettes) v *mifoka* mi-*fu*-kaa
soap *savony* saa-vu-ni
some *sasany* saa-saan
soon *atoato* aa-tu-aa-tu
sore throat *aretin-tenda* aa-re-tin-*ten*-daa
south *atsimo* aat-*si*-mu
souvenir shop *fivarotana fahatsiarovana*
fi-vaa-ru-taan faa-tsi-aa-*ru*-vaan
speak *miteny* mi-ten
spoon *sotro* su-tru
stamp *hajia* haad-zi
stand-by ticket *tapakila ho an'ny lisitra miandry*
taa-*paa*-kil waan-ni-*li*-si-traa mi-aan-dri
station (train) *gara* gaa-raa
stomach *vavony* vaa-vu-ni
stop v *mijanona* mid-*zaa*-nu-naa
stop (bus) n *fijanonana* fid-zaa-*nu*-naan
street *arabe* aa-raa-be
student *mpianatra* pi-*aa*-naa-traa
sunscreen *aro-masoandro* aa-ru-maa-su-*aan*-dru
swim v *milomano* mi-*lu*-maan

T

tampons *servieta hyjienika* se-ri-*vi*-e-taa hi-dzi-e-*ni*-kaa
teeth *nify* nif
telephone n *telefaonina* te-*le*-fon
television *televiziona* te-le-*vi*-zi-on
temperature (weather) *hafanana* haa-*faa*-naan
tent *lay* lai
that (one) *iny* i-ni
they *zareo* zaa-*re*-u
thirsty *mangetaheta* maan-ge-taa-*he*-taa
this (one) *ity* i-ti
throat *tenda* ten-daa
ticket *tapakila* taa-*paa*-kil
time *fotoana* fu-ton
tired *vizana* vi-zaan
tissues *mosoara* mu-*swaa*-raa
today *androany* aan-*dru*-aan
toilet *toerana fivoahana* tu-e-raan fi-vu-aa-haan
tonight *rahalina* raa-*haa*-li-naa
toothache *areti-nify* aa-re-ti-nif
toothbrush *borosynify* bu-*ru*-si-nif
toothpaste *dantifirisy* daan-ti-fris

torch (flashlight) *lampy de paosy* laam-pi de pos
tourist office *biraon'ny vahiny* bi-row-ni *vaa*-hin
towel *serivieta* se-ri-*vi*-e-taa
translate *mandika teny* maan-*di*-kaa ten
travel agency *birao mpandrindra dia*
bi-row *paan*-drin-draa di
travellers cheque *seky de voiazy* se-ki de *vo*-yaa-zi
trousers *pataloha* paa-taa-lu
twin beds *fandriana kely* faan-*dri*-naa kel
tyre *kodiarana* ku-di-aa-raan

U

underwear *atin 'akanjo* aa-ti-naa-*kaan*-dzu
urgent *maika* mai-kaa

V

vacant *malalaka* maa-*laa*-laa-kaa
vegetarian a *tsy misy hena* tsi mis *he*-naa
visa *vizà* vi-zaa

W

waiter *mpandroso sakafo* paan-*dru*-su *saa*-kaaf
walk v *mandeha tongotra* maan-de *tun*-gu-traa
wallet *paoketra kely* po-ke-traa kel
warm a *mafana* maa-faan
wash (something) *manasa* maa-naas
watch n *famataranandro* faa-maa-taa-*raa*-naan-dru
water *rano* *raa*-nu
we (including person addressed) *isika* i-sik
we (excluding person addressed) *izahay* i-*zaa*-hai
weekend *faran'ny herinandro* *faa*-raan-ni he-ri-naan-dru
west *andrefana* aan-dre-faan
wheelchair *sezan'ny kilemaina* se-zaan-ni ki-*le*-mai-naa
when *oviana* o-vi-naa
where *aiza* ai-zaa
who *iza* i-zaa
why *nahoana* naa-hon
window *varavarankely* vaa-raa-vaa-raan-kel
wine *divay* di-vai
with *miaraka amin'ny* mi-aa-raa-*kaa*-min-ni
without *tsy misy* tsi mis
woman *vehivavy* ve-*hi*-vaav
write *manoratra* maa-nu-raa-traa

Y

you sg *ianao* i-aa-now
you pl *ianareo* i-aa-naa-*re*-u

Portuguese

pronunciation

Vowels		Consonants	
Symbol	**English sound**	**Symbol**	**English sound**
a	run	b	bed
aa	father	d	dog
ai	aisle	f	fun
ay	say	g	go
e	bet	k	kit
ee	see	l	lot
o	pot	ly	million
oh	note	m	man
oo	zoo	n	not
ow	now	ng	ring (indicates the preceding vowel is nasal)
oy	boy		
		ny	canyon
		p	pet
		r	like 'tt' in 'butter' said fast
		rr	run (throaty)
		s	sun
		sh	shot
		t	top
		v	very
		w	win
		y	yes
		z	zero
		zh	pleasure

In this chapter, the Portuguese pronunciation is given in red after each word or phrase.

Each syllable is separated by a dot, and the syllable stressed in each word is italicised.

For example:
Olá. o-*laa*

PORTUGUÊS – pronunciation

114

language difficulties

Do you speak English?	*Fala inglês?*	faa·la eeng·*glesh*
Do you understand?	*Entende?*	eng·*teng*·de
I (don't) understand.	*(Não) Entendo.*	(nowng) eng·*teng*·doo
Could you please …?	*Podia …, por favor?*	poo·*dee*·a … poor fa·*vor*
repeat that	*repetir isto*	rre·pe·*teer* eesh·too
speak more slowly	*falar mais devagar*	fa·*laar* maish de·va·*gaar*
write it down	*escrever isso*	shkre·*ver* ee·soo

time, dates & numbers

What time is it?	*Que horas são?*	kee *o*·rash sowng
It's one o'clock.	*É uma hora.*	e *oo*·ma *o*·ra
It's (ten) o'clock.	*São (dez) horas.*	sowng (desh) *o*·rash
Quarter past (ten).	*(Dez) e quinze.*	(desh) e *keeng*·ze
Half past (ten).	*(Dez) e meia.*	(desh) e *may*·a
Quarter to (eleven).	*Quinze para as (onze).*	*keeng*·ze pa·ra ash (*ong*·ze)
At what time …?	*A que horas …?*	a ke *o*·rash …
At …	*À …*	aa …
It's (18 October).	*Hoje é dia (dezoito de Outubro).*	*o*·zhe e *dee*·a (de·*zoy*·too de oh·*too*·broo)

Monday	*segunda-feira*	se·*goong*·da·*fay*·ra
Tuesday	*terça-feira*	*ter*·sa·*fay*·ra
Wednesday	*quarta-feira*	*kwaar*·ta·*fay*·ra
Thursday	*quinta-feira*	*keeng*·ta·*fay*·ra
Friday	*sexta-feira*	*saysh*·ta·*fay*·ra
Saturday	*sábado*	*saa*·ba·doo
Sunday	*domingo*	doo·*meeng*·goo

yesterday	*ontem*	*ong*·teng
today	*hoje*	*o*·zhe
tomorrow	*amanhã*	aa·ma·*nyang*

numbers

0	zero	ze·roo	16	dezasseis	de·za·saysh
1	um	oong	17	dezassete	de·za·se·te
2	dois	doysh	18	dezoito	de·zoy·too
3	três	tresh	19	dezanove	de·za·no·ve
4	quatro	kwaa·troo	20	vinte	veeng·te
5	cinco	seeng·koo	21	vinte e um	veeng·te e oong
6	seis	saysh	22	vinte e dois	veeng·te e doysh
7	sete	se·te	30	trinta	treeng·ta
8	oito	oy·too	40	quarenta	kwa·reng·ta
9	nove	no·ve	50	cinquenta	seeng·kweng·ta
10	dez	desh	60	sessenta	se·seng·ta
11	onze	ong·ze	70	setenta	se·teng·ta
12	doze	do·ze	80	oitenta	oy·teng·ta
13	treze	tre·ze	90	noventa	no·veng·ta
14	catorze	ka·tor·ze	100	cem	seng
15	quinze	keeng·ze	1000	mil	meel

border crossing

I'm here ...	Estou ...	shtoh ...
in transit	em trânsito	eng trang·zee·too
on business	em negócios	eng ne·go·syoosh
on holiday	de férias	de fe·ree·ash

I'm here for ...	Vou ficar por ...	voh fee·kaar poor ...
(10) days	(dez) dias	(desh) dee·ash
(three) weeks	(três) semanas	(tresh) se·ma·nash
(two) months	(dois) meses	(doysh) me·zesh

I'm going to (Maputo).
Vou para (Maputo). voh pa·ra (ma·poo·to)

I'm staying at the (Panorama Hotel).
Estou no (Hotel Panorama). shtoh noo (o·tel pa·no·ra·ma)

tickets

One ... ticket (to Sofala), please.	Um bilhete de ... (para Sofala), por favor.	oong bee-*lye*-te de ... (pra so-*faa*-laa) poor fa-*vor*
one-way	ida	*ee*-da
return	ida e volta	*ee*-da ee *vol*-ta

Is there ...?	Tem ...?	teng ...
air conditioning	ar condicionado	aar kong-dee-syoo-*naa*-doo
a toilet	casa de banho	*kaa*-za de ba-nyoo

I'd like a ... seat, please.	Queria um lugar ... por favor.	ke-*ree*-a oong loo-*gaar* ... poor fa-*vor*
nonsmoking	de não fumadores	de nowng foo-ma-*do*-resh
smoking	para fumadores	pra foo-ma-*do*-resh

transport

Is this the ... to (Luanda)?	Este é o ... para (Luanda)?	*esh*-te e oo ... pra (*lwan*-da)
boat	barco	*baar*-koo
bus	autocarro	ow-to-*kaa*-rroo
train	comboio	kong-*boy*-oo

How much is it to ...?
Quanto custa até ao ...? — kwang-too *koosh*-ta a-*te* ow ...

Please take me to (this address).
Leve-me para (este endereço), por favor. — *le*-ve-me pa-ra (*esh*-te eng-de-*re*-soo) poor fa-*vor*

I'd like to hire a ...	Queria alugar ...	ke-*ree*-a a-loo-*gaar* ...
car (with air conditioning)	um carro (com ar condicionado)	oong *kaa*-rroo (kong aar kong-dee-syoo-*naa*-doo)
4WD	4WD	*kwaa*-troo poor *kwaa*-troo

directions

Where's the	Onde é o ...	ong·de e oo ...
nearest ...?	mais perto?	maish per·to
internet café	café da internet	ka·fe da eeng·ter·net
market	mercado	mer·kaa·doo
It's ...	É ...	e ...
behind ...	atrás de ...	a·traash de ...
in front of ...	em frente de ...	eng freng·te de ...
near (to ...)	perto (de ...)	per·too (de ...)
next to ...	ao lado de ...	ow laa·doo de ...
on the corner	na esquina	na shkee·na
opposite ...	do lado oposto ...	doo laa·doo oo·posh·too ...
straight ahead	em frente	eng freng·te
there	lá	laa

accommodation

I'd like to book a room, please.
Eu queria fazer uma   e·oo ke·ree·a fa·zer oo·ma
reserva, por favor.   rre·zer·va, por fa·vor

I'd like to stay for (three) nights.
Para (três) noites.   pa·ra (tresh) noy·tesh

Do you have	Tem um quarto ...?	teng oong kwaar·too ...
a ... room?		
single	de solteiro	de sol·tay·roo
double	de casal	de ka·zaal
twin	duplo	doo·ploo
How much is it per ...?	Quanto custa por ...?	kwang·too koosh·ta poor ...
night	noite	noy·te
person	pessoa	pe·so·a

banking & communications

I'd like to ...	Queria ...	ke·ree·a ...
change a travellers cheque	trocar traveller cheque	troo·kaar tra·ve·ler shek
change money	trocar dinheiro	troo·kaar dee·nyay·roo
get internet access	ter acesso à internet	ter a·se·soo aa eeng·ter·net
withdraw money	levantar dinheiro	le·vang·taar dee·nyay·roo

shopping

I'm looking for ...
Estou à procura de ...
shtoh aa proo·koo·ra de ...

How much is it?
Quanto custa?
kwang·too koosh·ta

Can you write down the price?
Pode escrever o preço?
po·de shkre·ver oo pre·soo

Do you accept ...?	Aceitam ...?	a·say·tang ...
credit cards	cartão de crédito	kar·towng de kre·dee·too
travellers cheques	travellers cheques	tra·ve·ler she·kesh

making conversation

Hello.	Olá.	o·laa
Good night.	Boa noite.	bo·a noy·te
Goodbye.	Adeus.	a·de·oosh

Mr	Senhor	se·nyor
Mrs	Senhora	se·nyo·ra
Ms	Menina	me·nee·na

How are you?	Como está?	ko·moo shta
Fine. And you?	Bem, e você?	beng e vo·se
What's your name?	Qual é o seu nome?	kwaal e oo se·oo no·me
My name's ...	O meu nome é ...	oo me·oo no·me e ...
I'm pleased to meet you.	Prazer em conhecê-lo/ conhecê-la. m/f	pra·zer eng koo·nye·se·lo/ koo·nye·se·la

This is my ...	*Este é o meu ... m*	*esh·te e oo me·oo ...*
	Esta é a minha ... f	*esh·ta e a mee·nya ...*
boyfriend	*namorado*	na·moo·*raa*·doo
daughter	*filha*	*fee*·lya
friend	*amigo/a* m/f	a·*mee*·goo/ga
girlfriend	*namorada*	na·moo·*raa*·da
husband	*marido*	ma·*ree*·doo
partner (intimate)	*companheiro/a* m/f	kong·pa·*nyay*·roo/a
son	*filho*	*fee*·lyoo
wife	*esposa*	*shpo*·za
I'm ...	*Eu sou ...*	e·oo soh ...
married	*casado/a* m/f	ka·*zaa*·doo/a
single	*solteiro/a* m/f	sol·*tay*·roo/a

Where are you from?	*De onde é?*	*dong*·de e
I'm from ...	*Eu sou ...*	e·oo soh ...
Australia	*da Austrália*	da owsh·*traa*·lya
Canada	*do Canadá*	doo ka·na·*daa*
New Zealand	*da Nova Zelândia*	da *no*·va ze·*lang*·dya
the UK	*do Reino Unido*	doo *ray*·noo oo·*nee*·doo
the USA	*dos Estados Unidos*	doosh *shtaa*·doosh oo·*nee*·doosh
Here's my ...	*Aqui está o meu ...*	a·*kee* shtaa oo *me*·oo ...
What's your ...?	*Qual é o seu ...?*	kwaal e oo *se*·oo ...
address	*endereço*	eng·de·*re*·soo
email address	*email*	ee·*mayl*
phone number	*número de telefone*	*noo*·me·roo de te·le·*fo*·ne
Can I take a photo (of you)?	*Posso(-lhe) tirar uma fotografia?*	*po*·soo(·lye) tee·*raar* *oo*·ma foo·too·graa·*fee*·a

120

eating out

I'd like ..., please.	Queria ..., por favor.	ke·ree·a ... poor fa·vor
the bill	a conta	a kong·ta
the menu	um menu	oong me·noo
a table for (five)	uma mesa para (cinco)	oo·ma me·za pa·ra (seeng·koo)
that dish	aquele prato	a·ke·le praa·too
Do you have vegetarian food?	Tem comida vegetariana?	teng koo·mee·da ve·zhe·ta·ree·aa·na
Could you prepare a meal without ...?	Pode preparar sem ...?	po·de pre·pa·raar seng ...
eggs	ovos	o·voosh
meat stock	caldo de carne	kaal·doo de kaar·ne

emergencies

Help!	Socorro!	soo·ko·rroo
Call ...!	Chame ...!	shaa·me ...
an ambulance	uma ambulância	oo·ma ang·boo·lang·sya
the police	a polícia	a poo·lee·sya

Could you help me, please?
Pode ajudar, por favor? po·de a·zhoo·daar poor fa·vor

Can I use the telephone?
Posso usar o seu telefone? po·soo oo·zaar oo se·oo te·le·fo·ne

I'm lost.
Estou perdido/a. m/f shtoh per·dee·doo/a

Where are the toilets?
Onde é a casa de banho? ong·de e a kaa·za de ba·nyoo

I've been assaulted.
Eu fui agredido/a. m/f e·oo fwee a·gre·dee·doo/a

I've been raped.
Eu fui violado/a. m/f e·oo fwee vee·oo·laa·doo/a

I've lost my ...	Eu perdi ...	e·oo per·dee ...
My ... was/were stolen.	Roubaram ...	rroh·baa·rang ...
bags	os meus sacos	oosh me·oosh saa·koosh
credit card	o meu cartão de crédito	oo me·oo kar·towng de kre·dee·too
handbag	a minha bolsa	a mee·nya bol·sa
jewellery	as minhas jóias	ash mee·nyash zhoy·ash
money	o meu dinheiro	oo me·oo dee·nyay·roo
passport	o meu passaporte	oo me·oo paa·sa·por·te
travellers cheques	os meus travellers cheques	oosh me·oosh tra·ve·ler she·kesh
wallet	a minha carteira	a mee·nya kar·tay·ra
I want to contact my ...	Eu quero contactar com ...	e·oo ke·roo kong·tak·taar kong ...
embassy	a minha embaixada	a mee·nya eng·bai·shaa·da
consulate	o meu consulado	oo me·oo kong·soo·laa·doo

medical needs

Where's the nearest ...?	Qual é ... mais perto?	kwaal e ... maish per·too
dentist	o dentista	oo deng·teesh·ta
doctor	o médico m	oo me·dee·koo
	a médica f	a me·dee·ka
hospital	o hospital	oo osh·pee·taal
pharmacist	a farmácia	a far·maa·sya

I need a doctor (who speaks English).
Eu preciso de um médico (que fale inglês).
e·oo pre·see·zoo de oong me·dee·koo (que faa·le eeng·glesh)

It hurts here.
Dói-me aqui.
doy·me a·kee

I'm allergic to (penicillin).
Eu sou alérgico/a a (penicilina). m/f
e·oo soh a·ler·zhee·koo/a a (pe·nee·see·lee·na)

PORTUGUÊS – medical needs

122

english–portuguese dictionary

Portuguese nouns and adjectives in this dictionary have their gender indicated with ⓜ (masculine) and ⓕ (feminine). If it's a plural noun, you'll see pl too. Words are also marked as v (verb), n (noun), a (adjective), pl (plural), sg (singular), inf (informal) and pol (polite) where necessary.

A

accommodation *hospedagem* ⓕ osh-pe-*daa*-zheng
after *depois* de-*poysh*
airport *aeroporto* ⓜ a-e-ro-*por*-too
alcohol *alcoól* ⓜ al-ko-ol
all a *todo/a* ⓜ/ⓕ *to*-doo/a
allergy *alergia* ⓕ a-ler-*zhee*-a
and *e* e
ankle *tornozelo* ⓜ toor-noo-*ze*-loo
antibiotics *antibióticos* ⓜ pl ang-tee-bee-*o*-tee-koosh
arm *braço* ⓜ *braa*-soo
aspirin *aspirina* ⓕ ash-pee-*ree*-na
asthma *asma* ⓕ *ash*-ma
ATM *caixa automático* ⓜ *kai*-sha ow-too-*maa*-tee-koo

B

baby *bebé* ⓜ&ⓕ be-*be*
back (body) *costas* ⓕ pl *kosh*-tash
backpack *mochila* ⓕ moo-*shee*-la
bad *mau/má* ⓜ/ⓕ *ma*-oo/maa
baggage claim *balcão de bagagens* ⓜ bal-*kowng* de ba-*gaa*-zhengsh
bank *banco* ⓜ *bang*-koo
bathroom *casa de banho* ⓕ *kaa*-za de ba-*nyoo*
battery *pilha* ⓕ *pee*-lya
beautiful *bonita/o* ⓜ/ⓕ boo-*nee*-too/a
bed *cama* ⓕ *ka*-ma
bee *abelha* ⓕ a-*be*-lya
beer *cerveja* ⓕ ser-*ve*-zha
before *antes* *ang*-tesh
bicycle *bicicleta* ⓕ bee-see-*kle*-ta
big *grande* ⓜ&ⓕ *grang*-de
blanket *cobertor* ⓜ koo-ber-*tor*
blood group *grupo sanguíneo* ⓜ *groo*-poo sang-*gwee*-nee-oo
bottle *garrafa* ⓕ ga-*rraa*-fa
bottle opener *saca-rolhas* ⓜ *saa*-ka-*rro*-lyash
boy *menino* ⓜ me-*nee*-noo
brake (car) *travão* ⓜ tra-*vowng*
breakfast *pequeno almoço* ⓜ pe-*ke*-noo aal-*mo*-soo

C

cancel *cancelar* kang-se-*laar*
can opener *abre latas* ⓜ *aa*-bre *laa*-tash
cash *dinheiro* ⓜ dee-*nyay*-roo
cell phone *telemóvel* ⓜ te-le-*mo*-vel
centre *centro* ⓜ *seng*-troo
cheap *barato/a* ⓜ/ⓕ ba-*raa*-too/a
check (bill) *conta* ⓕ *kong*-ta
chest *peito* ⓜ *pay*-too
child *criança* ⓜ&ⓕ kree-*ang*-sa
cigarette *cigarro* ⓜ see-*gaa*-rroo
city *cidade* ⓕ see-*daa*-de
clean a *limpo/a* ⓜ/ⓕ *leeng*-poo/a
closed *fechado/a* ⓜ/ⓕ fe-*shaa*-doo/a
cold a *frio/a* ⓜ/ⓕ *free*-oo/a
collect call *ligação a cobrar* ⓕ lee-ga-*sowng* a koo-*braar*
condom *preservativo* ⓜ pre-zer-va-*tee*-voo
constipation *prisão de ventre* ⓕ pree-*zowng* de *ven*-tre
contact lenses *lentes de contacto* ⓜ pl *leng*-tesh de kong-*taak*-too
cough *tosse* ⓕ *to*-se
currency exchange *câmbio* ⓜ *kang*-byoo
customs (immigration) *alfândega* ⓕ aal-*fang*-de-ga

D

dairy products *produtos lácteos* ⓜ pl pro-*doo*-toosh *laak*-tee-oosh
dangerous *perigoso/a* ⓜ/ⓕ pe-ree-*go*-zoo/a
day *dia* ⓜ *dee*-a
diaper *fralda* ⓕ *fraal*-da
diarrhoea *diarreia* ⓕ dee-a-*rray*-a
dinner *jantar* ⓜ zhang-*taar*
dirty *sujo/a* ⓜ/ⓕ *soo*-zhoo/a
disabled *deficiente* de-fee-see-*eng*-te
double bed *cama de casal* ⓕ *ka*-ma de ka-*zaal*
drink *bebida* ⓕ be-*bee*-da
drivers licence *carta de condução* ⓕ *kaar*-ta de kong-doo-*sowng*
drug (illicit) *droga* ⓕ *dro*-ga

E

ear *orelha* ⓕ o-re-lya
east *leste* lesh-te
economy class *classe económica* ⓕ
　klaa-se ee-koo-no-mee-ka
elevator *elevador* ⓜ ee-le-va-dor
email *email* ⓜ ee-mayl
English (language) *inglês* ⓜ eeng-glesh
exchange rate *taxa de câmbio* ⓕ taa-sha de kang-byoo
exit *saída* ⓕ saa-ee-da
expensive *caro/a* ⓜ/ⓕ kaa-roo/a

F

fast *rápido/a* ⓜ/ⓕ rraa-pee-doo/a
fever *febre* ⓕ fe-bre
finger *dedo* ⓜ de-doo
first-aid kit *estojo de primeiros socorros* ⓜ
　shto-zhoo de pree-may-roosh so-ko-rroosh
first class *primeira classe* ⓕ pree-may-ra klaa-se
fish *peixe* ⓜ pay-she
food *comida* ⓕ koo-mee-da
foot *pé* ⓜ pe
fork *garfo* ⓜ gaar-foo
free (of charge) *grátis* graa-teesh
funny *engraçado/a* ⓜ/ⓕ eng-gra-saa-doo/a

G

gift *presente* ⓜ pre-zeng-te
girl *menina* ⓕ me-nee-na
glass (drinking) *copo* ⓜ ko-poo
glasses *óculos* ⓜ pl o-koo-loosh
gluten *glúten* ⓜ gloo-teng
good *bom/boa* ⓜ/ⓕ bong/bo-a
gram *grama* ⓜ graa-ma
guide n *guia* ⓕ gee-a

H

hand *mão* ⓕ mowng
happy *feliz* ⓜ&ⓕ fe-leesh
have *ter* ter
he *ele* e-le
head *cabeça* ⓕ ka-be-sa
headache *dor de cabeça* ⓕ dor de ka-be-sa
heart *coração* ⓜ koo-ra-sowng

heart condition *problema de coração* ⓜ
　proo-ble-ma de koo-ra-sowng
heat *calor* ⓜ ka-lor
here *aqui* a-kee
high *alto/a* ⓜ/ⓕ aal-too/aa
highway *autoestrada* ⓕ ow-to-shtraa-da
homosexual n&a *homosexual* ⓜ&ⓕ
　o-mo-sek-soo-aal
hot *quente* keng-te
hungry *faminto/a* ⓜ/ⓕ fa-meeng-too/a

I

I *eu* e-oo
identification (card) *bilhete de identidade* ⓜ
　bee-lye-te de ee-deng-tee-daa-de
ill *doente* ⓜ&ⓕ doo-eng-te
important *importante* ⓜ&ⓕ eeng-por-tang-te
Internet *internet* ⓕ eeng-ter-net
interpreter *intérprete* ⓜ&ⓕ eeng-ter-pre-te

K

key *chave* ⓕ shaa-ve
kilogram *quilograma* ⓜ kee-loo-graa-ma
kitchen *cozinha* ⓕ koo-zee-nya
knife *faca* ⓕ faa-ka

L

laundry (place) *lavandaria* ⓕ la-vang-da-ree-a
lawyer *advogado/a* ⓜ/ⓕ a-de-voo-gaa-doo/a
left-luggage office *perdidos e achados* ⓜ pl
　per-dee-doosh ee aa-shaa-doosh
leg *perna* ⓕ per-na
lesbian n&a *lésbica* ⓕ lezh-bee-ka
less *menos* me-noosh
letter (mail) *carta* ⓕ kaar-ta
like v *gostar* goosh-taar
lost-property office *gabinete de perdidos e achados* ⓜ
　gaa-bee-ne-te de per-dee-doosh ee a-shaa-doosh
love v *amar* a-maar
lunch *almoço* ⓜ aal-mo-soo

M

man *homem* ⓜ o-meng
matches *fósforos* ⓜ pl fosh-foo-roosh
meat *carne* ⓕ kaar-ne
medicine *medicamentos* ⓜ pl me-dee-ka-meng-toosh

message *mensagem* ① meng-*saa*-zheng
mobile phone *telemóvel* ⓜ te-le-*mo*-vel
month *mês* ⓜ mesh
morning *manhã* ① ma-*nyang*
motorcycle *mota* ① *mo*-ta
mouth *boca* ① *bo*-ka
movie *filme* ⓜ *feel*-me
MSG *MSG* ⓜ e-me-e-se-*zhe*
museum *museu* ⓜ moo-ze-oo
music *música* ① *moo*-zee-ka

N

name *nome* ⓜ *no*-me
napkin *guardanapo* ⓜ gwar-da-*naa*-poo
nappy *fralda* ① *fraal*-da
national park *parque nacional* ⓜ
   paar-ke na-syoo-*naal*
nausea *náusea* ① *now*-zee-a
neck *pescoço* ⓜ pesh-*ko*-soo
new *novo/a* ⓜ/① *no*-voo/a
news *notícias* ① pl noo-*tee*-syash
newspaper *jornal* ⓜ zhor-*naal*
night *noite* ① *noy*-te
noisy *barulhento/a* ⓜ/① ba-roo-*lyeng*-too/a
nonsmoking *não-fumador* nowng-foo-ma-*dor*
north *norte* *nor*-te
nose *nariz* ⓜ na-*reesh*
now *agora* a-*go*-ra
number *número* ⓜ *noo*-me-roo
nuts *oleaginosas* ① pl o-lee-a-zhee-*no*-zash

O

oil (engine) *petróleo* ⓜ pe-*tro*-lyoo
OK *bem* beng
old *velho/a* ⓜ/① *ve*-lyoo/a
open a *aberto/a* ⓜ/① a-*ber*-too/a
outside *fora* *fo*-ra

P

package *embrulho* ⓜ eng-*broo*-lyoo
pain *dor* ① dor
paper *papel* ⓜ pa-*pel*
park (car) v *estacionar* shta-syoo-*naar*
passport *passaporte* ⓜ paa-sa-*por*-te
pay *pagar* pa-*gaar*
pen *caneta* ① ka-*ne*-ta
petrol *gasolina* ① ga-zoo-*lee*-na

pharmacy *farmácia* ① far-*maa*-sya
plate *prato* ⓜ *praa*-too
postcard *postal* ⓜ poosh-*taal*
post office *correio* ⓜ koo-*rray*-oo
pregnant *grávida* ① *graa*-vee-da

R

rain *chuva* ① *shoo*-va
razor *gilete* ① zhee-*le*-te
registered mail *correio registado* ⓜ
   koo-*rray*-oo re-zhee-*shtaa*-doo
rent v *alugar* a-loo-*gaar*
repair v *consertar* kong-ser-*taar*
reservation *reserva* ① rre-*zer*-va
restaurant *restaurante* ⓜ rresh-tow-*rang*-te
return v *voltar* vol-*taar*
road *estrada* ① *shtraa*-da
room *quarto* ⓜ *kwaar*-too

S

sad *triste* *treesh*-te
safe a *seguro/a* ⓜ/① se-*goo*-roo/a
sanitary napkin *penso higiénico* ⓜ
   peng-soo ee-zhee-e-nee-koo
seafood *marisco* ⓜ ma-*reesh*-koo
seat *assento* ⓜ a-*seng*-too
send *enviar* eng-vee-*aar*
sex *sexo* ⓜ *sek*-soo
shampoo *champô* ⓜ shang-*poo*
share (a dorm) v *partilhar* par-tee-*lyaar*
shaving cream *creme de barbear* ⓜ
   kre-me de bar-bee-*aar*
she *ela* *e*-la
sheet (bed) *lençol* ⓜ leng-*sol*
shirt *camisa* ① ka-*mee*-za
shoes *sapatos* ⓜ pl sa-*paa*-toosh
shop n *loja* ① *lo*-zha
shower n *chuveiro* ⓜ shoo-*vay*-roo
skin *pele* ① *pe*-le
skirt *saia* ① *sai*-a
sleep v *dormir* door-*meer*
small *pequeno/a* ⓜ/① pe-*ke*-noo/a
smoke (cigarettes) v *fumar* foo-*maar*
soap *sabonete* ⓜ sa-boo-*ne*-te
some *uns/umas* ⓜ/① pl oongsh/*oo*-mash
soon *em breve* eng *bre*-ve
sore throat *dores de garganta* ① pl
   do-resh de gar-*gang*-ta

south *sul* sool
souvenir shop *loja de lembranças* ①
  lo-zha de leng-*brang*-sash
speak *falar* fa-*laar*
spoon *colher* ① koo-*lyer*
stamp *selo* ① *se*-loo
stand-by ticket *bilhete sem garantia* ⓜ
  bee-*lye*-te seng ga-rang-*tee*-a
station (train) *estação* ① shta-*sowng*
stomach *estômago* ⓜ *shto*-ma-goo
stop ∨ *parar* pa-*raar*
stop (bus) *paragem* ① pa-*raa*-zheng
street *rua* ① *rroo*-a
student *estudante* ⓜ&① shtoo-*dang*-te
sunscreen *protecção anti-solar* ①
  proo-te-*sowng* ang-tee-soo-*laar*
swim ∨ *nadar* na-*daar*

T

tampons *tampões* ⓜ pl tang-*powngsh*
teeth *dentes* ⓜ pl *deng*-tesh
telephone *telefone* ① te-le-*fo*-ne
television *televisão* ① te-le-vee-*zowng*
temperature (weather) *temperatura* ①
  teng-pe-ra-*too*-ra
tent *tenda* ① *teng*-da
that one *aquele/a* ⓜ/① a-*ke*-le/a
they *eles/elas* ⓜ/① *e*-lesh/e-*lash*
thirsty *sedento/a* ⓜ/① se-*deng*-too/a
this one *este/a* ⓜ/① *esh*-te/a
throat *garganta* ① gar-*gang*-ta
ticket *bilhete* ⓜ bee-*lye*-te
time *tempo* ⓜ *teng*-poo
tired *cansado/a* ⓜ/① kang-*saa*-doo/a
tissues *lenços de papel* ⓜ pl *leng*-soosh de pa-*pel*
today *hoje* o-*zhe*
toilet *casa de banho* ① *kaa*-za de ba-*nyoo*
tonight *hoje à noite* o-zhe aa *noy*-te
toothache *dor de dentes* ① dor de *deng*-tesh
toothbrush *escova de dentes* ① *shko*-va de *deng*-tesh
toothpaste *pasta de dentes* ① *paash*-ta de *deng*-tesh
torch (flashlight) *lanterna eléctrica* ①
  lang-*ter*-na e-*le*-tree-ka
tourist office *escritório de turismo* ⓜ
  shkree-*to*-ryoo de too-*reezh*-moo
towel *toalha* ① *twaa*-lya
translate *traduzir* tra-doo-*zeer*

travel agency *agência de viagens* ①
  a-*zheng*-sya de vee-*aa*-zhengsh
travellers cheque *travellers cheque* ⓜ *tra*-ve-ler shek
trousers *calças* ① pl *kaal*-sash
twin beds *camas gémeas* ① pl *ka*-mash *zhe*-me-ash
tyre *pneu* ⓜ *pe*-ne-oo

U

underwear *roupa interior* ① *rroh*-pa eeng-te-ree-*or*
urgent *urgente* ⓜ&① oor-*zheng*-te

V

vacant *vago/a* ⓜ/① *vaa*-goo/a
vegetable *legume* ⓜ le-*goo*-me
vegetarian a *vegetariano/a* ⓜ/① ve-zhe-ta-ree-*a*-noo/a
visa *visto* ⓜ *veesh*-too

W

waiter *criado/a de mesa* ⓜ/① kree-*aa*-doo/a de *me*-za
walk ∨ *caminhar* ka-mee-*nyaar*
wallet *carteira* ① kar-*tay*-ra
warm a *morno/a* ⓜ/① *mor*-noo/a
wash (something) *lavar* la-*vaar*
watch *relógio* ⓜ rre-*lo*-zhyoo
water *água* ① *aa*-gwa
we *nós* nosh
weekend *fim-de-semana* ⓜ feeng-de-se-*ma*-na
west *oeste* o-*esh*-te
wheelchair *cadeira de rodas* ① ka-*day*-ra de *rro*-dash
when *quando* *kwang*-doo
where *onde* *ong*-de
who *quem* keng
why *porquê* poor-*ke*
window *janela* ① zha-*ne*-la
wine *vinho* ⓜ *vee*-nyoo
with *com* kong
without *sem* seng
woman *mulher* ① moo-*lyer*
write *escrever* shkre-*ver*

Y

you inf sg/pl *tu/vocês* too/vo-*sesh*
you pol sg/pl *você/vós* vo-*se*/vosh

Shona

pronunciation

Vowels		Consonants	
Symbol	**English sound**	**Symbol**	**English sound**
aa	father	b	bed
e	bet	b′	strong b with air sucked inward
ee	see	ch	cheat
o	pot	d	dog
oo	zoo	d′	strong d with air sucked inward
		dz	adze
		f	fun
		g	go
		h	hat
		j	jar
		k	kit
		m	man
		n	not
		ng	ring
		ny	canyon
		p	pet
		r	run (trilled)
		s	sun
		sh	shot
		t	top
		ts	lets
		v	very
		w	win
		y	yes
		z	zero
		zh	pleasure

In this chapter,
the Shona pronunciation
is given in orange after each phrase.

Each syllable is separated
by a dot. For example:

Mazviita.   maa·zvee·ta

Shona's glottalised consonants,
simplified as b′ and d′
in our pronunciation guide,
are made by tightening and releasing
the space between the vocal cords
when you pronounce them.
Both sounds are 'implosive' – instead of
breathing out to make the sound, you
breathe in.

SHONA
chishona

introduction

'Saunter', 'stroll', 'amble', 'march': a few of the English variations on 'walk'. Shona (*ChiShona* chee-sho-na) beats English hands down in this department, though – what about 'walk with buttocks shaking' (*mbwembwera* mbwe-mbwe-raa), 'walk squelchingly through mud' (*chakwaira* chaa-kwaa-ee-raa), 'walk with a stick' (*donzva* d'o-nzvaa), 'walk a long way' (*panha* paa-nhaa) or 'walk in a very short dress' (*pushuka* poo-shoo-kaa)? And that's just a sample of the more than 200 words Shona has for this everyday activity. Shona, a member of the Bantu language family, is spoken by about 11 million people, mainly in the southern African countries of Mozambique, Botswana and Zambia, in addition to a large number in the diaspora. The vast majority of speakers, however, are in Zimbabwe: the three official languages are English, Shona and Ndebele, but Shona is spoken by about 80 per cent of the population. The language has a flourishing literary culture, including novels, short stories, plays and journalism, and an enormous output of poetry – in fact, due to the metaphorical nature of the language, it's as though every Shona speaker is a poet.

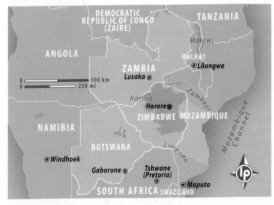

■ shona (native language) ■ shona (generally understood)

introduction – SHONA

language difficulties

Do you speak English?	Munotaura chiNgezi here?	moo·no·taa·oo·raa chee·nge·zee he·re
Do you understand?	Munonzvisisa here?	moo·no·nzvee·see·saa he·re
I understand.	Ndinonzvisisa.	ndee·no·nzvee·see·saa
I don't understand.	Handinzvisisi.	haa·ndee·nzvee·see·see
Could you please ...?	Munga ... wo here?	moo·ngaa ... wo he·re
repeat that	dzokorora izvozvo	dzo·ko·ro·raa i·zvo·zvo
speak more	taurisa	taa·oo·ree·saa
slowly	zvinyoronyoro	zvee·nyo·ro·nyo·ro
write it down	zvinyorei pasi	zvee·nyo·re·ee paa·see

time, dates & numbers

In time and date expressions, Shona uses English-style numbers.

What time is it?	Inguvai?	ee·ngoo·vaa·ee
It's (two) o'clock.	I(tu) kiroko.	ee·(too) kee·ro·ko
Quarter past (one).	Kota pasiti (hwani).	ko·taa paa·see·tee (hwaa·nee)
Half past (one).	Hafu pasiti (hwani).	haa·foo paa·see·tee (hwaa·nee)
Quarter to (eight).	Kota tu(eyiti).	ko·taa too·(e·yee·tee)
At what time ...?	Nenguvai ...?	ne·ngoo·vaa·ee ...
At ...	Na ...	naa ...
It's (15 December).	Ndi (15 Dhisemba).	ndee (fee·fee·tee·nee dee·se·mbaa)

yesterday	nezuro	ne·zoo·ro
today	nhasi	nhaa·see
tomorrow	mangwana	maa·ngwaa·naa

Monday	Muvhuro	moo·vhoo·ro
Tuesday	Chipiri	chee·pee·ree
Wednesday	Chitatu	chee·taa·too
Thursday	China	chee·naa
Friday	Chishanu	chee·shaa·noo
Saturday	Mugovera	mu·go·ve·raa
Sunday	Svondo	svo·ndo

numbers

0	*ziro*	zee-ro	20	*makumi*	ma-koo-mee
1	*-mwe*	-mwe		*maviri*	maa-vee-ree
2	*-viri*	-vee-ree	21	*makumi*	ma-koo-mee
3	*-tatu*	-taa-too		*maviri*	maa-vee-ree
4	*-na*	-naa		*neimwe*	ne-ee-mwe
5	*-shanu*	-shaa-noo	22	*makumi*	ma-koo-mee
6	*-tanhatu*	-taa-nhaa-too		*maviri*	maa-vee-ree
7	*-nomwe*	-no-mwe		*nembiri*	ne-mbee-ree
8	*-sere*	-se-re	30	*makumi*	maa-koo-mee
9	*-pfumbamwe*	-pfoo-mbaa-mwe		*matatu*	maa-taa-too
10	*gumi*	goo-mee	40	*makumi*	maa-koo-mee
11	*gumi neimwe*	goo-mee ne-ee-mwe		*mana*	maa-naa
12	*gumi*	goo-mee	50	*makumi*	maa-koo-mee
	nembiri	ne-mbee-ree		*mashanu*	maa-shaa-noo
13	*gumi*	goo-mee	60	*makumi*	maa-koo-mee
	nenhatu	ne-nhaa-too		*matanhatu*	maa-taa-nhaa-too
14	*gumi nena*	goo-mee ne-naa	70	*makumi*	maa-koo-mee
15	*gumineshanu*	goo-mee-ne-shaa-noo		*manomwe*	maa-no-mwe
16	*gumi*	goo-mee	80	*makumi*	maa-koo-mee
	nenhanhatu	ne-nhaa-nhaa-too		*masere*	maa-se-re
17	*gumi*	goo-mee	90	*makumi*	maa-koo-mee
	nenomwe	ne-no-mwe		*mapfu-*	maa-pfoo-
18	*gumi nesere*	goo-mee ne-se-re		*mbamwe*	mbaa-mwe
19	*gumi nepfu-*	goo-me ne-pfoo-	100	*zana*	zaa-naa
	mbamwe	mbaa-mwe	1000	*chiuru*	chee-oo-roo

border crossing

I'm here ...	*Ndiri muno ...*	ndee-ree moo-no ...
in transit	*patiranziti*	paa-tee-ra-nzee-tee
on business	*nezve bhizinesi*	ne-zve bee-zee-ne-see
on holiday	*pahorodhi*	paa-ho-ro-dee
I'm here for ...	*Ndiri muno kwe ...*	ndee-ree moo-no kwe ...
(10) days	*mazuva (gumi)*	maa-zoo-vaa (goo-mee)
(three) weeks	*mavhiki (matatu)*	maa-vhee-kee (maa-ta-too)
(two) months	*mwedzi (miviri)*	mwe-dzee (mee-vee-ree)

I'm going to (Gweru).
Ndiri kuenda ku (Gweru).
ndee·ree koo·e·ndaa koo (gwe·roo)

I'm staying at the (Midland Hotel).
Ndiri kugara pa (Midland Hotera).
ndee·ree koo·gaa·raa paa (mee·dlaand ho·te·raa)

tickets

One ... ticket (to Bulawayo), please.	*Ndinodawo tiketi rimwe ... (roku Bhuruwayo).*	ndee·no·daa·wo tee·ke·tee ree·mwe ... (ro·koo boo·roo·waa·yo)
one-way	*rehwaniweyi*	re·hwaa·nee·we·yee
return	*rokuenda ndichidzoka*	ro·koo·e·ndaa ndee·chee·dzo·kaa
I'd like to ... my ticket, please.	*Ndinodawo ku ... tiketi rangu.*	ndee·no·daa·wo koo ... tee·ke·tee raa·ngoo
cancel	*kanzura*	kaa·nzoo·raa
change	*chinja*	chee·njaa
collect	*korekita*	ko·re·kee·ta
Is there a ...?	*Pane ... here?*	paa·ne ... he·re
toilet	*chimbudzi*	che·mboo·dzee
air conditioning	*eya kondishina*	e·yaa ko·ndee·shee·naa

I'd like a smoking/nonsmoking seat, please.
Ndingadawo pasiti panoputirwa/ pasingaputirwi.
ndee·ngaa·daa·wo paa·see·tee paa·no·poo·tee·rwaa/ paa·see·ngaa·poo·tee·rwee

How long does the trip take?
Pane mufambo wakadii?
paa·ne moo·faa·mbo waa·kaa·dee·ee

Is it a direct route?
Iyi ndiyo nzira inonanga ikoko here?
ee·yee ndee·yo nzee·raa ee·no·naa·ngaa ee·ko·ko he·re

transport

Where does the flight (to Victoria Falls) arrive/depart?
Ndege ye (kuVictoria Falls)   nde·ge ye (koo·vee·kee·to·ree·yaa fols)
inosvikira/inosimukira   ee·no·svee·kee·raa/ee·no·see·moo·kee·raa
kupi?   koo·pee

How long will it be delayed?
Ichanonoka zvakadii?   ee·chaa·no·no·kaa zva·kaa·d'ee·ee

Is this the bus to (Chivhu)?
Iri ndiro bhazi roku   ee·ree ndee·ro baa·zee ro·koo
(Chivhu) here?   (chee·vhoo) he·re

Is this the train to (Mutare)?
Ichi ndicho chitima chokwa   ee·che ndee·cho chee·tee·maa cho·kwaa
(Mutare) here?   (moo·taa·re) he·re

How much is it to ...?
Kunoita marii kuenda ku ...?   koo·no·ee·taa maa·ree·ee koo·e·ndaa koo ...

Please take me to (this address).
Nditakureiwo kuenda   ndee·taa·koo·re·ee·wo koo·e·ndaa
ku (adhiresi iyi).   koo (aa·dee·re·see ee·yee)

I'd like to hire a ...   *Ndinoda kuhaya ...*   ndee·no·d'a koo·haa·yaa ...
(with air conditioning).   *(ine eya kondishina).*   (ee·ne e·yaa ko·ndee·shee·naa)
   car   *motokari*   mo·to·kaa·ree
   4WD   *ye fohwiri*   ye fo·hwee·ree
     dhiraivhi   dee·raa·ee·vhe

How much is it for (three) days/weeks?
Inoita marii kwemazuva/   ee·no·ee·taa maa·ree·ee kwe·maa·zoo·vaa/
mavhiki (matatu)?   maa·vhee·kee (maa·taa·too)

directions

Where's the (nearest) internet café?
Ko indaneti kafe   ko ee·ndaa·ne·tee kaa·fe
(iri pedyo pedyo) iri kupi?   (ee·ree pe·jgo pe·jgo) ee·ree koo·pee

Where's the (nearest) market?
Ko musika (uri pedyo pedyo)   ko moo·see·kaa (oo·ree pe·jgo pe·jgo)
uri kupi?   oo·ree koo·pee

Is this the road to (Mozambique)?

Uyu ndiwo mugwagwa woku (Mozambiki) here?   oo·yoo ndee·wo moo·gwaa·gwaa wo·koo (mo·zaa·mbee·kee) he·re

Can you show me (on the map)?

Munganditaridzawo (pamepu) here?   moo·ngaa·ndee·taa·ree·dzaa·wo (paa·me·poo) he·re

What's the address?	*Kero yacho ndiyani?*	ke·ro yaa·cho ndee·yaa·nee
How far is it?	*Kure zvakadii?*	koo·re zvaa·kaa·d'ee·ee
How do I get there?	*Ndinosvikako sei?*	ndee·no·svee·kaa·ko se·ee
Turn left/right.	*Konera kuruboshwe/ kurudyi.*	ko·ne·raa koo·roo·bo·shwe/ koo·roo·jgee

It's ...	*Iri ...*	ee·ree ...
behind ...	*seri ...*	se·ree ...
in front of ...	*mberi kwe ...*	mbe·ree kwe ...
near (to ...)	*pedyo (ne ...)*	pe·jgo (ne ...)
next to ...	*padivi pe ...*	pa·d'ee·vee pe ...
on the corner	*pakona*	paa·ko·naa
opposite ...	*pakatarisana ne ...*	paa·kaa·taa·ree·saa·naa ne ...
straight ahead	*nanga mberi*	naa·nga mbe·ree
there	*apo*	aa·po

accommodation

Where's a ...?	*Ndokupi ...?*	ndo·koo·pee ...
camping ground	*kunokembwa*	koo·no·ke·mbwaa
guesthouse	*kuimba yavaenzi*	koo·ee·mbaa yaa·vaa·e·nzee
hotel	*kuhotera*	koo·ho·te·raa
youth hostel	*kuhositeri*	koo·ho·see·te·ree

Can you recommend somewhere cheap/good?

Ungarekomenda kumwe kwakachipa/kwakanaka?   oo·ngaa·re·ko·me·ndaa koo·mwe kwaa·kaa·chee·paa/kwaa·kaa·naa·kaa

I'd like to book a room, please.

Ndinokumbirawo kubhuka rumu.   ndee·no·koo·mbee·raa·wo koo·boo·kaa roo·moo

I have a reservation.

Ndakarizevha.   ndaa·kaa·ree·ze·vha

Do you have	Mune rumu	moo-ne roo-moo
a ... room?	... here?	... he-re
single	yomunhu mumwe	yo-moo-nhoo moo-mwe
double	yavanhu vaviri	yaa-vaa-nhoo vaa-vee-ree
twin	ine mibhedha miviri	ee-ne mee-be-daa mee-vee-ree

How much is it per (night/person)?
Imarii pa(zuva/munhu)? ee-maa-ree-ee paa-(zoo-vaa/moo-nhoo)

I'd like to stay for (two) nights.
Ndingada kugara ndee-ngaa-daa koo-gaa-raa
kweusiku (huviri). kwe-oo-see-koo (hoo-vee-ree)

What time is check-out?
Cheki auti iriko nenguvai? che-kee aa-oo-tee ee-ree-ko ne-ngoo-vaa-ee

Am I allowed to camp here?
Ndinobvumirwa kukemba ndee-no-bvoo-mee-rwaa koo-ke-mbaa
panohere? paa-no-he-re

banking & communications

I'd like to ...	Ndinoda ku-...	ndee-no-daa koo-...
arrange a transfer	ronga zvetiranzifeya	ro-ngaa zve-tee-raa-nzee-fe-yaa
cash a cheque	kesha cheki	ke-shaa che-kee
change a travellers	chinja macheki	chee-njaa maa-che-kee
cheque	okufambisa	o-koo-faa-mbee-saa
change money	chinja mari	chee-njaa maa-ree
withdraw money	dhirowa mari	dee-ro-waa maa-ree

I want to ...	Ndinoda ku-...	ndee-no-daa koo-...
buy a phonecard	tenga kadhi refoni	te-ngaa kaa-dee re-fo-nee
call (Singapore)	fonera (kuSingapo)	fo-ne-raa (koo-see-ngaa-po)
reverse the charges	rivhesa machaji	ree-vhe-saa maa-chaa-jee
use a printer	shandisai purinda	shaa-ndee-saa-ee poo-ree-ndaa
use the internet	shandisai indaneti	shaa-ndee-saa-ee ee-ndaa-ne-tee

How much is it per hour?
Imarii paawa? ee-maa-ree-ee paa-aa-waa

How much does a (three-minute) call cost?
Kufona kwe (maminitsi matatu) koo-fo-naa kwe (maa-mee-nee-tsee maa-taa-too)
kunoita marii? koo-no-ee-taa maa-ree-ee

(One dollar) per minute/hour.
(Dhora rimwe) paminiti/paawa. (do-raa ree-mwe) paa-mee-nee-tee/paa-aa-waa

tours

When's the next ...?	Ko ... rini?	ko ... ree·nee
day trip	rwendo rwanhasi	rwe·ndo rwaa·nhaa·see
	runotevera ruriko	roo·no·te·ve·raa roo·re·ko
tour	tuwa inotevera	too·waa ee·no·te·ve·raa
	iriko	ee·ree·ko
Is ... included?	Ko ...-kasanganiswa here?	ko ...·kaa·saa·ngaa·nee·swaa he·re
accommodation	pokurara pa	po·koo·raa·raa paa
the admission charge	mari yokupindisa ya	maa·ree yo·koo·pee·ndee·saa yaa
food	mari yokudya ya	maa·ree yo·koo·jgaa yaa
transport	mari yokufambisa ya	maa·ree yo·koo·faa·mbee·saa yaa

How long is the tour?
Tuwa ichatora nguva yakadii? too·waa ee·chaa·to·raa ngoo·vaa yaa·kaa·d'ee·ee

What time should we be back?
Tinofanira kudzoka nenguvaii? tee·no·faa·nee·raa koo·dzo·kaa ne·ngoo·vaa·ee·ee

shopping

I'm looking for ...
Ndiri kutsvaga ... ndee·ree koo·tsvaa·gaa ...

I need film for this camera.
Ndinoda firimu rekamera iyi. ndee·no·da fee·ree·moo re·kaa·me·raa ee·yee

Can I listen to this?
Ndingateererawo kune izvi here? ndee·ngaa·te·e·re·raa·wo koo·nee ee·zvee he·re

Can I have my ... repaired?
Ndingagadzirirwa ... yangu here? ndee·ngaa·gaa·dzee·ree·rwaa ... yaa·ngoo he·re

When will it be ready?
Inenge yapera rinhi? ee·ne·nge yaa·pe·raa ree·nee

How much is it?
Inoita marii? ee·o·ee·taa maa·ree·ee

Can you write down the price?
Unganyora mutengo wacho pasi here? oo·ngaa·nyo·raa moo·te·ngo waa·cho paa·see he·re

What's your lowest price?
    Mutengo wakachipisa ndoupi?   moo·te·ngo waa·kaa·chee·pee·saa ndo·oo·pee

I'll give you (five) dollars.
    Ndinokupai madhora (mashanu).   ndee·no·koo·paa·ee maa·do·raa (maa·shaa·noo)

There's a mistake in the bill.
    Pane chakanganiswa pabhiri.   pa·ne chaa·kaa·ngaa·nee·swaa paa·bee·ree

It's faulty.
    Rakanyangara.   raa·kaa·nyaa·ngaa·raa

I'd like a receipt/refund, please.
    Ndinodawo risiti/rifandi.   ndee·no·daa·wo ree·see·tee/ree·faa·ndee

Do you accept …?	*Munobvuma … here?*	moo·no·bvoo·maa … he·re
credit cards	*makiredhiti kadzi*	maa·kee·re·dee·tee kaa·dzee
debit cards	*madhebhiti kadzi*	ma·de·bee·tee ka·dzee
travellers cheques	*macheki*	maa·che·kee
	okufambisa	oo·koo·faa·mbee·saa

Could you …?	*Munga … here?*	moo·nga … he·re
burn a CD from	*pisa CD kubva*	pee·sa see·dee koo·bvaa
my memory card	*mumemori*	moo·me·mo·ree
	kadhi rangu	kaa·dee raa·ngoo
develop this film	*dhivheropai*	dee·vhe·ro·pa·ee
	firimu iri	fee·ree·moo ee·ree

making conversation

Hello.	*Mhoroi.*	mho·ro·ee
Good night.	*Rarai zvakanaka.*	raa·raa·ee zvaa·kaa·naa·kaa
Goodbye.	*Tichaonana.*	tee·chaa·o·naa·naa
Mr	*Va-*	vaa·
Mrs	*Mai*	maa·ee
Ms/Miss	*Muzvare*	moo·zvaa·re
How are you?	*Makadii?*	maa·kaa·d'ee·ee
Fine, and you?	*Ndiripo makadiiwo?*	ndee·ree·po maa·kaa·d'ee·ee·wo
What's your name?	*Zita renyu ndiani?*	zee·taa re·nyoo ndee·aa·nee
My name's …	*Zita rangu ndinonzi …*	zee·taa raa·ngoo ndee·no·nzee …
I'm pleased to	*Ndinofara*	ndee·no·faa·raa
meet you.	*kukuzivai.*	koo·koo·zee·vaa·ee

This is my ...

boyfriend	*Uyu mukomana wangu.*	oo·yoo moo·ko·maa·naa waa·ngoo
daughter	*Uyu mwanasikana wangu.*	oo·yoo mwaa·naa·naa·see·kaa·naa waa·ngoo
father	*Ava ndi-baba wangu.*	aa·vaa ndee·b'aa·b'aa vaa·ngoo
friend	*Iyi ishamwari yangu.*	ee·yee ee·shaa·mwaa·ree yaa·ngoo
girlfriend	*Uyu musikana wangu.*	oo·yoo moo·see·kaa·naa waa·ngoo
husband	*Uyu murume wangu.*	oo·yoo moo·roo·me waa·ngoo
mother	*Ava ndi-amai vangu.*	aa·vaa ndee·aa·maa·ee vaa·ngoo
sibling (of the opposite sex)	*Iyi ihanzvadzi yangu.*	ee·yee ee·haa·nzvaa·dzee yaa·ngoo
sibling (elder of the same sex)	*Uyu mukoma wangu.*	oo·yoo moo·ko·maa waa·ngoo
sibling (younger of the same sex)	*Uyu munin'ina wangu.*	oo·yoo moo·nee·ngee·naa waa·ngoo
son	*Uyu mwanakomana wangu.*	oo·yoo mwaa·naa·ko·maa·naa waa·ngoo
wife	*Ava vadzimai vangu.*	aa·vaa vaa·dzee·maa·ee vaa·ngoo

Here's my ...	*Heyi ... yangu.*	he·yee ... yaa·ngoo
What's your ...?	*Ko ... yenyu ndiani?*	ko ... ye·nyoo ndee·aa·nee
(email) address	*(imeiri) adhiresi*	(ee·me·ree) a·dee·re·see
phone number	*nhamba yefoni*	nhaa·mbaa ye·fo·nee

Where are you from?	*Munobva kupi?*	moo·no·bvaa koo·pee

I'm from ...	*Ndinobva ku ...*	ndee·no·bvaa koo ...
Australia	*Ositireriya*	o·see·tee·re·ree·yaa
Canada	*Kanadha*	kaa·naa·daa
New Zealand	*Nyuzirandi*	nyoo·zee·raa·ndee

I'm married. m	*Ndakaroora.*	ndaa·kaa·ro·o·raa
I'm married. f	*Ndakaroorwa.*	ndaa·kaa·ro·o·rwaa
I'm not married. m	*Handina kuroora.*	haa·ndee·naa koo·ro·o·raa
I'm not married. f	*Handina kuroorwa.*	haa·ndee·naa koo·ro·o·rwaa
Can I take a photo (of you)?	*Ndingatora pikicha (inewe) here?*	ndee·ngaa·to·raa pee·kee·chaa (ee·ne·we) he·re

eating out

Can you recommend a ...?	Munga-rekomenda ... here?	moo-nga-re-ko-me-ndaa ... he-re
bar	bhawa	baa-waa
dish	chokudya	cho-koo-jgaa
place to eat	nzvimbo yokudyira	nzvee-mbo yo-koo-jgee-raa
I'd like ..., please.	Ndingadawo ...	ndee-ngaa-daa-wo ...
the bill	bhiri	bee-ree
the menu	minyu	mee-nyoo
a table for (two)	tebhuru ye (vaviri)	te-boo-roo ye (vaa-vee-ree)
that dish	chikafu icho	chee-kaa-foo ee-cho
Do you have vegetarian food?	Mune kudya kwechivhegiterieni here?	moo-ne koo-jga kwe-chee-vhe-gee-te-ree-e-nee he-re
Could you prepare a meal without ...?	Mungagadzira kudya kusina ... here?	moo-ngaa-gaa-dzee-raa koo-jga koo-see-naa ... he-re
eggs	mazai	maa-zaa-ee
meat stock	muto wenyama	mo-to we-nyaa-maa
(cup of) coffee/tea ...	(kapu ye-)kofi/tii ...	(kaa-poo ye-)ko-fee/tee-ee ...
with milk	ine mukaka	ee-ne moo-kaa-kaa
without sugar	isina shuga	ee-see-naa shoo-gaa
(boiled) water	mvura (yakavidzwa)	mvoo-raa (yaa-kaa-vee-dzwaa)

emergencies

Call ...!	Daidzai ...!	d'aa-ee-dzaa-ee ...
an ambulance	ambhurenzi	aam-boo-re-nzee
a doctor	dhokotera	do-ko-te-raa
the police	mapurisa	maa-poo-ree-saa

Could you help me, please?
Mungandibatsirawo here? moo-ngaa-ndee-b'aa-tsee-raa-wo he-re

Where are the toilets?
Zvimbudzi zviri kupi? zvee-mboo-dzee zvee-ree koo-pee

I want to report an offence.
Ndinoda kumhan'ara mhosva. ndee-no-daa koo-mha-ngaa-raa mho-svaa

I have insurance.
Ndine ishuwarenzi. ndee·ne ee·shoo·waa·re·nzee

I want to contact my consulate/embassy.
Ndinoda kutaura neEmbasi ndee·no·d'aa koo·taa·oo·raa ne·e·mba·see
yangu. yaa·ngoo

My bags were stolen.
Mabhegi angu abiwa. maa·bhe·gee aa·ngoo aa·b'ee·waa

My passport was stolen.
Pasipoti rangu rabiwa. paa·see·po·tee raa·ngoo raa·b'ee·waa

My wallet was stolen.
Chikwama changu chabiwa. chee·kwaa·maa chaa·ngoo chaa·b'ee·waa

I've been assaulted. *Ndarohwa.* ndaa·roh·waa
I've been raped. *Ndabatwa chibharo.* ndaa·baa·twaa chee·ba·ro
I've been robbed. *Ndabirwa.* ndaa·bee·rwaa

medical needs

Where's the nearest dentist?
Chiremba wemazino ari chee·re·mbaa we·maa·zee·no aa·ree
pedyo pedyo ari kupi? pe·jgo pe·jgo aa·ree koo·pee

Where's the nearest doctor?
Dhokotera ari pedyo do·ko·te·raa aa·ree pe·jgo
pedyo ari kupi? pe·jgo aa·ree koo·pee

Where's the nearest pharmacist?
Famasi iri pedyo pedyo iri kupi? faa·maa·see ee·ree pe·jgo pe·jgo ee·ree koo·pee

I need a doctor (who speaks English).
Ndinoda dhokotera ndee·no·d'aa do·ke·te·raa
(anotaura chiNgezi). (aa·no·taa·oo·raa chee·nge·zee)

Could I see a female doctor?
Ndingaonawo dhokotera ndee·ngaa·o·naa·wo do·ko·te·raa
wechikadzi here? we·chee·kaa·dzee he·re

It hurts here.
Panorwadza ndapapa. paa·no·rwaa·dzaa ndaa·paa·paa

I'm allergic to (penicillin).
Muviri wangu unosema moo·vee·ree waa·ngoo oo·no·se·maa
(penesirini). (pe·ne·see·ree·nee)

140

english–shona dictionary

In this dictionary, words are marked as n (noun), a (adjective), v (verb), sg (singular), pl (plural), inf (informal) and pol (polite) where necessary.

A

accommodation *pokurara* po-koo-raa-raa
adaptor *adhaputa* aa-daa-poo-taa
after *musure* moo-soo-re
airport *nhandare yendege* nhaa-ndaa-re ye-nde-ge
alcohol *hwahwa* hwaa-hwaa
all *-ose* -o-se
allergy *rusemo* roo-se-mo
and *na-* naa-
ankle *ziso regumbo* zee-so re-goo-mbo
antibiotics *mapiritsi okudzivirira*
  maa-pee-ree-tsee o-koo-dzee-vee-ree-raa
arm *ruoko* roo-o-ko
asthma *asima* a-see-maa
ATM *ATM* ay-tee-em

B

baby *mucheche* moo-che-che
back (body) *musana* moo-saa-naa
backpack *nhava yokumusana*
  nhaa-vaa yo-koo-moo-saa-naa
bad *-ipa* -ee-paa
baggage claim *kunotorwa mabhegi*
  koo-no-to-rwaa maa-be-gee
bank *bhangi* baa-ngee
bathroom *imba yokugezera* ee-mbaa yo-koo-ge-ze-ra
battery *bhatiri* baa-tee-ree
beautiful *kunaka* koo-naa-kaa
bed *mubhedha* moo-be-daa
beer *doro* do-ro
bees *nyuchi* nyoo-chee
before *pasure* paa-soo-re
bicycle *bhasikoro* baa-see-ko-ro
big *-kuru* -koo-roo
blanket *jira* jee-raa
blood group *chikamu cheropa* chee-kaa-moo che-ro-paa
bottle *bhodhoro* bo-do-ro
bottle opener *chivhuro chebhodhoro*
  chee-vhoo-ro che-bo-do-ro
boy *mukomana* moo-ko-maa-naa
brakes (car) *mabhureki* maa-boo-re-kee
breakfast *bhurekifasi* boo-re-kee-faa-see
bronchitis *chirwere chemapapu*
  chee-rwe-re che-maa-paa-pu

C

café *kafe* kaa-fe
cancel *kanzura* kaa-nzoo-raa
can opener *chivhuro chegaba*
  chee-vhoo-ro che-gaa-b'aa
cash n *keshi* ke-shee
cell phone *serifoni* se-ree-fo-nee
centre n *pakati* paa-kaa-tee
cheap *chipa* chee-paa
check (bill) *cheki* che-kee
check-in n *pokuchekaini* po-koo-che-kaa-ee-nee
chest *chipfuva* chee-pfoo-vaa
child *mwana* mwaa-naa
cigarette *mudzanga* moo-dzaa-ngaa
city *guta* goo-taa
clean a *chena* che-naa
closed *vharwa* vhaa-rwaa
cold a *-tonhora* -to-nho-raa
collect call *rivhesi chaji* ree-ve-see chaa-jee
condom *kondomu* ko-ndo-moo
constipation *kupatirwa* koo-paa-tee-rwaa
contact lenses *makondakiti renzi*
  maa-ko-ndaa-kee-tee re-nzee
cough n *-kosora* -ko-so-raa
currency exchange *kuchinjiwa kwemari*
  koo-chee-njee-waa kwe-maa-ree
customs (immigration) *kupinda nokubuda*
  koo-pee-ndaa no-koo-b'oo-d'aa

D

dairy products *zvine mukaka* zvee-ne moo-ka-ka
dangerous *-ne ngozi* -ne ngo-zee
date (time) *musi we (nguva)* moo-see we (ngoo-vaa)
day *zuva* zoo-vaa
diaper *napukeni* naa-poo-ke-nee
diarrhoea *manyoka* maa-nyo-kaa
dinner *zvokudya* zo-koo-jgaa
dirty *tsvina* tsvee-naa
disabled *chikosha* chee-ko-shaa
double bed *mubhedha wevanhu vaviri*
  moo-be-daa we-vaa-nhoo vaa-vee-ree
drink n *chokunwa* cho-koo-nwaa
drivers licence *raisenzi yemotokari*
  raa-ee-se-nzee ye-mo-to-kaa-ree
drug (illicit) *dhiragi* dee-raa-gee

E

ear *nzeve* nze-ve
east *madokero* maa-do-ke-ro
economy class *mbhombhera* mbo-mbe-raa
elevator *rifuti* ree-foo-tee
email n *imeri* ee-me-ree
English (language) *chiNgezi* chee-nge-zee
exchange rate *reti yokochinja mari*
 re-tee yo-ko-chee-njaa maa-ree
exit n *pokubuda napo* po-koo-b'oo-d'aa naa-po
expensive *-dhura* -doo-raa
eye *ziso* zee-so

F

fast *-kurumidza* -koo-roo-mee-dzaa
fever *hosha* ho-shaa
finger *munwe* moo-nwe
first-aid kit *bhokisi refesiti eidhi*
 bo-kee-see re-fe-see-tee e-ee-dee
first class *kutopa* koo-to-paa
fish n *hove* ho-ve
food *kudya* koo-jgaa
foot *tsoka* tso-kaa
fork *foroko* fo-ro-kaa
free (of charge) *mahara* ma-haa-raa
fruit *muchero* moo-che-ro
funny *-setsa* -se-tsaa

G

game park *gemupaki* maa-ge-moo-paa-kee
gift *chipo* chee-po
girl *musikana* moo-see-kaa-naa
glass (drinking) *girazi* gee-raa-zee
glasses *magirazi* ma-gee-raa-zee
gluten *-rembuka* -re-mboo-kaa
good *-naka* -na-kaa
gram *giramu* gee-raa-moo
guide n *mutungamiriri* moo-too-ngaa-mee-ree-ree

H

hand *ruoko* roo-o-ko
happy *-fara* -faa-raa
have *-ne* -ne
he *a-* aa-
head *musoro* moo-so-ro
headache *kutemwa nemusoro* koo-te-mwaa ne-moo-so-ro
heart *moyo* mo-yo

heart condition *chirwere chemoyo* chee-rwe-re che-mo-yo
heat n *kudziya* koo-dzee-yaa
here *pano* paa-no
high *-refu* -re-foo
highway *mugwagwa* moo-gwaa-gwaa
homosexual n *ngochani* ngo-chaa-nee
homosexual a *hungochani* hoo-ngo-chaa-nee
hot *-pisa* -pee-saa
hungry *-ne nzara* -ne nzaa-raa

I

I *Ini* ee-nee
identification (card) *chitupa* chee-too-paa
ill *-rwara* -rwaa-raa
important *-kosha* -ko-shaa
internet *Indaneti* ee-ndaa-ne-tee
interpreter *muturikiri* moo-too-ree-kee-ree

K

key *kiyi* kee-yee
kilogram *kirogiramu* kee-ro-gee-raa-moo
kitchen *imba yokubikira* ee-mbaa yo-koo-b'ee-kee-raa
knife *banga* b'aa-ngaa

L

laundry (place) *imba yokuwachira*
 ee-mbaa yo-koo-waa-chee-raa
lawyer *gweta* gwe-taa
left-luggage office *pahofisi panosiiwa nhumbi*
 paa-ho-fee-see pa-no-see-ee-waa nhoo-mbee
leg *gumbo* goo-mbo
lesbian n *ngochani* ngo-chaa-nee
lesbian a *hungochani* hoo-ngo-chaa-nee
less *hafuka* haa-foo-ka
letter (mail) *tsamba* tsaa-mbaa
like v *-da* -d'aa
lost-property office
 pahofisi panochengetedzwa zvakarasika
 paa-hof-ee-see paa-no-che-nge-te-dzwa
 zva-kaa-raa-see-kaa
love v *-da* -daa
lunch *ranji* raa-njee

M

man *murume* moo-roo-me
matches *machisi* maa-chee-see
meat *nyama* nyaa-maa

medicine *mushonga* moo-sho-ngaa
message *shoko* sho-ko
mobile phone *serifoni* se-ree-fo-nee
month *mwedzi* mwe-dzee
morning *mangwanani* ma-ngwaa-naa-nee
motorcycle *mudhudhudhu* moo-doo-doo-doo
mouth *muromo* moo-ro-mo
movie *firimu* fee-ree-moo
MSG *MSG* em-es-jee
museum *muziyamu* moo-zee-ya-moo
music *mumanzi* moo-maa-nzee

N

name n *zita* zee-taa
napkin *napukeni* naa-poo-ke-nee
nappy *mutambo* moo-taa-mbo
national park *neshinari paki* ne-shee-naa-ree paa-kee
nausea *chisvoto* chee-swo-to
neck *huro* hoo-ro
new *-tsva* -tsvaa
news *nhau* nha-oo
newspaper *bepanhau* be-paa-nha-oo
night *usiku* oo-see-koo
nightclub *naiti kirabhu* na-ee-tee kee-raa-bu
noisy *ruzha* roo-zha
nonsmoking *hapaputirwi fodya*
    haa-paa-poo-tee-rwee fo-jgaa
north *maodzanyemba* ma-o-dzaa-nye-mbaa
nose *mhino* m-hee-no
now *ikozvino* ee-ko-zvee-no
number *nhamba* nhaa-mbaa
nuts *nzungu* nzoo-ngoo

O

oil (engine) *oiri* o-ee-ree
OK *okeyi* o-ke-yee
old *tsaru* tsaa-roo
open a *vhurika* vhoo-ree-kaa
outside *panze* paa-nze

P

package *pakeji* paa-ke-jee
pain *chirwadzo* chee-rwaa-dzo
palace *dzimbabwe* dzee-mbaa-bwe
paper *bepa* b'e-paa
park (car) v *-paka* -paa-kaa
passport *pasipoti* paa-see-po-tee
pay *-bhadhara* -baa-daa-raa
pen *chinyoreso* chee-nyo-re-so

petrol *peturo* pe-tu-ro
pharmacy *famasi* faa-maa-see
plate *ndiro* ndee-ro
postcard *positikadhi* po-see-tee-kaa-dee
post office *hofisi yetsamba* ho-fee-see ye-tsaa-mbaa
pregnant *-ne nhumbu* -ne noo-mboo

R

rain n *mvura* mvoo-ra
registered mail *tsamba yaka rejisitiwa*
    tsaa-mbaa yaa-kaa re-jee-see-tee-waa
rent v *-renda* -re-ndaa
repair v *-gadzira* -gaa-dzee-raa
reservation *kurizevho* koo-ree-ze-vhaa
restaurant *resitorendi* re-see-to-re-ndee
return v *-dzoka* -dzo-kaa
road *mugwagwa* moo-gwaa-gwaa
room *imba* ee-mbaa

S

sad *-suruvara* -soo-roo-vaa-raa
safe a *banya* baa-nyaa
sanitary napkin *chidhende* chee-de-nde
seafood *chokudya chomumvura*
    cho-koo-jgaa cho-moo-mvoo-raa
seat *chigaro* chee-gaa-ro
send *-tuma* -too-maa
(have) sex *-svirana* -swee-raa-naa
shampoo *shambu* shaa-mboo
share (a dorm, etc) *kusheya* koo-she-yaa
shaving cream *kirimu yokushevha*
    kee-ree-moo yo-koo-she-vhaa
she a- aa-
sheet (bed) *shiti (bhedha)* shee-tee (be-daa)
shirt *hembe* he-mbe
shoes *shangu* shaa-ngoo
shop n *chitoro* chee-to-ro
shower n *shawa* shaa-waa
skin *ganda* gaa-ndaa
skirt *siketi* see-ke-tee
sleep v *-rara* -raa-raa
small *-diki* -d'ee-kee
smoke (cigarettes) v *-puta* -poo-taa
soap *sipo* see-po
some *-mwe* -mwe
soon *iko zvino* ee-ko zvee-no
sore throat *-karakata* -kaa-raa-kaa-taa
south *chamhembe* chaa-mhe-mbe
souvenir shop *chitoro chesuvheniya*
    chee-to-ro che-soo-vhe-nee-yaa

speak *-taura* -taa·oo·raa
spoon *chipunu* chee·poo·noo
stamp n *chitambi* chee·taa·mbee
station (train) *chiteshi chechitima*
   chee·te·shee che·chee·tee·maa
stomach *dumbu* d'oo·mboo
stop v *-mira* -mee·raa
stop (bus) n *chiteshi chebhazi* chee·te·shee che·baa·zee
street *mugwagwa* moo·gwaa·gwaa
student *mudzidzi* moo·dzee·dzee
sunscreen *mafuta okudzivirira zuva*
   maa·foo·taa o·koo·dzee·vee·ree·raa zoo·vaa
swim v *-shambira* -shaa·mbee·raa

T

tampons *matambuni* maa·taa·mboo·nee
teeth *mazino* maa·zee·no
telephone n *foni* fo·nee
television *terevhizhini* te·re·vhee·zhee·nee
temperature (weather) *temburicha* te·mboo·ree·chaa
tent *tende* te·nde
that (one) *icho* ee·cho
they (lit: people) *Ivo* ee·vo
thirsty *-ne nyota* -ne nyo·taa
this (one) *ichi* ee·chee
throat *huro* hoo·ro
ticket *tikiti* tee·kee·tee
time *nguva* ngoo·vaa
tired *-neta* -ne·taa
tissues *matishu* maa·tee·shoo
today *nhasi* nhaa·see
toilet *chimbudzi* chee·mboo·dzee
tonight *usiku hwuno* oo·see·koo hwoo·no
toothache *kurwadza kwezino* koo·rwaa·dza kwe·zee·no
toothbrush *bhurashi remazino* boo·raa·shee re·maa·zee·no
toothpaste *mushonga wemazino*
   moo·sho·ngaa we·maa·zee·no
torch (flashlight) *tochi* to·chee
tourist office *hofisi yetuwarizimu*
   ho·fee·see ye·too·waa·ree·zee·moo
towel *tauro* taa·oo·ro
translate *-turikira* -too·ree·kee·raa
travel agency *tiraveri ajendi* tee·raa·ve·ree aa·je·ndee
travellers cheque *macheki okufambisa*
   maa·che·kee o·koo·faa·mbee·saa
trousers *mabhurukwa* maa·boo·roo·kwaa

twin beds *imba ine mibhedha miviri*
   ee·mba ee·ne mee·be·daa mee·vee·ree
tyre *taya* taa·yaa

U

underwear *nduwe* ndoo·we
urgent *kukurumidza* koo·koo·roo·mee·dzaa

V

vacant *pane nzvimbo* paa·ne nvee·mbo
vegetable n *muriwo* moo·ree·wo
vegetarian a *muvhejiteriyeni* moo·vhe·jee·te·ree·ye·nee
visa *vhiza* vhee·zaa

W

waiter *hweta* hwe·taa
walk v *-famba* -faa·mbaa
wallet *chikwama* chee·kwaa·maa
warm a *-dziya* -dzee·yaa
wash (something) *-geza* -ge·zaa
watch n *wachi* waa·chee
water *mvura* mvoo·raa
we *ti-* tee-
weekend *hwikendi* hwee·ke·ndee
west *madokero* maa·d'o·ke·ro
wheelchair *hwiricheya* hwee·ree·che·yaa
when *rini* ree·nee
where (at what place) *papi* paa·pee
where (in what place) *mupi* moo·pee
where (to where) *kupi* koo·pee
who *ani* aa·nee
why *sei* se·ee
window *hwindo* hwee·ndo
wine *waini* waa·ee·nee
with *ne-* ne-
without *-sina* -see·naa
woman *mukadzi* moo·kaa·dzee
write *nyora* nyo·raa

Y

you sg inf/pol *iwe/imi* ee·we/ee·mee
you pl inf&pol *imi* ee·mee

Swahili

pronunciation

Vowels		Consonants	
Symbol	**English sound**	**Symbol**	**English sound**
aa	father	b	bed
ee	see	ch	cheat
ey	as in 'bet', but longer	d	dog
oh	note	dh	that
oo	zoo	f	fun
		g	go
		h	hat
		j	jar
		k	kit
		l	lot
		m	man
		n	not
In this chapter, the Swahili pronunciation is given in brown after each phrase.		ng	ring
		ny	canyon
Each syllable is separated by a dot, and the syllable stressed in each word is italicised.		p	pet
		r	run (but softer, more like a light 'd')
For example:		s	sun
Habari. haa-*baa*-ree		sh	shot
		t	top
		th	thin
		v	very
		w	win
		y	yes
		z	zero

SWAHILI
kiswahili

introduction

Swahili (*kiswahili* kee-swa-*hee*-lee) is one of the most widely spoken African languages, with an estimated 50 million-plus speakers throughout East Africa. Though it's the mother tongue of only about 4 to 5 million people, it's used as a second language or a lingua franca by speakers of many other African languages. Swahili is the national language of Tanzania and Kenya and is widely used in Uganda, Rwanda and Burundi, as well as in the eastern part of the Democratic Republic of Congo and on the Indian Ocean islands of Zanzibar and the Comoros. There are speakers of Swahili in the southern parts of Ethiopia and Somalia, the north of Mozambique and Zambia, and even on the northwestern coast of Madagascar. Swahili belongs to the Bantu group of languages from the Niger-Congo family and can be traced back to the first millenium AD. Standard Swahili developed from the urban dialect of Zanzibar City, dominant from precolonial times. Although there are many dialects of Swahili, you'll be understood if you stick to the standard coastal form, as used in this book.

 swahili (native language)    swahili (generally understood)

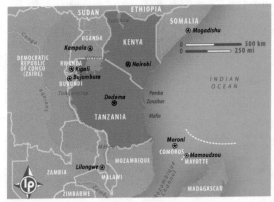

language difficulties

Do you speak (English)?	Unasema (Kiingereza)?	oo-naa-sey-maa (kee-een-gey-rey-zaa)
Do you understand?	Unaelewa?	oo-naa-ey-ley-waa
I understand.	Naelewa.	naa-ey-ley-waa
I don't understand.	Sielewi.	see-ey-ley-wee

Could you please ...?	Tafadhali ...	taa-faa-dhaa-lee ...
repeat that	sema tena	sey-maa tey-naa
speak more slowly	sema pole pole	sey-maa poh-ley poh-ley
write it down	andika	aan-dee-kaa

time, dates & numbers

What time is it?	Ni saa ngapi?	nee saa n-gaa-pee
It's one o'clock.	Ni saa saba.	nee saa saa-baa
It's (two) o'clock.	Ni saa (nane).	nee saa (naa-ne)
Quarter past (one).	Ni saa (saba) na robo.	nee saa (saa-baa) naa roh-boh
Half past (one).	Ni saa (saba) na nusu.	nee saa (saa-baa) naa noo-soo
Quarter to (ten).	Ni saa (nne) kasarobo.	nee saa (n-ney) kaa-saa-roh-boh
At what time ...?	... saa ngapi?	... saa n-gaa-pee
At ...	Saa ...	saa ...
It's (18 October).	Ni (tarehe kumi na nane, mwezi wa kumi). (lit: date eighteen, month tenth)	nee (taa-rey-hey koo-mee naa naa-ney mwey-zee waa koo-mee)

yesterday	jana	jaa-naa
today	leo	ley-oh
tomorrow	kesho	key-shoh

Monday	Jumatatu	joo-maa-taa-too
Tuesday	Jumanne	joo-maa-n-ney
Wednesday	Jumatano	joo-maa-taa-noh
Thursday	Alhamisi	aal-haa-mee-see
Friday	Ijumaa	ee-joo-maa
Saturday	Jumamosi	joo-maa-moh-see
Sunday	Jumapili	joo-maa-pee-lee

numbers

0	*sifuri*	see-*foo*-ree	17	*kumi na saba*	*koo*-mee naa *saa*-baa
1	*moja*	*moh*-jaa	18	*kumi na nane*	*koo*-mee naa *naa*-ney
2	*mbili*	m-*bee*-lee	19	*kumi na tisa*	*koo*-mee naa *tee*-saa
3	*tatu*	*taa*-too	20	*ishirini*	ee-shee-*ree*-nee
4	*nne*	*n*-ney	21	*ishirini*	ee-shee-*ree*-nee
5	*tano*	*taa*-noh		*na moja*	naa *moh*-jaa
6	*sita*	*see*-taa	22	*ishirini*	ee-shee-*ree*-nee
7	*saba*	*saa*-baa		*na mbili*	naa m-*bee*-lee
8	*nane*	*naa*-ney	30	*thelathini*	they-laa-*thee*-nee
9	*tisa*	*tee*-saa	40	*arobaini*	aa-roh-baa-ee-nee
10	*kumi*	*koo*-mee	50	*hamsini*	haam-*see*-nee
11	*kumi na moja*	*koo*-mee naa *moh*-jaa	60	*sitini*	see-*tee*-nee
12	*kumi na mbili*	*koo*-mee naa m-*bee*-lee	70	*sabini*	saa-*bee*-nee
13	*kumi na tatu*	*koo*-mee naa *taa*-too	80	*themanini*	they-maa-*nee*-nee
14	*kumi na nne*	*koo*-mee naa *n*-ney	90	*tisini*	tee-*see*-nee
15	*kumi na tano*	*koo*-mee naa *taa*-noh	100	*mia moja*	*mee*-aa *moh*-jaa
16	*kumi na sita*	*koo*-mee naa *see*-taa	1000	*elfu*	*eyl*-foo

border crossing

I'm ...	*Mimi ni ...*	*mee*-mee nee ...
in transit	*safarini*	saa-faa-*ree*-nee
on business	*kwa biashara*	kwaa bee-aa-*shaa*-raa
on holiday	*kwa likizo*	kwaa lee-*kee*-zoh
I'm here for ...	*Nipo kwa ...*	*nee*-poh kwaa ...
(three) days	*siku (tatu)*	*see*-koo (*taa*-too)
(two) weeks	*wiki (mbili)*	*wee*-kee (m-*bee*-lee)
(four) months	*miezi (minne)*	mee-*ey*-zee (mee-*n*-ney)

I'm going to (Malindi).
Naenda (Malindi). naa-*eyn*-daa (maa-*leen*-dee)

I'm staying at (the Pendo Inn).
Nakaa (Pendo Inn). naa-*kaa* (*peyn*-doh een)

tickets

One … ticket to (Iringa), please.	*Tiketi moja ya … kwenda (Iringa).*	tee·*key*·tee *moh*·jaa yaa … *kweyn*·daa (ee·*reen*·gaa)
one-way	*kwenda tu*	*kweyn*·daa too
return	*kwenda na kurudi*	*kweyn*·daa naa koo·*roo*·dee
I'd like to … my ticket, please.	*Nataka … tiketi yangu, tafadhali.*	naa·*taa*·kaa … tee·*key*·tee *yaan*·goo taa·faa·*dhaa*·lee
cancel	*kufuta*	koo·*foo*·taa
change	*kubadilisha*	koo·baa·dee·*lee*·shaa
confirm	*kuhakikisha*	koo·haa·kee·*kee*·shaa

I'd like a smoking/nonsmoking seat, please.
Nataka kiti kuvuta/kutovuta sigara. — naa·*taa*·kaa *kee*·tee koo·*voo*·taa/koo·toh·*voo*·taa see·*gaa*·raa

Is there a toilet?
Kuna choo? — *koo*·naa choh

Is there a air conditioning?
Kuna a/c? — *koo*·naa ey·*see*

How long does the trip take?
Safari huchukua muda gani? — saa·*faa*·ree hoo·choo·*koo*·aa *moo*·daa *gaa*·nee

Is it a direct route?
Njia ni moja kwa moja? — n·*jee*·aa nee *moh*·jaa kwaa *moh*·jaa

transport

Where does flight (number 432) arrive/depart?
Ndege (namba mia nne thelathini na mbili) itafika/itaondoka wapi? — n·*dey*·gey (*naam*·baa *mee*·aa *n*·ney they·laa·*thee*·nee naa m·*bee*·lee) ee·taa·*fee*·kaa/ee·taa·ohn·*doh*·kaa *waa*·pee

How long will it be delayed?
Itachelewa kwa muda gani? — ee·taa·chey·*ley*·waa kwaa *moo*·daa *gaa*·nee

Is this the ...	Hii ni ... kwenda	hee nee ... kweyn-daa
to (Mombasa)?	(Mombasa)?	(mohm-baa-saa)
boat	Boti	boh-tee
bus	Basi	baa-see
plane	Ndege	n-dey-gey
train	Treni	trey-nee

How much is it to ...?
Ni bei gani kwenda ...?　　nee bey gaa-nee kweyn-daa ...

Please take me to (this address).
Tafadhali niendeshe　　taa-faa-dhaa-lee nee-eyn-dey-shey
mpaka (anwani hii).　　m-paa-kaa (aan-waa-nee hee)

I'd like to hire a car/4WD (with air conditioning).
Nataka kukodi gari/　　naa-taa-kaa koo-koh-dee gaa-ree/
forbaifor (kwenye a/c).　　fohr-baa-ee-fohr (kwey-nyey ey-see)

How much is it for (three) days/weeks?
Ni bei gani kwa siku/wiki (tatu)?　　nee bey gaa-nee kwaa see-koo/wee-kee (taa-too)

directions

Where's the	... hapo karibuni	... haa-poh kaa-ree-boo-nee
nearest ...?	iko wapi?	ee-koh waa-pee
internet café	Intaneti Kafe	een-taa-ney-tee kaa-fey
market	Soko	soh-koh

Is this the road to (Embu)?
Hii ni barabara kwenda (Embu)?　　hee nee baa-raa-baa-raa kweyn-daa (eym-boo)

Can you show me (on the map)?
Unaweza kunionyesha　　oo-naa-wey-zaa koo-nee-oh-nyey-shaa
(katika ramani)?　　(kaa-tee-kaa raa-maa-nee)

What's the address?
Anwani ni nini?　　aan-waa-nee nee nee-nee

How far is it?
Ni umbali gani?　　nee oom-baa-lee gaa-nee

How do I get there?
Nifikaje?　　nee-fee-kaa-jey

Turn left/right.
Geuza kushoto/kulia.　　gey-oo-zaa koo-shoh-toh/koo-lee-aa

It's ...	Iko ...	ee·koh ...
behind ...	nyuma ya ...	nyoo·maa yaa ...
in front of ...	mbele ya ...	m·bey·ley yaa ...
near ...	karibu na ...	kaa·ree·boo naa ...
next to ...	jirani ya ...	jee·raa·nee yaa ...
on the corner	pembeni	peym·bey·nee
opposite ...	ng'ambo ya ...	ng·aam·boh yaa ...
straight ahead	moja kwa moja	moh·jaa kwaa moh·jaa
there	hapo	haa·poh

accommodation

Where's a ...?	... iko wapi?	... ee·koh waa·pee
camping ground	Uwanja wa	oo·waan·jaa waa
	kambi	kaam·bee
guesthouse	Gesti	gey·stee
hotel	Hoteli	hoh·tey·lee
youth hostel	Hosteli ya	hoh·stey·lee yaa
	vijana	vee·jaa·naa

Can you recommend somewhere cheap/good?

Unaweza kunipendeke   oo·naa·wey·zaa koo·nee·peyn·dey·key
zea malazi rahisi/nzuri?   zey·aa maa·laa·zee raa·hee·see/n·zoo·ree

I'd like to book a room, please.

Nataka kufanya   naa·taa·kaa koo·faa·nyaa
buking, tafadhali.   boo·keeng taa·faa·dhaa·lee

I have a reservation.

Nina buking.   nee·naa boo·keeng

How much is it per night/person?

Ni bei gani kwa usiku/mtu?   nee bey gaa·ne kwaa oo·see·koo/m·too

Do you have a ... room? *Kuna chumba kwa ...?* koo·naa choom·baa kwaa ...

single	mtu mmoja	m·too m·moh·jaa
double	watu wawili,	waa·too waa·wee·lee
	kitanda kimoja	kee·taan·daa kee·moh·jaa
twin	watu wawili,	waa·too waa·wee·lee
	vitanda viwili	vee·taan·daa vee·wee·lee

I'd like to stay for (two) nights.
Nataka kukaa kwa   naa-*taa*-kaa koo-*kaa* kwaa
usiku (mbili).   oo-*see*-koo (m-*bee*-lee)

What time is check-out?
Muda wa kuachia   moo-daa waa koo-aa-*chee*-aa
chumba ni saa ngapi?   choom-baa nee saa n-*gaa*-pee

Am I allowed to camp here?
Naweza kuwa hapa kwa usiku?   naa-*wey*-zaa koo-waa *haa*-paa kwaa oo-*see*-koo

banking & communications

I'd like to ...	*Nataka ...*	naa-*taa*-kaa ...
cash a cheque	*kulipwa fedha*	koo-*leep*-waa *fey*-dhaa
	kutokana na hundi	koo-toh-*kaa*-naa naa *hoon*-dee
change a travellers	*kubadilisha*	koo-baa-dee-*lee*-shaa
cheque	*hundi ya msafiri*	*hoon*-dee yaa m-saa-*fee*-ree
change money	*kubadilisha hela*	koo-baa-dee-*lee*-shaa *hey*-laa
transfer money	*kufikisha hela*	koo-fee-*kee*-shaa *hey*-laa
withdraw money	*kuondoa hela*	koo-ohn-*doh*-aa *hey*-laa

I want to ...	*Nataka ...*	naa-*taa*-kaa ...
buy a phonecard	*kununua kadi*	koo-noo-*noo*-aa *kaa*-dee
	ya simu	yaa *see*-moo
call (Singapore)	*kupiga simu kwa*	koo-*pee*-gaa *see*-moo kwaa
	(Singapore)	(seen-gaa-*pohr*)
reverse the charges	*kugeuza gharama*	koo-gey-*oo*-zaa gaa-*raa*-maa
use a printer	*kutumia printa*	koo-too-*mee*-aa *preen*-taa
use the internet	*kutumia intaneti*	koo-too-*mee*-aa een-taa-*ney*-tee

How much is it per hour?
Ni bei gani kwa saa?   nee bey *gaa*-nee kwaa saa

How much does a (three)-minute call cost?
Kupiga simu kwa dakika   koo-*pee*-gaa *see*-moo kwaa daa-*kee*-kaa
(tatu) ni bei gani?   (*taa*-too) nee bey *gaa*-nee

(1000 shillings) per minute/hour.
(Shilingi elfu moja) kwa   (shee-*leen*-gee *eyl*-foo moh-jaa) kwaa
dakika/saa.   daa-*kee*-kaa/saa

tours

When's the next ...?	... ijayo itakuwa lini?	... ee·*jaa*·yoh ee·taa·*koo*·waa *lee*·nee
day trip	Safari ya siku moja	saa·*faa*·ree yaa *see*·koo moh·jaa
tour	Safari	saa·*faa*·ree

Is ... included?	Inazingatia ...?	ee·naa·zeen·gaa·*tee*·aa ...
accommodation	malazi	maa·*laa*·zee
food	chakula	chaa·*koo*·laa
the park entrance fee	ada za hifadhi	*aa*·daa zaa hee·*faa*·dhee
transport	usafiri	oo·saa·*fee*·ree

How long is the tour?
Safari itachukua muda gani?
saa·*faa*·ree ee·taa·choo·*koo*·aa *moo*·daa *gaa*·nee

What time should we be back?
Turudi saa ngapi?
too·*roo*·dee saa n·*gaa*·pee

shopping

I'm looking for ...
Natafuta ...
naa·taa·*foo*·taa ...

I need film for this camera.
Nahitaji filamu kwa kemra hii.
naa·hee·*taa*·jee fee·*laa*·moo kwaa *keym*·raa hee

Can I listen to this?
Naomba tusikilize.
naa·*ohm*·baa too·see·kee·*lee*·zey

Can I have my ... repaired?
Mnaweza kutengeneza ... yangu hapa?
m·naa·*wey*·zaa koo·teyn·gey·*ney*·zaa ... *yaan*·goo *haa*·paa

When will it be ready?
Itakuwa tayari lini?
ee·taa·*koo*·waa taa·*yaa*·ree *lee*·nee

How much is it?
Ni bei gani?
ni bey *gaa*·nee

Can you write down the price?
Andika bei.　　　　　　　　　　aan-*dee*-kaa bey

What's your lowest price?
Niambie bei ya mwisho.　　　　nee-aam-*bee*-ey bey *yaa*-koh yaa *mwee*-shoh

I'll give you (500 shillings).
Nitakupa (shilingi mia tano).　nee-taa-*koo*-paa (shee-*leen*-gee mee-aa *taa*-noh)

There's a mistake in the bill.
Kuna kosa kwenye bili.　　　　koo-naa koh-saa kweyn-yey *bee*-lee

It's faulty.
Haifanyi kazi.　　　　　　　　haa-ee-*faa*-nyee *kaa*-zee

I'd like a receipt, please.
Naomba risiti, tafadhali.　　　naa-*ohm*-baa ree-*see*-tee taa-faa-*dhaa*-lee

I'd like a refund, please.
Nataka unirudishie　　　　　　naa-*taa*-kaa oo-nee-roo-dee-*shee*-ey
hela, tafadhali.　　　　　　　*hey*-laa taa-faa-*dhaa*-lee

Do you accept …?	*Mnakubali …*	m-naa-koo-*baa*-lee …
credit cards	*kadi ya benki*	*kaa*-dee yaa *beyn*-kee
travellers cheques	*hundi ya msafiri*	*hoon*-dee yaa m-saa-*fee*-ree

Could you …?	*Mnaweza …?*	m-naa-*wey*-zaa …
burn a CD from	*kurekodi CD*	koo-ree-*koh*-dee see-*dee*
my memory card	*kutoka kadi ya*	koo-*toh*-kaa *kaa*-dee yaa
	kunakili ya	koo-naa-*kee*-lee yaa
	kemra yangu	*keym*-raa *yaan*-goo
develop this film	*kusafisha*	koo-saa-*fee*-shaa
	picha hizi	*pee*-chaa *hee*-zee

making conversation

Hello.	*Habari.*	haa-*baa*-ree
Good night.	*Usiku mwema.*	oo-*see*-koo *mwey*-maa
Goodbye.	*Tutaonana.*	too-taa-oh-*naa*-naa
Mr	*Bwana*	*bwaa*-naa
Mrs	*Bi*	bee
Ms/Miss	*Bibi*	*bee*-bee

How are you?	Habari?	haa-*baa*-ree
Fine, and you?	Nzuri, wewe je?	n-*zoo*-ree *wey*-wey jey
What's your name?	Jina lako nani?	*jee*-naa *laa*-koh naa-nee
My name's ...	Jina langu ni ...	*jee*-naa *laan*-goo nee ...
I'm pleased to	Nafurahi	naa-foo-*raa*-hee
meet you.	kukufahamu.	koo-koo-faa-*haa*-moo

This is my ...	Huyu ni ...	*hoo*-yoo nee ...
boyfriend	mpenzi wangu	m-*peyn*-zee *waan*-goo
brother	kakangu	*kaa*-kaan-goo
daughter	binti yangu	*been*-tee *yaan*-goo
father	babangu	*baa*-baan-goo
friend	rafiki yangu	raa-*fee*-kee *yaan*-goo
girlfriend	mpenzi wangu	m-*peyn*-zee *waan*-goo
husband	mume wangu	*moo*-mey *waan*-goo
mother	mamangu	*maa*-maan-goo
sister	dadangu	*daa*-daan-goo
son	mwanangu	*mwaa*-naan-goo
wife	mke wangu	m-*key waan*-goo

Here's my ...	Hii ni ... yangu.	hee nee ... *yaan*-goo
address	anwani	aan-*waa*-nee
email address	anwani ya	aan-*waa*-nee yaa
	barua pepe	baa-*roo*-aa *pey*-pey
phone number	simu	*see*-moo

| Where are you from? | Unatoka wapi? | oo-naa-*toh*-kaa waa-*pee* |

I'm from ...	Natoka ...	naa-*toh*-kaa ...
Australia	Australia	aa-oo-*straa*-lee-aa
Canada	Kanada	*kaa*-naa-daa
New Zealand	Nyuzilandi	nyoo-zee-*laan*-dee
the UK	Uingereza	oo-een-gey-*rey*-zaa
the USA	Marekani	maa-rey-*kaa*-nee

I'm married.	Nimeoa. m	nee-mey-*oh*-aa
	Nimeolewa. f	nee-mey-oh-*ley*-waa
I'm single.	Mimi sina mpenzi.	*mee*-mee *see*-naa m-*peyn*-zee
Can I take a photo	Ni sawa nikipiga	nee *saa*-waa nee-kee-*pee*-gaa
(of you)?	picha (ya wewe)?	*pee*-chaa (yaa *wey*-wey)

eating out

Can you	*Unaweza*	oo·naa·*wey*·zaa
recommend a ...?	*kupendekeza ...?*	koo·peyn·dey·*key*·zaa ...
bar	*baa*	baa
dish	*chakula*	chaa·*koo*·laa
place to eat	*hoteli kwa*	hoh·*tey*·lee kwaa
	chakula	chaa·*koo*·laa
I'd like ...,	*Naomba ...,*	naa·*ohm*·baa ...
please.	*tafadhali.*	taa·faa·*dhaa*·lee
the bill	*bili*	*bee*·lee
the menu	*menyu*	*mey*·nyoo
a table for (two)	*meza kwa (wawili)*	*mey*·zaa kwaa (wa·*wee*·lee)
that dish	*chakula kile*	cha·*koo*·la *kee*·ley
Do you have	*Mna chakula*	m·naa chaa·*koo*·laa
vegetarian food?	*bila nyama?*	*bee*·laa *nyaa*·maa
Could you prepare	*Unaweza kuandaa*	oo·naa·*wey*·zaa koo·aan·*daa*
a meal without ...?	*mlo bila ...?*	m·loh *bee*·laa ...
eggs	*mayai*	maa·*yaa*·ee
meat stock	*supu ya nyama*	*soo*·poo yaa *nyaa*·maa
(cup of)	*(kikombe cha)*	(kee·*kohm*·bey chaa)
coffee/tea ...	*kahawa/chai ...*	kaa·*haa*·waa/*chaa*·ee ...
with milk	*na maziwa*	naa maa·*zee*·waa
without sugar	*bila sukari*	*bee*·laa soo·*kaa*·ree
(boiled) water	*maji (ya kuchemshwa)*	*maa*·jee (yaa koo·*cheym*·shwaa)

emergencies

Call an ambulance!	*Ita gari la hospitali.*	ee·taa *gaa*·ree laa ho·spee·*taa*·lee
Call a doctor!	*Mwite daktari.*	m·*wee*·tey daak·*taa*·ree
Call the police!	*Waite polisi.*	waa·*ee*·tey poh·*lee*·see
Help me, please.	*Saidia, tafadhali.*	saa·ee·*dee*·aa taa·faa·*dhaa*·lee
I'm lost.	*Nimejipotea.*	nee·mey·jee·poh·*tey*·aa
Where are the toilets?	*Vyoo viko wapi?*	vyoh *vee*·ko *waa*·pee

I have insurance.
Nina bima. nee·naa *bee*·maa

I want to contact my consulate/embassy.
Nataka kuwasiliana naa·*taa*·kaa koo·waa·see·lee·*aa*·naa
na ubalozi wangu. naa oo·baa·*loh*·zee waan·goo

I've been assaulted. *Nilishambuliwa.* nee·lee·shaam·boo·*lee*·waa
I've been raped. *Nilibakwa.* nee·lee·*baa*·kwaa
I've been robbed. *Niliibiwa.* nee·lee·ee·*bee*·waa

I've lost my ...	*Nilipoteza ...*	nee·lee·poh·*tey*·zaa ...
bags	*mizigo yangu*	mee·zee·goh *yaan*·goo
credit card	*kadi ya benki*	*kaa*·dee yaa *beyn*·kee
handbag	*mkoba wangu*	m·*koh*·baa *waan*·goo
jewellery	*vipuli vyangu*	vee·*poo*·lee *vyaan*·goo
money	*pesa yangu*	*pey*·saa *yaan*·goo
passport	*pasipoti yangu*	paa·see·*poh*·tee *yaan*·goo
travellers	*hundi za msafiri*	*hoon*·dee zaa m·saa·*fee*·ree
cheques	*zangu*	*zaan*·goo
wallet	*pochi ya pesa*	*poh*·chee ya *pey*·sa

medical needs

Where's the	... *hapo karibuni*	... *haa*·poh kaa·ree·*boo*·nee
nearest ...?	*iko wapi?*	ee·koh waa·pee
dentist	*Daktari wa meno*	daak·*taa*·ree waa *mey*·noh
doctor	*Daktari*	daak·*taa*·ree
hospital	*Hospitali*	hoh·spee·*taa*·lee
pharmacist	*Duka la madawa*	*doo*·kaa laa maa·*daa*·waa

I need a doctor (who speaks English).
Nahitaji daktari naa·hee·*taa*·jee daak·*taa*·ree
(anayesema Kiingereza). (aa·naa·yey·*sey*·maa kee·een·gey·*rey*·zaa)

Could I see a female doctor?
Inawezekana nione ee·naa·wey·zey·*kaa*·naa nee·*oh*·ney
daktari mwanamke? daak·*taa*·ree mwaa·*naam*·key

It hurts here.
Inauma hapa. ee·naa·*oo*·maa *haa*·paa

I'm allergic to (penicillin).
Nina mzio wa (penisilini). nee·naa m·*zee*·oh waa (pey·nee·see·*lee*·nee)

english–swahili dictionary

Swahili verbs are shown in their root (basic) forms, with a hyphen in front. To express a series of functions in a sentence, the verb can have several elements added: prefixes, infixes and suffixes. Some adjectives also have a hyphen in front, as they take different prefixes depending on the characteristics of the thing described. Words are also marked as a (adjective), n (noun), v (verb), sg (singular) or pl (plural) as necessary.

A

accommodation *malazi* maa-*laa*-zee
adaptor *adapta* aa-*daap*-taa
after *baada ya* baa-*aa*-daa yaa
airport *uwanja wa ndege* oo-*waan*-jaa waa n-*dey*-gey
alcohol *kilevi* kee-*lev*-vee
all *zote* zoh-tey
allergy *mzio* m-*zee*-oh
and *na* naa
ankle *kiwiko cha mguu* kee-wee-koh chaa m-*goo*
antibiotic *kiuavijasumu* kee-oo-aa-vee-*jaa-soo*-moo
arm *mkono* m-*koh*-noh
aspirin *aspirini* aa-spee-*ree*-nee
asthma *pumu* poo-moo
ATM *mashine ya kutolea pesa*
      maa-*shee*-ney yaa koo-toh-*ley*-aa *pey*-saa

B

baby *mtoto mchanga* m-*toh*-toh m-*chaan*-gaa
back (body) *mgongo* m-*gohn*-goh
backpack *shanta* shaan-taa
bad *mbaya* m-*baa*-yaa
bank *benki* beyn-kee
bathroom *bafuni* baa-*foo*-nee
battery *betri* bey-tree
beautiful *ya kupendeza* yaa koo-peyn-*dey*-zaa
bed *kitanda* kee-*taan*-daa
beer *bia* bee-aa
bee *nyuki* nyoo-kee
before *kabla* kaa-blaa
bicycle *baisikeli* baa-ee-see-*key*-lee
big *kubwa* koob-waa
blanket *blanketi* blaan-key-tee
blood group *aina ya damu* aa-ee-naa yaa *daa*-moo
bottle *chupa* choo-paa
bottle opener *kifungua chupa* kee-foon-*goo*-aa choo-paa
boy *mvulana* m-voo-*laa*-naa
brakes (car) *breki* brey-kee
breakfast *chai ya asubuhi* chaa-ee yaa aa-soo-*boo*-hee

C

café *mgahawa* m-gaa-*haa*-waa
cancel -*futa* -*foo*-taa
can opener *opena ya kopo* oh-*pey*-naa yaa *koh*-poh
cash n *fedha* fey-dhaa
cell phone *simu ya mkononi* see-moo yaa m-koh-*noh*-nee
centre n *katikati* kaa-tee-*kaa*-tee
cheap *rahisi* raa-*hee*-see
check (bill) *bili* bee-lee
check-in n *mapokezi* maa-poh-*key*-zee
chest *kufua* koo-*foo*-aa
child *mtoto* m-*toh*-toh
cigarette *sigara* see-*gaa*-raa
clean a *safi* saa-fee
closed *ya kufungwa* yaa koo-*foon*-gwaa
cold a *baridi* baa-*ree*-dee
condom *kondom* kohn-dohm
constipation *uyabisi wa tumbo*
      oo-yaa-bee-see waa *toom*-boh
contact lenses *lenzi mboni* leyn-zee m-*boh*-nee
cough n *kikohozi* kee-koh-*hoh*-zee
currency exchange *kubadilisha hela*
      koo-baa-dee-*lee*-shaa hey-laa
customs (immigration) *forodha* foh-*roh*-dhaa

D

dairy products *mazao ya maziwa*
      maa-*zaa*-oh yaa maa-*zee*-waa
dangerous *hatari* haa-*taa*-ree
day *siku* see-koo
diaper *nepi* ney-pee
diarrhoea *kuhara* koo-*haa*-raa
dinner *chakula cha jioni* chaa-koo-laa chaa jee-*oh*-nee
dirty *chafu* chaa-foo
disabled *wasiojiweza* waa-see-oh-jee-*wey*-zaa
drink n *kinywaji* kee-*nywaa*-jee
drug (illicit) *madawa (ya kulevya)*
      maa-*daa*-waa (yaa koo-*ley*-vyaa)

E

ear *sikio* see-kee-oh
east *mashariki* maa-shaa-ree-kee
economy class *daraja la tatu* daa-raa-jaa laa taa-too
elevator *lifti* leef-tee
email *barua pepe* baa-roo-aa pey-pey
English (language) *Kiingereza* kee-een-gey-rey-zaa
exit n *kutoka* koo-toh-kaa
expensive *ghali* gaa-lee
eye *jicho* jee-choh

F

fast *ya kasi* yaa kaa-see
fever *homa* hoh-maa
finger *kidole* kee-doh-ley
first class *daraja la kwanza* daa-raa-jaa laa kwaan-zaa
fish n *samaki* saa-maa-kee
food *chakula* chaa-koo-laa
foot *mguu* m-goo
fork *uma* oo-maa
free (of charge) *bure* boo-rey
fruit *tunda* toon-daa
funny *ya kuchekesha* yaa koo-chey-key-shaa

G

game park *hifadhi ya wanyama* hee-fad-dhee yaa waa-nyaa-maa
gift *zawadi* zaa-waa-dee
girl *msichana* m-see-chaa-naa
glass (drinking) *glesi* gley-see
glasses *miwani* mee-waa-nee
good *nzuri* n-zoo-ree
gram *gramu* graa-moo
guide n *kiongozi* kee-ohn-goh-zee

H

hand *mkono* m-koh-noh
happy *mwenye furaha* mwey-nyey foo-raa-haa
have *-wa na* -waa naa
he *yeye* yey-yey
head *kichwa* keech-waa
headache *maumivu ya kichwa* maa-oo-mee-voo yaa keech-waa
heart *moyo* moh-yoh

heart condition *ugonjwa wa moyo* oo-gohn-jwaa waa moh-yoh
heat n *joto* joh-toh
here *hapa* haa-paa
high *juu* joo
highway *barabara* baa-raa-baa-raa
homosexual *msenge* m-seyn-gey
hot *joto* joh-toh
hungry *njaa* n-jaa

I

I *mimi* mee-mee
identification (card) *kitambulisho* e-taam-boo-lee-shoh
ill *mgonjwa* m-gohn-jwaa
important *muhimu* moo-hee-moo
internet *intaneti* een-taa-ney-tee
interpreter *mkalimani* m-kaa-lee-maa-nee

K

key *ufunguo* oo-foon-goo-oh
kilogram *kilo* kee-loh
kitchen *jiko* jee-koh
knife *kisu* kee-soo

L

laundry (place) *udobi* oo-doh-bee
lawyer *mwanasheria* mwaa-naa-shey-ree-aa
leg *mguu* m-goo
lesbian *msagaji* m-saa-gaa-jee
less *chache* chaa-chey
letter (mail) *barua* baa-roo-aa
like v *-penda* -peyn-daa
love v *-penda* -peyn-daa
lunch *chakula cha mchana* chaa-koo-laa chaa m-chaa-naa

M

man *mwanamume* mwaa-naa-moo-mey
matches *vibiriti* vee-bee-ree-tee
meat *nyama* nyaa-maa
medicine *dawa* daa-waa
message *ujumbe* oo-joom-bey
mobile phone *simu ya mkononi* see-moo yaa m-koh-noh-nee
month *mwezi* mwey-zee
morning *asubuhi* aa-soo-boo-hee

motorcycle *pikipiki* pee-kee-*pee*-kee
mouth *mdomo* m-*doh*-moh
movie *filamu* fee-*laa*-moo
MSG *msg* eym-eys-gee
museum *makumbusho* maa-koom-*boo*-shoh
music *muziki* moo-*zee*-kee

N

name n *jina* jee-*naa*
napkin *kitambaa cha mkono*
   kee-*taam*-baa chaa m-*koh*-noh
nappy *nepi* ney-pee
national park *hifadhi ya wanyama*
   hee-*faa*-dhee yaa waa-*nyaa*-maa
nausea *kichefuchefu* kee-chey-foo-*chey*-foo
neck *shingo* sheen-goh
new *mpya* m-pyaa
news *habari* haa-*baa*-ree
newspaper *gazeti* gaa-zey-tee
night *usiku* oo-see-koo
nightclub *klabu ya usiku* klaa-boo yaa oo-see-koo
noisy *yenye kelele* yey-nyey key-ley-ley
nonsmoking *hakuna sigara* haa-koo-naa see-*gaa*-raa
north *kaskazini* kaas-kaa-zee-nee
nose *pua* poo-aa
now *sasa* saa-saa
number *namba* naam-baa
nut *kokwa* kohk-waa

O

oil (engine) *mafuta* maa-*foo*-taa
OK *sawa tu* saa-waa too
old *ya zamani* yaa zaa-*maa*-nee
open a *wazi* waa-zee
outside *nje* n-jey

P

package *furushi* foo-*roo*-shee
pain *maumivu* maa-oo-*mee*-voo
paper *karatasi* kaa-raa-*taa*-see
park (car) v *-egesha* -ey-*gey*-shaa
passport *pasipoti* paa-see-*poh*-tee
pay *-lipa* -*lee*-paa
pen *kalamu* kaa-*laa*-moo
petrol *mafuta* maa-*foo*-taa
pharmacy *duka la dawa* doo-kaa laa *daa*-waa

plate *sahani* saa-*haa*-nee
postcard *postikadi* poh-stee-*kaa*-dee
post office *posta* poh-staa
pregnant *mjamzito* m-jaa-m-zee-toh

R

rain n *mvua* m-*voo*-aa
razor *wembe* weym-bey
registered mail *barua ya rejista*
   baa-*roo*-aa yaa rey-jee-staa
rent v *-kodi* -koh-dee
repair v *-tengeneza* -teyn-gey-ney-zaa
reservation *buking* boo-keeng
restaurant *mgahawa* m-gaa-haa-waa
return v *-rudi* -roo-dee
road *barabara* baa-raa-*baa*-raa
room *chumba* choom-baa

S

sad *masikitiko* maa-see-kee-*tee*-koh
safe a *salama* saa-*laa*-maa
sanitary napkin *sodo* soh-doh
seafood *vyakula kutoka baharini*
   vyaa-*koo*-laa koo-*toh*-kaa baa-haa-*ree*-nee
seat *kiti* kee-tee
send *-peleka* -pey-*ley*-kaa
sex *mapenzi* maa-*peyn*-zee
shampoo *shampuu* shaam-*poo*
share (a dorm, etc) *-gawana* -gaa-*waa*-naa
shaving cream *sabuni ya kunyolea*
   saa-*boo*-nee yaa koo-nyoh-*ley*-aa
she *yeye* yey-yey
sheet (bed) *shuka* shoo-kaa
shirt *shati* shaa-tee
shoes *viatu* vee-*aa*-too
shop n *duka* doo-kaa
shower n *bafuni* baa-*foo*-nee
skin *ngozi* n-goh-zee
skirt *skati* skaa-tee
sleep v *-sinzia* -seen-*zee*-aa
small *-dogo* -doh-goh
smoke (cigarettes) v *-vuta* -*voo*-taa
soap *sabuni* saa-*boo*-nee
some *kadhaa* kaa-dhaa
soon *sasa hivi* saa-saa *hee*-vee
sore throat *koo lenye maumivu*
   koh *ley*-nyey maa-oo-*mee*-voo

south *kusini* koo-see-nee
souvenir shop *duka la kumbukumbu*
  doo-kaa laa koom-boo-*koom*-boo
speak -*sema* -*sey*-maa
spoon *kijiko* kee-*jee*-koh
stamp v *stempu* steym-poo
station (train) *stesheni* stey-*shey*-nee
stomach *tumbo* toom-boh
stop v -*simama* -see-*maa*-maa
stop (bus) n *kituo* kee-*too*-oh
street *njia* n-*jee*-aa
student *mwanafunzi* mwaa-naa-*foon*-zee
sunscreen *dawa la kukinga jua*
  daa-waa laa koo-*keen*-gaa joo-aa
swim v -*ogelea* -oh-gey-*ley*-aa

T

tampon *sodo* soh-doh
teeth *meno* mey-noh
telephone n *simu* see-moo
television *televisheni* tey-ley-vee-*shey*-nee
temperature (weather) *halijoto* haa-lee-*joh*-toh
tent *hema* hey-maa
that (one) *hiyo* hee-yoh
they *wao* waa-oh
(to be) thirsty (-*sikia*) *kiu* (-see-kee-aa) *kee*-oo
this (one) *hii* hee
throat *koo* koh
ticket *tiketi/tikiti* tee-*key*-tee/tee-*kee*-tee
time *saa* saa
tired *ya kuchoka* yaa koo-*choh*-kaa
tissues *karatasi za shashi* kaa-raa-*taa*-see zaa *shaa*-shee
today *leo* ley-oh
toilet *choo* choh
tonight *usiku huu* oo-*see*-koo hoo
toothache *maumivu ya jino*
  maa-oo-*mee*-voo yaa *jee*-noh
toothbrush *mswaki* m-*swaa*-kee
toothpaste *dawa la meno* daa-waa laa *mey*-noh
torch (flashlight) *tochi* toh-chee
tourist office *ofisi ya watalii* o-*fee*-see yaa waa-*taa*-lee
towel *taulo* taa-oo-loh
translate -*tafsiri* -taaf-*see*-ree
travel agency *uwakala wa safari*
  oo-waa-*kaa*-laa waa saa-*faa*-ree
travellers cheque *hundi ya msafiri*
  hoon-dee yaa m-saa-*fee*-ree

trousers *suruali* soo-roo-*aa*-lee
twin beds *vitanda viwili* vee-*taan*-daa vee-*wee*-lee
tyre *tairi* taa-ee-ree

U

underwear *chupi* choo-pee
urgent *muhimu sana* moo-*hee*-moo *saa*-naa

V

vacant *tupu* too-poo
vegetable a *mboga* m-*boh*-gaa
vegetarian a *mlaji wa mboga za majani tu*
  m-*laa*-jee waa m-*boh*-gaa zaa maa-*jaa*-nee too
visa *viza/visa* vee-zaa/vee-saa

W

waiter *mhudumu* m-hoo-*doo*-moo
walk v -*tembea* -teym-*bey*-aa
warm a *ya joto* yaa joh-toh
wash (something) -*osha* -oh-shaa
watch n *saa* saa
water *maji* maa-jee
we *sisi* see-see
weekend *wikendi* wee-*keyn*-dee
west *magharibi* maa-ghaa-*ree*-bee
wheelchair *kiti cha magurudumu*
  kee-tee chaa maa-goo-roo-*doo*-moo
when *wakati* waa-*kaa*-tee
where *wapi* waa-pee
who *nani* naa-nee
why *kwa nini* kwaa *nee*-nee
window *dirisha* dee-*ree*-shaa
wine *mvinyo* m-vee-nyoh
with *na* naa
without *bila* bee-laa
woman *mwanamke* mwaan-*aam*-key
write -*andika* -aan-*dee*-kaa

Y

you sg *wewe* wey-wey
you pl *nyinyi* nyee-nyee

Wolof

pronunciation

Vowels		Consonants	
Symbol	**English sound**	**Symbol**	**English sound**
a	act	b	bed
aa	father	ch	cheat
ai	aisle	d	dog
aw	law	f	fun
ay	say	g	go
e	bet	h	hat
ee	see	j	jar
ey	as in 'bet', but longer	k	kit
i	hit	kh	as the 'ch' in the Scottish *loch*
o	pot	l	lot
oh	cold	m	man
oo	zoo	n	not
ow	now	ng	ring
u	put	ny	canyon
uh	ago	p	pet

In this chapter, the Wolof pronunciation is given in dark brown after each phrase.

Each syllable is separated by a dot, and the syllable stressed in each word is italicised.

For example:

Mangi.   maan-gee

r	run (trilled)
s	sun
t	top
w	win
y	yes

introduction

Dig this, man: there's an intriguing, though controversial, theory that Wolof-speaking West Africans introduced words like 'hip', 'dig' and 'jive' to American English while they were enslaved in North America in the 17th century. The origin of the name 'Wolof' (*wolof wo-*lof) itself is hotly debated, too, but perhaps the most likely suggestion is that it comes from the name of the area called 'Lof'. The Lebu people, to whom Wolof is commonly linked, were one of a number of different ethnic groups who joined together and founded the Jolof Empire in Lof at the end of the 14th century. Wolof is a member of the West Atlantic group of the Niger-Congo language family, and is the lingua franca of the northwestern African nations of Senegal and Gambia, where it's spoken by about 80 per cent of their inhabitants (eight million people) as a first or second language. It's also spoken on a smaller scale in the neighbouring countries of Mauritania, Mali and Guinea.

 wolof (native language)   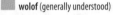 wolof (generally understood)

language difficulties

Do you speak English?	*Ndax dégg nga angale?*	ndakh deg nguh *an*·ga·ley
Do you understand?	*Dégg nga?*	deg nguh
I understand.	*Dégg naa.*	deg naa
I don't understand.	*Dégguma.*	*deg*·goo·ma
Could you	*Ndax mën nga …*	ndakh muhn nga …
please …?	*su la neexee?*	soo luh *ney*·khey
repeat that	*ko waxaat*	koh *wa*·khaat
speak more slowly	*wax ndànk*	wakh ndank
write it down	*ko bind*	koh bind

time, dates & numbers

What time is it?	*Ban waxtu moo jot?*	ban *wakh*·too moh jot
It's one o'clock.	*Benn waxtu moo jot.*	ben *wakh*·too moh jot
It's (two) o'clock.	*(Ñaari) waxtu moo jot.*	(nyaa·ree) *wakh*·too moh jot
Quarter past (one).	*(Benn) waxtu teggalna fukki miniit ak juróom.*	(ben) *wakh*·too *teg*·gal·na *fuk*·kee mi·*neet* ak *joo*·rohm
Half past (one).	*(Benn) waxtu ak xaaj.*	(ben) *wakh*·too ak khaaj
Quarter to (eight).	*(Juróom ñetti) waxtu des na fukki miniit ak juróom.*	(joo·rohm *nyet*·tee) *wakh*·too des nuh *fuk*·kee mi·*neet* ak *joo*·rohm
At what time …?	*Ban waxtu …?*	ban *wakh*·too …
It's (15 December).	*Tey la (fukkeeli fan ak juróom ci weeru desaambar).*	tay luh (*fuk*·key·lee fan ak *joo*·rohm chee *wey*·roo dey·*saam*·bar)
yesterday	*démb*	*dem*·buh
today	*tey*	tay
tomorrow	*suba*	*soo*·ba
Monday	*altine*	*al*·ti·ney
Tuesday	*talaata*	ta·*laa*·ta
Wednesday	*àllarba*	al·*lar*·ba
Thursday	*alxames*	al·*kha*·mes
Friday	*àjjuma*	*aj*·ju·ma
Saturday	*gaawu*	*gaa*·woo
Sunday	*dibéer*	dee·*beyr*

numbers

0	*tus*	toos	18	*fukk ak*	fuk ak	
1	*benn*	ben		*juróom ñett*	*joo*-rohm nyet	
2	*ñaar*	nyaar	19	*fukk ak*	fuk ak	
3	*ñett*	nyet		*juróom ñeent*	*joo*-rohm nyeynt	
4	*ñeent*	nyeynt	20	*ñaar fukk*	nyaar fuk	
5	*juróom*	*joo*-rohm	21	*ñaar fukk ak*	nyaar fuk ak	
				benn	ben	
6	*juróom benn*	*joo*-rohm ben	22	*ñaar fukk ak*	nyaar fuk ak	
7	*juróom ñaar*	*joo*-rohm nyaar		*ñaar*	nyaar	
8	*juróom ñett*	*joo*-rohm nyet	30	*fan weer*	fan weyr	
9	*juróom ñeent*	*joo*-rohm nyeynt	40	*ñeent fukk*	nyeynt fuk	
10	*fukk*	fuk	50	*juróom fukk*	*joo*-rohm fuk	
11	*fukk ak benn*	fuk ak ben	60	*juróom benn*	*joo*-rohm ben	
12	*fukk ak ñaar*	fuk ak nyaar		*fukk*	fuk	
13	*fukk ak ñett*	fuk ak nyet	70	*juróom ñaar*	*joo*-rohm nyaar	
14	*fukk ak ñeent*	fuk ak nyeynt		*fukk*	fuk	
15	*fukk ak juróom*	fuk ak *joo*-rohm	80	*juróom ñett*	*joo*-rohm nyet	
				fukk	fuk	
16	*fukk ak*	fuk ak	90	*juróom ñent*	*joo*-rohm nyent	
	juróom benn	*joo*-rohm ben	90	*fukk*	fuk	
17	*fukk ak*	fuk ak	100	*téeméer*	*tey*-meyr	
	juróom ñaar	*joo*-rohm nyaar	1000	*junni*	*jun*-nee	

border crossing

I'm here ...	*Mangi fii ...*	*maan*-gee fee ...
in transit	*ci transit*	chee *tran*-seet
on business	*ndax afeer*	ndakh a-*feyr*
on holiday	*ci vacances*	chee wa-*kaans*
I'm here for ...	*Mangi fii ba ...*	*maan*-gee fee buh ...
(10) days	*(fukki) fan*	*(fuk*-kee) fan
(three) weeks	*(ñetti) ay bés*	*(nyet*-tee) ai bes
(two) months	*(ñaari) weer*	*(nyaa*-ree) weyr

I'm going to (Dakar).

Maangi dem (Ndakaaru).   *maan*-gee dem (nda-*kaa*-roo)

I'm staying at the (Ganalé Hotel).

Maangi dal ci (oteelu Ganale).   *maan*-gee dal chee (oh-*tey*-lu *ga*-na-le)

tickets

One ... ticket (to Tambacounda), please.	*Benn ... tike (ba Tambakunda) bu la neexee.*	ben ... ti·ke (ba tam·ba·kun·da) boo la *ney*·khey
one-way	*benn yoon*	ben yawn
return	*dem ak dikk*	dem ak dik
I'd like to ... my ticket, please.	*Dama bëgga ... sama tike, bu la neexee.*	da·ma buhg·ga ... *sa*·ma ti·ke boo la *ney*·khey
cancel	*far*	far
change	*soppi*	sop·pee
collect	*jél*	jel
I'd like a ... seat, please.	*Dama bëgga palaas fuñu ... bu la neexee.*	da·ma buhg·ga pa·*laas* foo·nyoo ... boo la *ney*·khey
nonsmoking	*dul tóxe*	dul toh·khe
smoking	*mëna tóx*	muh·na tokh

Is there a toilet/air conditioning?
Ndax am na wanag/kilimaatisër?   ndakh am na *wa*·nak/ki·li·maa·ti·*suhr*

How long does the trip take?
Ñaata waxtu la tukki bi di jél?   nyaa·ta *wakh*·too la *tuk*·kee bee dee jel

Is it a direct route?
Ndax amul taxaaw?   ndakh *a*·mul *ta*·khow

transport

Where does flight (Air France 07) arrive/depart?
Fan la volu (Air France juróom ñaar)   fan la *vo*·loo (er *fa*·raans *joo*·rohm nyaar)
di eggsi/deme?   dee *eg*·see/*de*·mey

How long will it be delayed?
Ñaata waxtu lañu xaar   nyaa·ta *wakh*·tu *la*·nyoo khaar
balaa muy dem?   ba·*laa* mu·ee dem

Is this the ... to (Foundiougne)?	Ndax bii ... mooy dem (Funjuñ)?	ndakh bee ... mohy dem (fun·juny)
boat	gaal	gaal
bus	kaar	kaar
plane	awiyon	a·wee·yong
train	saxaar	sa·khaar

How much is it to ...?
Paasu fii ba ... ñaata la? paa·soo fee ba ... nyaa·ta la

Please take me to (this address).
Yóbbu ma ci (adres bii). yob·boo ma chee (ad·res bee)

I'd like to hire a car/4WD (with air conditioning).
Begg naa luwe oto/kat-kat buhg naa lu·we o·to/kat·kat
(bu am kilimaatisër). (boo am ki·li·maa·tee·suhr)

How much is it for (three) days/weeks?
Ñaata lay jar suma ko bëggee nyaa·ta lai jar su·ma koh buhg·gey
luwe (ñetti) fan/ay bés? lu·we (nyet·tee) fan/ai bes

directions

Where's the (nearest) ...?	... (bi gëna jege fii), fan la feete?	... (bee guh·na je·gey fee) fan la fey·te
internet café	Siberkafe	see·ber·ka·fey
market	Marse	mar·sey

Is this the road to (Banjul)?
Ndax yoon bii yoonu (Banjul) la? ndakh yawn bee yaw·nu (ban·jul) la

Can you show me (on the map)?
Ndax mën nga ma ndakh muhn nga ma
ko won(ci kart bi)? koh won (chee kart bee)

What's the address?
Lan mooy adres bi? lan mohy ad·res bee

Is it far?
Ndax sore na? ndakh so·re na

How do I get there?
Naka laa fay yegge? na·ka laa fai yeg·ge

Turn left/right.
Jaddal ci sa càmmoñ/ndeyjoor. jad·dal chee sa cham·mony/nday·johr

It's ...	Mungi ...	mun·gee ...
behind ...	ci ginnaaw ...	chee gin·naaw ...
in front of ...	ci kanamu ...	chee ka·na·moo ...
near (to ...)	jégena ak ...	je·ge·na ak ...
next to ...	ci wetu ...	chee we·tu ...
on the corner	ci angal bi	chee an·gal bee
opposite ...	jàkkaarlook ...	jaak·kaar·lohk ...
straight ahead	ci sa kanam	chee sa ka·nam
there	fële	fuh·le

accommodation

Where's a ...?	Fan la ... nekk?	fan la ... nek
camping ground	kampamaan bi	kam·pa·maan bee
guesthouse	auberge bi	oh·beyrs bee
hotel	oteel	oh·teyl
youth hostel	auberge de jeunesse	oh·beyrs duh juh·nes

Can you recommend somewhere cheap/good?
Ndax mën nga ma digal	ndakh muhn nga ma dig·uhl
fu yomb/baax?	foo yomb/baakh

I'd like to book a room, please.
Bëgg naa jél ab néeg,	buhg naa jel ab neyg
su la neexee.	soo la ney·khey

I have a reservation.
Am naa reserwaasiyon ba pare.	am naa rey·ser·waa·see·yon ba pa·re

Do you have	Am ngeen	am ngeyn
a ... room?	néeg ...?	neyg ...
single	pur kenn	pur ken
double	pur ñaari nit	pur nyaa·ree nit
twin	bu am ñaari lal	bu am nyaa·ree lal

How much is it per night?
Benn bés, ñaata lay jar?	ben bes nyaa·ta lai jar

How much is it per person?
Ku nekk, ñaata lay fey?	ku nek nyaa·ta lai fay

I'd like to stay for (two) nights.
Dinaa fii nekk (ñaari) fan.	dee·naa fee nek (nyaa·ree) fan

What time is check-out?
Ban waxtu laa wara
delloo caabi bi?

ban *wakh*·too laa *wa*·ra
del·loh *chaa*·bee bee

Am I allowed to camp here?
Ndax mën naa kampe fii?

ndakh muhn naa *kam*·pey fee

banking & communications

Note that prices in Senegal are calculated in lots of five CFA francs – so *téeméer tey*·meyr means '100', but in the context of money it translates as 500 CFA francs.

I'd like to ...	*Bëgg naa ...*	buhg naa ...
arrange a transfer	*jàllale xaalis*	*jaal*·la·le *khaa*·lis
cash a cheque	*aankese sek bi*	*an*·ke·sey sek bee
change a travellers	*aankese*	*an*·ke·sey
cheque	*traveler bi*	*tra*·ve·ler bee
change money	*saanse xaalis*	*saan*·sey *khaa*·lis
withdraw money	*génne xaalis*	*gen*·ney *khaa*·lis

I want to ...	*Bëgg naa ...*	buhg naa ...
buy a phonecard	*jénd kart telefoniik*	jend kart te·le·fo·*neek*
call (the US)	*woote ci (Ameriik)*	*woh*·te chee (a·me·*reek*)
reverse the charges	*moom mu fey*	mohm moo fay
use a printer	*jëfandikoo*	juh·*fan*·di·koh
	amprimaan bi	*am*·pree·maan bee
use the internet	*jëfandikoo*	juh·*fan*·di·koh
	anternet bi	*an*·ter·net bee

How much is it per hour?
Benn waxtu, ñaata lay jar?

ben *wakh*·too nyaa·ta lai jar

How much does a (three-minute) call cost?
Wooteek (ñetti miniit), ñaata lay jar?

woh·teyk (*nyet*·tee mi·*neet*) nyaa·ta lai jar

(1000 CFA francs) per minute/hour.
Waxtu/Miniit bu nekk,
(ñaari téeméer) la.

wakh·too/mi·*neet* bu nek
(nyaa·ree *tey*·meyr) la

tours

When's the ...?	... kañ la?	kany la ...
next day trip	Beneen	ben·eyn
	exkursiyon bi	ek·skur·si·yon bee
next tour	Beneen wisiit bi	ben·eyn wi·seet bee
Is ... included?	Ndax ... dafa ci bokk?	ndakh ... da·fa chee bok
accommodation	oteel bi	oh·teyl bee
the admission charge	antere	an·te·rey
food	lekk	lek
transport	tukki	tuk·kee

How long is the tour?
Wisiiit bi ñaata waxtu lay jël? wi·seet bee nyaa·ta wakh·too lai jel

What time should we be back?
Ban waxtu lañu wara ñibbsi? ban wakh·too la·nyoo wa·ra nyib·see

shopping

I'm looking for ...
... laay wut. ... lai wut

I need film for this camera.
Pelikiil laa soxla pur aparee bii. pe·lee·keel laa sokh·la pur a·pa·rey bee

Can I listen to this?
Ndax mën naa dégglu lii? ndakh muhn naa deg·loo lee

Can I have my ... repaired?
Ndax mën nga ma jagalal sama ...? ndakh muhn nga ma ja·ga·lal sa·ma ...

When will it be ready?
Kañ lay pare? kany lai pa·re

How much is it?
Ñaata lay jar? nyaa·ta lai jar

Can you write down the price?
Ndax mën nga bind piri bi? ndakh muhn nga bind pee·ree bee

What's your lowest price?
Lan mooy sa derñe piri? lan mohy sa der·nye pi·ri

I'll give you (500) CFA francs.		
(Téeméer) laa mën.		(tey·meyr) laa muhn

There's a mistake in the bill.		
Dangeen juum ci adisiyon bi.		dan·geyn joom chi a·di·si·yon bee

It's faulty.		
Baaxul.		baa·khul

I'd like a receipt, please.		
Bindal ma resi bu la neexee.		bin·duhl ma re·si boo la ney·khey

I'd like a refund.		
Begg naa nga delloo ma sama xaalis.		buhg naa nga del·loh ma sa·ma khaa·lis

Do you accept ...?	*Dingeen nangu ...?*	din·geyn nan·goo ...
credit cards	*kart keredi*	kart ke·re·dee
debit cards	*kart bankeer*	kart ban·keyr
travellers cheques	*traveleer*	tra·ve·leer

Could you ...?	*Ndax mën ngeen ...?*	ndakh muhn ngeyn ...
burn a CD from	*sottil ma foto*	sot·til ma fo·to
my memory card	*yi ci CD*	yee chee se·de
develop this film	*sottil foto yi*	sot·til fo·to yee

making conversation

Hello.	*Salaam aleekum.*	sa·laam a·ley·kum
Good night.	*Fanaanleen jàmm.*	fa·naan·leyn jam
Goodbye.	*Mangi dem.*	maan·gee dem
Mr	*Góor gi*	gohr gee
Mrs	*Soxna si*	sokh·na see
Miss (young girl)	*Janq bi*	jank bee
How are you?	*Na nga def?*	na nga def
Fine, and you?	*Mangi fi rekk, na nga def?*	maan·gee fee rek na nga def
What's your name?	*Noo tudd?*	noh tud
My name's ...	*... laa tudd.*	... laa tud

This is my ...	Kii, sama ... la.	kee sa-ma ... la
boyfriend	far	far
brother (older)	mag	mak
brother (younger)	rakk	rak
daughter	doom bu jigéen	dohm boo ji-geyn
father	baay	ba-ai
friend	xarit	kha-rit
girlfriend	coro	cho-ro
husband	jëkkër	juhk-kuhr
mother	yaay	yaai
sister (older)	mag bu jigéen	mak boo ji-geyn
sister (younger)	rakk bu jigéen	rak boo ji-geyn
son	doom bu góor	dohm boo gohr
wife	jabar	ja-bar

Here's my ...	Sama ... angi.	sa-ma ... an-gee
What's your ...?	Lan mooy sa ...?	lan mohy sa ...
address	adres	ad-res
email address	imel	ee-mel
phone number	nimero telefon	ni-me-ro te-le-fon

Where are you from?	Fan nga joge?	fan nga jo-ge

I'm from ...	... laa joge.	... laa jo-ge
Australia	Ostrali	os-tra-lee
New Zealand	Nuwel Selaand	nu-wel se-laand
the UK	Anglateer	an-gla-teyr
the USA	Ameriik	a-me-reek

I'm married. m	Am naa Jëkër.	am naa juh-kuhr
I'm married. f	Am naa jabar.	am naa ja-bar
I'm not married.	Séyaguma.	say-a-gu-ma
Can I take a photo of you?	Ndax mën naa la foto?	ndakh muhn naa la fo-to
Can I take a photo of this?	Ndax mën naa foto lii?	ndakh muhn naa fo-to lee

eating out

Can you	Mën nga ma	muhn nga ma
recommend a ...?	digal ...	dig-uhl ...
bar	baar	baar
dish	benn palaat	ben pa-laat
place to eat	benn restoraan	ben res-to-raan

I'd like …, please.	Dama bëgg …	da·ma buhg …
the bill	adisiyon	a·di·si·yon
the menu	kart bi	kart bee
a table for (two)	taabalu (ñaari) nit	taa·ba·lu (nyaa·ree) nit
that dish	palaat bale	pa·laat ba·le

Do you have vegetarian food?	Ndax am ngeen palaat yu wejetariyan?	ndakh am ngeyn pa·laat yoo we·je·ta·ri·yan

Could you prepare a meal without …?	Ndax men nga togg ñam bu andul ak …	ndakh muhn nga tog nyam boo an·dul ak …
eggs	nen	nen
meat stock	soos yàpp	sohs yaap

(cup of) coffee …	(kaasu) kafe …	(kaa·su) ka·fe …
(cup of) Senegalese tea …	(kaasu) àttaaya …	(kaa·su) at·tai·ya …
(cup of) regular tea …	(kaasu) lipton …	(kaa·su) lip·ton …
with milk	ak meew	ak meyw
without sugar	bu amul suukar	boo a·mul soo·kuhr

(boiled) water	ndox mu (ñu baxal ba pare)	ndokh moo (nyoo ba·khal ba pa·re)

emergencies

Help!	Wóoy!	wohy

Call …!	Wooyal ma …!	woh·yal ma …
an ambulance	ambilaans bi	am·bi·laans bee
a doctor	doktoor	dok·tohr
the police	alkaati	al·kaa·tee

Could you help me, please?		
Mën nga ma dimmali, bu la neexee?		muhn nga ma dim·ma·lee boo la ney·khey

I'm lost.		
Dama réer.		da·ma reyr

Where are the toilets?		
Ana wanag wi?		a·na wa·nak wee

I have insurance.		
Am naa asiraans.		am naa a·si·raans

I've ...	Dañu ...	da-nyoo ...
been assaulted	dal sama kow	dal sa-ma koh
had my pockets picked	ma tafu	ma ta-foo
been raped	ma yakkataan	ma yak-ka-taan
been robbed	ma sàcc	ma sach

I've lost my ...	Sama ... daf ma réer.	sa-ma ... daf ma reyr
My ... was/were stolen.	Dañu sàcc sama ...	da-nyoo sach sa-ma ...
bags	sak yi	sak yee
credit card	kart keredi	kart ke-re-dee
handbag	sak bi	sak bee
jewellery	takkukaay	tak-koo-kaiy
money	xaalis	khaa-lis
passport	paspoor	pas-pohr
travellers cheques	traveler	tra-ve-leyr
wallet	kalpe	kal-pe

I want to contact my consulate/embassy.

Bëgg naa yéganteek sama   buhg naa ye-gan-teyk sa-ma
konsulaa/ambasaad.   kon-su-laa/am-ba-saad

medical needs

Where's the nearest ...?	... bi gëna jege fii, fan la feete?	... bee guh-na je-ge fee fan la fey-te
dentist	Daantist	daan-teest
doctor	Doktoor	dok-tohr
hospital	Opitaal	o-pi-taal
pharmacist	Farmasyeng	far-mas-yeng

I need a doctor (who speaks English).

Dama soxla doktoor   da-ma sokh-la dok-tohr
(bu dégg angale)   (boo deg an-ga-le)

Could I see a female doctor?

Ndax mën naa gis doktoor   ndakh muhn naa gis dok-tohr
bu jigéen?   boo ji-geyn

It hurts here.

Fii lay metti.   fee ley met-tee

I'm allergic to (penicillin).

Dama am alersi ci (penisilin).   da-ma am a-ler-see chee (pe-ni-si-lin)

english–wolof dictionary

In this dictionary, words are marked as n (noun), a (adjective), v (verb), sg (singular) and pl (plural) where necessary.

A

accommodation *dal* dal
adaptor *adaptër* a-dap-tuhr
airport *ayropoor* ai-roh-pawr
alcohol *sàngara* saan-ga-ra
all *lépp/yépp* sg/pl lip/yip
all (people) *ñépp* nyip
allergy *alersi* a-ler-see
and *ak* ak
ankle *waq* waak
antibiotics *antibiyotik* an-tee-bee-yoh-teek
anti-inflammatories *antianflamatwaar* an-tee-an-fla-mat-waar
arm *loxo* lo-kho
aspirin *aspiriin* as-pee-reen
asthma *asma* as-ma
ATM *masiinu xaalis* ma-see-noo khaa-lis

B

baby *bebe* be-be
back (body) *diggu-gannaaw* dig-goo-gan-now
backpack *sakado* sa-ka-doh
bad *bon* bon
baggage claim *teerukaayu bagaas* tey-roo-kai-yoo ba-gaas
bank *bank* baank
bathroom *wanag* wa-nak
battery *piil* peel
beautiful *rafet* ra-fet
bed *lal* lal
beer *beer* beyr
bees *yamb* yamb
before *balaa* ba-laa
bicycle *velo* ve-loh
big *réy* ray
blanket *mbàjj* mbaaj
blood group *xeetu deret* khey-too de-ret
bottle *butéel* boo-teyl
bottle opener *ubbikaayu butéel* ub-bee-kai-yoo boo-teyl
boy *xale bu góor* kha-le boo gohr
brakes (car) *fere* fe-re
breakfast *ndekki* ndek-kee
bronchitis *bronsiit* bron-seet

C

café *kafe* ka-fay
cancel *bayyi* baiy-yee
can opener *ubbikaayu pot* ub-bee-kai-yoo pot
cash n *espes* es-pes
cell phone *portaabal* por-taa-bal
centre n *biir* beer
cheap *yomb* yomb
check (bill) *adisiyon* a-di-see-yon
check-in n *jël caabi* juhl chaa-bee
chest *dënn* duhn
child *xale* kha-le
cigarette *sigaret* see-ga-ret
city *dëkk* duhk
clean a *set* set
closed *téj* tij
codeine *kodeyin* koh-de-yeen
cold a *sedd* sed
collect call *PCV* pe-se-ve
condom *preservatif* prey-seyr-va-teef
constipation *seere* sey-re
contact lenses *lanti* lan-tee
cough n *sëgët* suh-kuht
currency exchange *dëwiis* duh-wees
customs (immigration) *duwaan* doo-waan

D

dairy products *lu jóge ci meew* loo joh-ge chee meyw
dangerous *dansërë* daa-suh-ruh
date (time) *dat* dat
day *bës* buhs
diaper *ngemb* ngemb
diarrhoea *biir buy daw* beer boo-ee dow
dinner *reer* reyr
dirty *tilim* ti-lim
disabled (person) *andikape* an-dee-ka-pey
double bed *lalu ñaari nit* la-loo nyaa-ree nit
drink n *buwaason* boo-waa-son
drivers licence *permi kondiir* per-mee kon-deer
drug (illicit) *dorog* do-rog

E

ear *nopp* nop
east *penku* pen-koo
economy class *kalaas bu yomb* ka-laas boo yomb
elevator *asansëër* a-san-suuhr
email n *imel* ee-mel
English (language) *angale* an-ga-ley
exchange rate *kuru weccee* koo-roo we-chey
exit n *bunt* bunt
expensive *jafe* ja-fe
eye *bët* buht

F

fast *gaaw* gow
fever *yaram wuy tàng* ya-ram woo-ee taang
finger *baaraam* baa-raam
first class *përëmiyeer kalas* puh-ruh-mee-yeyr ka-*las*
fish n *jën* juhn
food *lekk* lek
foot *tank* taank
fork *furset* fur-set
free (of charge) *amul fey* a-mul fay
fruit *furwi* fur-wee
funny *reetaanlu* rey-taan-loo

G

game park *reserv* rey-serv
gift *kado* ka-do
girl *xale bu jigéen* kha-le boo ji-geyn
glass (drinking) *kaas* kaas
glasses *linet* li-net
good *baax* baakh
gram *garam* ga-ram
guide n *njiit* njeet

H

hand *loxo* lo-kho
happy *kontaan* kon-taan
have *am* am
he *moom* mohm
head *bopp* bop
headache *bopp buy metti* bop boo-ee met-tee
heart *xol* khol
heart condition *feebaru xol* fey-ba-roo khol
heat n *tàngaay* taan-gaai
here *fii* fee
high *kawe* ka-we
highway *otoruut* ot-to-root

homosexual n&a *góor-jigéen* gohr-ji-geyn
hot *tàng* taang
hungry *xiif* kheef

I

I *man* maan
identification (card) *dantite* dan-tee-te
ill *wopp* wop
important *am solo* am so-lo
Internet *anternet* an-ter-net
interpreter *lapto* lap-to

J

job *ligéey* li-gay

K

key *caabi* chaa-bee
kilogram *kilo* kee-lo
kitchen *waañ* waany
knife *paaka* paa-ka

L

laundry (place) *fóotukaay* foh-too-kaai
lawyer *awokaa* a-woh-kaa
left-luggage office *konseeñ* kon-seeny
leg *tank* taank
lesbian n&a *lesbiyen* les-bee-yen
letter (mail) *bataaxal* ba-taa-khal
like v *bëgg* buhg
love v *nob* nob
lunch *añ* any

M

man *góor* gohr
matches *almet* al-met
meat *yàpp* yaap
medicine *garab* ga-rab
message *yóbbante* yohb-ban-te
mobile phone *portaabal* por-taa-bal
month *weer* weyr
morning *suba* soo-ba
motorcycle *moto* mo-to
mouth *gémmiñ* gem-meeny
movie *film* film
museum *mise* mee-se
music *misik* mee-seek

DICTIONARY

178

N

name (first) *tur* tur
name (surname) n *sant* sant
napkin *serwiyet* ser-wee-yet
nappy *ngemb* ngemb
national park *park nasyonaal*
  park nas-yo-naal
nausea *xel mu teey* khel moo tey
neck *baat* baat
new *bees* beys
news *xabaar* kha-baar
newspaper *surnaal* sur-naal
night *guddi* gud-dee
nightclub *bwat* bwat
noisy *bare coow* ba-re choh
nonsmoking *fu kenn dul tóx*
  foo ken dul tohkh
north *bëj-gànnaar*
  buhj-gaan-naar
nose *bakkan* bak-kan
now *léegi* ley-gee
number *nimero* nee-me-ro
nuts (peanuts) *gerte* ger-te

O

oil (engine) *iwil* ee-weel
OK *baax na* baakh na
old *màgget* maag-get
open a *ubbi* ub-bee
outside *ci biti* chee bee-tee

P

package *paket* pa-ket
pain *mettit* met-teet
palace *pale* pa-le
paper *këyit* kuh-yit
park (car) v *gaare* gaa-re
passport *paaspoor* paas-pawr
pay v *fey* fay
pen *bindukaay* bin-doo-kai
petrol *esaas* e-saas
pharmacy *farmasi* far-ma-see
plate *palaat* pa-laat
postcard *kart postaal*
  kart poh-staal
post office *post* post
pregnant *ëmb* uhmb

Q

quiet *teey* teey

R

rain n *taw* tow
razor *raasuwaar* raa-su-waar
registered mail *leetar rekomande* lee-tar re-ko-man-de
rent v *luwe* loo-we
repair v *defar* de-far
reservation *reserwaasiyon* rey-ser-waa-see-yon
restaurant *restoraan* res-to-raan
return v *dellu* del-loo
road *yoon* yawn
room *néeg* nayg

S

sad *trist* treest
safe a *wóor* woohr
sanitary napkin *fridom* free-dom
seat *toogu* taw-gu
send (someone) *yónni* yon-nee
send (something) *yónnee* yon-ney
(to have) sex *tëdd ak* tuhd ak
shampoo *sampowe* sam-po-we
share (a dorm) *bokk (néeg)* bok (neyyg)
shaving cream *krem pur watu* krem pur wa-too
she *moom* mohm
sheet (bed) *darab* da-rap
shirt *simis* si-mis
shoes *dàll* daal
shop n *bitik* bee-teek
shower (place) n *sanguwaay* san-goo-waai
skin *der* der
skirt *siip* seep
sleep v *nelaw* ne-low
small *tuuti* too-tee
smoke (cigarettes) v *tóx* tohkh
soap *saabu* saa-boo
some (a little) *tuuti* too-tee
soon *léegi* ley-gee
sore throat *baat bu metti* baat boo met-tee
south *bëj-saalum* buhj-saa-loom
souvenir shop *bitiku suweniir* bee-tee-koo soo-we-neer
speak *wax* wakh
speak (a language) *dégg* deg
spoon *kuddu* kood-doo
stamp *tambar* tam-bar
station (train) *gaar* gaar
stomach *biir* beer

stop v *taxaw* ta-khow
stop (bus) n *are kaar* a-re kaar
street *mbedd* mbed
student *jàngkat* jaang-kat
sunscreen *krem soleer* krem so-leyr
swim v *féey* faay

T

tampons *tampong* tam-pong
teeth *bëñ* buhny
telephone n *telefon* te-le-fon
television *telewisyon* te-le-wis-yon
temperature (weather) *tamperatir* tam-pe-ra-teer
tent *xayma* khai-ma
that (one) *bee* bey
that (one over there) *bële* buh-le
they *ñoom* nyohm
thirsty *mar* mar
this (one) *bii* bee
throat *put* put
ticket (admission) *tike* ti-ke
ticket (transport) *biye* bee-ye
time (for something) *jot* jot
time (o'clock) *waxtu wakh*-too
tired *sonn* son
tissues *muswaar* mus-waar
today *tey* tay
toilet *wanag* wa-nak
tonight *tey ci guddi* tay chee gud-dee
toothache *bëñ buy metti* buhny boo-ee met-tee
toothbrush *borosada* bo-ro-sa-da
toothpaste *kolgat* kol-gat
torch (flashlight) *lampu tors* lam-poo tors
tourist office *sandika dinisiativ*
    san-dee-ka dee-nee-see-ya-teev
towel *serwiyet* ser-kee-yet
translate *tekki* tek-kee
travel agency *asansu woyaas* a-saan-su wo-yaas
travellers cheque *traveleer* tra-ve-leyr
trousers *tubéy* too-bay
twin beds *lal* lal
tyre *pënë* puh-nuh

U

underwear (underpants) *silip* si-lip
urgent *jamp* jamp

V

vegetable n *lejum* le-jum
vegetarian a *nit ku dul lekk yàpp*
    nit koo dul lek yaap
visa *visa* vee-sa

W

waiter *servër* seyr-vuhr
walk v *dox* dokh
wallet *kalpe* kal-pe
warm a *tàng* taang
wash (something) *raxas* ra-khas
watch n *montar* mon-tar
water n *ndox* ndokh
we *ñun* nyun
weekend *wikend* wee-kend
west *sowu* soh-woo
wheelchair *puus-puus*
    poos-poos
when *kañ* kany
where *fan* fan
who *kan* kan
why *lutax* loo-takh
window *palanteer* pa-lan-teyr
wine *biiñ* beeny
with *ak* ak
without *bu amul* boo a-mul
woman *jigéen* ji-geyn
write *bind* bind

Y

you sg *yow* yohw
you pl *yeen* yeyn

DICTIONARY

Xhosa

pronunciation

Vowels		Consonants	
Symbol	**English sound**	**Symbol**	**English sound**
aa	father	b	as in **rib-punch**
aw	law	b'	strong b with air sucked in
e	bet	ch'	as in 'let-show', but spat out'
ee	see	d	as in 'hard-times'
u	put	dl	like a voiced hl
		f	fun
		g	as in 'big-kick'
		h	hat
		hl	as in the Welsh 'llewellyn'
		j	jar
		k	kit
		k'	strong k
		l	lot
		m	man
		n	not
		ng	finger
		ny	canyon
		p	pet
		p'	popping p
		r	run (rolled)
		s	sun
		sh	shot
		t	top
		t'	spitting t
		ts'	as in 'lets', but spat out
		v	very
		w	win
		y	yes
		z	zero

In this chapter,
the Xhosa pronunciation
is given in teal after each phrase.

Each syllable is separated
by a dot, and the syllable stressed in
each word is italicised.

For example:

Enkosi.   e-*nk'aw*-see

Xhosa's glottalised consonants,
simplified as b', ch', k', p', t' and ts'
in our pronunciation guide,
are made by tightening and releasing
the space between the vocal cords
when you pronounce the sound,
a bit like combining it with the
sound in the middle of the word 'uh-
oh'. The sound b' has an extra twist –
instead of breathing out to make the
sound, you breathe in.

For information on Xhosa's distinctive
click sounds, see the box on page 184.

The term 'voiced' used in relation to
the dl sound means that it's produced
with the vocal cords vibrating.

introduction

Learn some Xhosa (*Funda isiXhosa* fu·*ndaa* ee·see·*kh¦aw*·saa) words and not only will you be able to communicate with the Xhosa people in their own language, but you'll have something in common with one of Africa's greatest heroes. Nelson Mandela is arguably the world's most famous Xhosa speaker – incidentally, his Xhosa name is the somewhat prophetic *Rolihlahla* raw·lee·*hlaa*·hlaa (troublemaker). Xhosa is the most widely distributed African language in South Africa (although most of its speakers live in the southeastern Cape Province) and one of the country's official languages. About 18 per cent of South Africans, or six and a half million people, speak Xhosa. It belongs to the Nguni subfamily of the Bantu languages, along with Zulu, Swati and Ndebele. The Bantu-speaking groups migrated south over the centuries along the coast of East Africa and through Central Africa. In southern Africa, they encountered Khoisan-speaking people and borrowed elements of their language – in particular, the 'click' sounds, a distinctive feature of Xhosa and other South African languages.

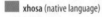 **xhosa** (native language)   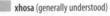 **xhosa** (generally understood)

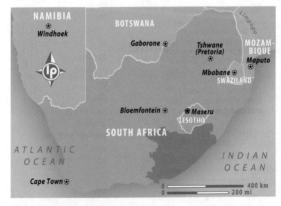

language difficulties

Do you speak English?	Uyasithetha isingesi?	u·yaa-see-*te*-taa ee-see-*nge*-see
Do you understand?	Uyaqonda?	u·yaa-*kjaw*-ndaa
I (don't) understand.	(Andi)qondi.	(aa-ndee-)*kjaw*-ndee

Could you please ...?	Unakho ukunceda ...?	u·naa-*kaw* u·k'u·n!e-daa ...
repeat that	khawuphinde	kaa-wu-*pee*-nde
speak more	thetha ngoku	*te*-taa ngaw-k'u
slowly	cothisisa	*k!aw*-tee-see-saa
write it down	yibhale phantsi	yee-*baa*-le paa-nts'ee

click sounds

Xhosa has a series of click sounds: some clicks are against the front teeth (like a 'tsk' sound), some are against the roof of the mouth at the front (like a 'tock' sound) and some are against the side teeth (like the chirrup you make to get a horse to start walking).

front teeth	roof of the mouth	side teeth	description
k!	kj	k!¦	voiceless
kh!	khj	kh!¦	aspirated (with a puff of air)
g!	gj	g!¦	voiced
n!	nj	n!¦	nasalized voiceless
gn!	gnj	gn!¦	nasalised voiced

time, dates & numbers

What time is it?	Ngubani ixesha?	ngu-*b'aa*-nee ee-k¦e-shaa
It's one o'clock.	Nguwani.	ngu-*waa*-nee
It's (two) o'clock.	Ngu(thu).	ngu-(*tu*)
Quarter past (one).	Yikota pasti (wani).	yee-*k'aw*-t'aa p'aa-*st'ee* (*waa*-nee)
Half past (one).	Yihaf pasti (wani).	yee-*haaf* p'aa-st'ee (*waa*-nee)
Quarter to (eight).	Yikota thu(eyiti).	yee-*k'aw*-t'aa tu-(e-*yee*-t'ee)
At what time ...?	Ngobani ixesha ...?	ngaw-*b'aa*-nee ee-k¦e-shaa ...
At ...	Ngo ...	ngaw ...
It's (15 December).	Yi(fiftini kaDisemba).	yee-(feef-*t'ee*-nee k'aa-*dee*-se-mbaa)

yesterday	*izolo*	ee·*zaw*·law
today	*namhlanje*	naam·*hlaa*·nje
tomorrow	*ngomso*	ngaw·msaw
Monday	*mvulo*	mvu·*law*
Tuesday	*lwesibini*	lwe·see·*b'ee*·nee
Wednesday	*lwesithathu*	lwe·see·*taa*·tu
Thursday	*lwesine*	lwe·see·*ne*
Friday	*lwesihlanu*	lwe·see·*hlaa*·nu
Saturday	*mgqibelo*	m·*gjee*·b'e·law
Sunday	*cawa*	k!aa·waa

numbers

In Xhosa, numbers borrowed from English are commonly used and will be understood. They're also given in this chapter, rather than the more complex Xhosa forms. Numbers one to 10 are given below.

1	*wani*	waa·nee	6	*siksi*	seek'·see
2	*thu*	tu	7	*seveni*	se·ve·nee
3	*thri*	tree	8	*eyithi*	e·yee·tee
4	*fo*	faw	9	*nayini*	naa·yee·nee
5	*fayifu*	faa·yee·fu	10	*teni*	t'e·nee

border crossing

I'm here ...	*Ndilapha ...*	ndee·*laa*·paa ...
in transit	*ngothutho*	ngaw·*tu*·taw
on business	*shishina*	shee·shee·naa
on holiday	*eholideyini*	e·*haw*·lee·de·yee·nee
I'm here for ...	*Ndilapha ka ...*	ndee·*laa*·paa k'aa ...
(10) days	*(teni) imini*	(t'e·nee) ee·*mee*·nee
(three) weeks	*(thri) iveki*	(tree) ee·*ve*·k'ee
(two) months	*(thu) inyanga*	(tu) ee·*nyaa*·ngaa

I'm going to (Cintsa).
Ndiya kwidolophu (eCintsa).   ndee·yaa k'wee·*daw*·law·pu (e·*lee*·nts'aa)

I'm staying at the (Buccaneer's).
Ndihlala kwihotele
(eBuccaneer's).   ndee·*hlaa*·laa k'wee·*haw*·t'e·le
(e·b'u·*k!aa*·ners)

tickets

A ... ticket (to Mdantsane), please.	Linye ... itikiti (eliya eMdantsane), nceda.	lee·nye ... ee·t'ee·k'ee·t'ee (e·lee·yaa e·mdaa·nts'aa·ne) n!e·daa
one-way	ndlelanye	ndle·laa·nye
return	buyela	b'u·ye·laa

I'd like to ... my ticket, please.	Ndingathanda uku ... itikiti lam, ndiyacela.	ndee·ngaa·taa·ndaa u·k'u ... ee·t'ee·k'ee·t'ee laam ndee·yaa·le·laa
cancel	rhoxisa	khaw·k¦ee·saa
change	tshintsha	ch'ee·ntshaa
collect	qokelela	¡aw·k'e·le·laa

I'd like a ... seat, please.	Ndingathanda ... esihlalweni, ndiyacela.	ndee·ngaa·taa·ndaa ... e·see·hlaa·lwe·nee ndee·yaa·le·laa
nonsmoking	ukutshaya	u·k'u·ch'aa·yaa
smoking	ukungatshayi	u·k'u·ngaa·ch'aa·yee

Is there a toilet/air conditioning?
Ikhona ithoyilethi/umoya ogudileyo?
ee·kaw·naa ee·taw·yee·le·tee/u·maw·yaa aw·gu·dee·le·yaw

How long does the trip take?
Luthatha kangakanani uhambo?
lu·taa·taa k'aa·ngaa·k'aa·naa·nee u·haa·mb'aw

Is it a direct route?
Yindlela ethe tse?
yee·ndle·laa e·te ts'e

transport

Where does flight (SAA59) arrive/depart?
Iflayithi (SAA fifti nayini) ifika/ihamba phi?
ee·flaa·yee·tee (s·aa·aa feef·t'ee naa·yee·nee) ee·fee·k'aa/ee·haa·mb'aa pee

How long will it be delayed?
Izakulibazisa kangakanani?
ee·zaa·k'u·lee·b'aa·zee·saa k'aa·ngaa·k'aa·naa·nee

Is this the ... to (Port Elizabeth)?	Yile ... eya (eBhayi)?	yee·*le* ... e·*yaa* (e·*baa*·yee)?
boat	iphenyane	ee·*pe*·nyaa·ne
bus	ibhasi	ee·*baa*·see
plane	inqwelomoya	ee·*njwe*·law·maw·yaa
train	uloliwe	u·*law*·lee·we

How much is it to ...?
Kuxabisa njani u ...?   ku·k¦*aa*·b'ee·saa *njaa*·ne u ...

Please take me to (this address).
Ndicela undise (kule dilesi).   ndee·*k!e*·laa u·*ndee*·se (k'u·*le* dee·le·see)

I'd like to hire a car/4WD (with air conditioning).
Ndifuna ukuhayarisha   ndee·*fu*·naa u·k'u·*haa*·yaa·ree·shaa
imoto/4WD   ee·*maw*·t'aw/ee·*faw*·weel·*draa*·yee·vu
(ibe nomoya ogudileyo).   (ee·*b'e* naw·*maw*·yaa aw·*gu*·dee·le·yaw)

How much is it for (three) days/weeks?
Ixabisa kangakanani   ee·k¦*aa*·b'ee·saa k'aa·ngaa·*k'aa*·naa·nee
iintsuku (eziyithri)/iiveki?   ee·*nts'u*·k'u (e·zee·yee·*tree*)/ee·*ve*·k'ee

directions

Where's the (nearest) ...?	Iphi e(kufutshane) ...?	ee·*pee* e·(k'u·*fu*·ch'aa·ne) ...
internet café	ikhefi	ee·*ke*·fee
	yeintanethi	ye·ee·*nt'aa*·ne·tee
market	imakhethi	ee·*maa*·ke·tee

Is this the road to (Grahamstown)?
Ingaba lendlela iya (eRhini)?   ee·*ngaa*·b'aa le·*ndle*·laa ee·yaa (e·*khee*·nee)

Can you show me (on the map)?
Ungandibonisa (kwimaphu)?   ungaa·ndee·*b'aw*·nee·saa (k'wee·*maa*·pu)

What's the address?
Ithini idilesi?   ee·*tee*·nee ee·*dee*·le·see

How far is it?
Kukude kangakanani?   k'u·k'u·*de* k'aa·ngaa·*k'aa*·naa·nee

How do I get there?
Ndifika njani apho?   ndee·*fee*·k'aa *njaa*·nee aa·*paw*

Turn left/right.
Jika ekhohlo/ekunene.   jee·k'aa e·*kaw*·hlaw/e·k'u·*ne*·ne

It's ...	I ...	ee ...
behind ...	emva ...	e·*mvaa* ...
in front of ...	ngaphambi ko ...	ngaa·*paa*·mb'ee k'aw ...
near (to ...)	kufutshane ...	k'u·*fu*·ch'aa·ne ...
next to ...	landelayo ...	laa·*nde*·laa·yaw ...
on the corner	ekoneni	e·*kaw*·ne·nee
opposite ...	chaseneyo ...	kh!aa·se·ne·yaw ...
straight ahead	nkqo-ngaphambili	nkjaw·ngaa·*paa*·mb'ee·lee
there	apho	aa·*paw*

accommodation

Where's a ...?	Iphi i ...?	ee·*pee* ee ...
camping ground	ibala lokukhempisha	ee·*b'aa*·laa law·k'u·*ke*·mp'ee·shaa
guesthouse	indlu yamandwendwe	ee·*ndlu* yaa·maa·*ndwe*·ndwe
hotel	ihotele	ee·*haw*·t'e·le
youth hostel	ihostele yolutsha	ee·*haw*·st'e·le yaw·lu·*ch'aa*

Can you recommend somewhere cheap/good?
Ungancoma naphina
tshipu/kakuhle?

u·ngaa·*nk!aw*·maa naa·*pee*·naa
ch'*ee*·p'u/k'aa·k'u·*hle*

I'd like to book a room, please.
Ndingathanda ukubhukisha
igumbi, ndiyacela.

ndee·ngaa·*taa*·ndaa u·k'u·*bu*·k'ee·shaa
ee·*gu*·mb'ee ndee·yaa·*k!e*·laa

I have a reservation.
Ndinamalungiselelo.

ndee·naa·maa·*lu*·ngee·se·le·law

Do you have a ... room?	Unalo igumbi ...?	u·*naa*·law ee·*gu*·mb'ee ...
single	kanye	k'aa·*nye*
double	kabini	k'aa·*b'ee*·nee
twin	wele	*we*·le

How much is it per night/person?
Yimalini ubusuku/umntu?

yee·*maa*·lee·nee u·*b'u*·su·k'u/*um*·nt'u

I'd like to stay for (two) nights.
Ndingathanda ukuhlala
ubusuku ka(bini).

ndee·ngaa·*taa*·ndaa u·k'u·*hlaa*·laa
u·*b'u*·su·k'u k'aa·(*b'ee*·nee)

What time is check-out?
Lithini ixesha   lee-*tee*-nee ee-*k!e*-shaa
lokuphonononga phandle?   law-k'u-*paw*-naw-naw-ngaa *paa*-ndle

Am I allowed to camp here?
Ndivumelekile   ndee-*vu*-me-le-k'ee-le
ukukhempisha apha?   u-k'u-*ke*-mp'ee-shaa aa-*paa*

banking & communications

I'd like to ...	*Ndingathanda ...*	ndee-ngaa-*taa*-ndaa ...
arrange a transfer	*cwangcisela*	k!waa-*ng!ee*-se-laa
	utshintsho	u-*ch'ee*-nch'aw
cash a cheque	*itsheki yemali*	ee-*ch'e*-k'ee ye-*maa*-lee
change a travellers cheque	*tshintsha itsheki yabahambi*	*ch'ee*-nch'aa ee-*ch'ee*-k'ee yaa-b'aa-*haa*-mb'ee
change money	*tshintsha imali*	*ch'ee*-nch'aa ee-*maa*-lee
withdraw money	*tsala imali*	*ts'aa*-laa ee-*maa*-lee

I want to ...	*Ndifuna uku ...*	ndee-*fu*-naa u-*k'u* ...
buy a phonecard	*thenga ikhadi*	*te*-ngaa ee-*kaa*-dee
	lokufowuna	law-k'u-*faw*-wu-naa
call (Singapore)	*fowuna e (Singapore)*	*faw*-wu-naa e (see-ngaa-p'aw-re)
reverse the charges	*buyisela i ntlawulo*	b'u-*yee*-se-laa ee ee-*ntlaa*-wu-law
use a printer	*sebenzisa iprinta*	se-b'e-*nzee*-saa ee-*pree*-nt'aa
use the internet	*sebenzisa i intanethi*	se-b'e-*nzee*-saa ee ee-*nt'aa*-ne-tee

How much is it per hour?
Ingaxabisa   ee-ngaa-*k!aa*-b'ee-saa
kangakanani ngeawari?   k'aa-ngaa-*k'aa*-naa-nee *nge*-aa-waa-ree

How much does a (three-minute) call cost?
Ingaba ixabisa   ee-*ngaa*-b'aa ee-*k!aa*-b'ee-saa
kangakanani (imizuzu   k'aa-ngaa-*k'aa*-naa-nee (ee-*mee*-zu-zu
eyithri) yocingo?   e-yee-*tree*) yaw-*k!ee*-ngaw

(One rand) per minute/hour.
(Wani randi)   (waa-nee *raa*-ndee)
umzuzu/ngeawari.   um-*zu*-zu/nge-aa-*waa*-ree

tours

When's the	Yeyiphi	ye·yee·pee
next ...?	landelayo ...?	laa·nde·laa·yaw ...
day trip	usuku lohamba	u·su·k'u law·haa·mb'aa
tour	ukhenketho	u·ke·nk'e·taw

Is ... included?	I ... idityanisiwe?	ee ... dee·ty'aa·nee·see·we
accommodation	indawo	ee·ndaa·waw
	yokuhlala	yaw·k'u·hlaa·laa
the admission	ixabiso	ee·k¦aa·b'ee·saw
charge	elibizwayo	e·lee·b'ee·zwaa·yaw
	intlawulo	ee·ntlaa·wu·law
food	ukutya	u·k'u·ty'aa
transport	isithuthi	ee·see·tu·tee

How long is the tour?
Lude kangakanani ukhenketho? — lu·de k'aa·ngaa·k'aa·naa·nee u·ke·nk'e·taw

What time should we be back?
Ngubani ixesha — ngu·b'aa·nee ee·k¦e·shaa
esinokubuya ngalo? — e·see·naw·k'u·b'u·yaa ngaa·law

shopping

I'm looking for ...
Ndifuna ... — ndee·fu·naa ...

I need film for this camera.
Ndifuna ifilimu yekhamera. — ndee·fu·naa ee·fee·lee·mu ye·kaa·me·raa

Can I listen to this?
Ndingamamela le? — ndee·ngaa·maa·me·laa le

Can I have my ... repaired?
Ndiyafuna ilungisiwe ...? — ndee·yaa·fu·naa ee·lu·ngee·swe ...

When will it be ready?
Izakulunga nini? — ee·zaa·k'u·lu·ngaa nee·nee

How much is it?
Yimalini? — yee·maa·li·nee

Can you write down the price?
Ungabhala phantsi ixabiso? — u·ngaa·baa·laa paa·nts'ee ee·k¦aa·b'ee·saw

What's your lowest price?		
Lithini ixabiso elingezantsi?		lee-*tee*-nee ee-*k¦aa*-b'ee-saw e-lee-nge-*zaa*-nts'ee

I'll give you (five) rand.		
Ndizakunika (ifayifu) randi.		ndee-*zaa*-k'u-nee-k'aa (ee-*faa*-yee-fu) *raa*-ndee

There's a mistake in the bill.		
Ikhona impazamo kwibhili.		ee-*kaw*-naa ee-*mp'aa*-zaa-maw k'wee-*bee*-lee

It's faulty.		
Iyaphazama.		ee-ya-*paa*-zaa-maa

I'd like a receipt/refund, please.		
Ndingathanda irisiti/		ndee-ngaa-*taa*-ndaa ee-*ree*-see-t'ee/
irifandi, ndiyacela.		ee-ree-*faa*-ndee ndee-yaa-*k!e*-laa

Do you accept ...?	*Uyayamkela ...?*	u-yaa-*yaam*-k'e-laa ...
credit cards	*ikhredithi khadi*	ee-kre-*dee*-tee *kaa*-dee
debit cards	*idebhithi khadi*	ee-de-*bee*-tee *kaa*-dee
travellers	*itsheki*	ee-*ch'e*-k'ee
cheques	*zabahambi*	zaa-b'aa-*haa*-mb'ee

Could you ...?	*Ungakwazi uku ...?*	u-ngaa-*k'waa*-zee u-*k'u* ...
burn a CD from	*tshisa isidi*	*ch'ee*-saa ee-*see*-dee
my memory card	*kweyam imemori*	k'we-*yam* ee-*me*-maw-ree
	khadi	*ka*-dee
develop this film	*phucula le ifilimu*	pu-*k!u*-laa le ee-*fee*-lee-mu

making conversation

Hello.	*Molo.*	*maw*-law
Good night.	*Ubusuku benzolo.*	u-*b'u*-su-k'u b'e-*nzaw*-law
Goodbye.	*Usale ngoxolo.*	u-*saa*-le ngaw-*k¦aw*-law

Mr	*Mhlekazi*	mhle-k'*aa*-zee
Mrs	*Nkosazana*	nk'*aw*-saa-zaa-naa
Ms/Miss	*Nenekazi*	ne-ne-k'*aa*-zee

How are you?	*Kunjani?*	k'u-*njaa*-nee
Fine, and you?	*Ndiyaphila,*	ndee-yaa-*pee*-laa
	unjani wena?	u-*njaa*-nee *we*-naa
What's your name?	*Ngubani*	ngu-*b'aa*-nee
	igama lakho?	ee-*gaa*-maa laa-*kaw*
My name's ...	*Igama lam ngu ...*	ee-*gaa*-maa laam ngu ...

I'm pleased to meet you.	Ndiyavuya ukukwazi.	ndee·yaa·*vu*·ya u·k'u·*k'waa*·zee
This is my ...	Yeyam le ...	ye·*yaam* le ...
boyfriend	inkwenkwe	ee·*nk'we*·nk'we
brother	mntakwethu	mnt'aa·*k'we*·tu
daughter	intombazana	ee·*nt'aw*·mb'aa·zaa·naa
father	utata	u·*t'aa*·t'aa
friend	umhlobo	um·*hlaw*·b'aw
girlfriend	intokazi	ee·*nt'aw*·k'aa·zee
husband	umyeni	u·*mye*·nee
mother	umama	u·*maa*·maa
sister	udade	u·*daa*·de
son	unyana	u·*nyaa*·naa
wife	umfazi	um·*faa*·zee
Here's my ...	Nantsi i ...	*naa*·nts'ee ee ...
What's your ...?	Ithini i ...?	ee·*tee*·nee ee ...
(email) address	idilesi (yeimeyli)	ee·*dee*·le·see (ye·*ee*·mey·lee)
phone number	inombolo	ee·naw·*mb'aw*·law
	yefowni	ye·*faw*·wu·nee
Where are you from?	Ungowaphi?	u·*ngaw*·waa·pee
I'm from ...	Ndingowase ...	ndee·*ngaw*·waa·se ...
Australia	Ostreliya	*aw*·stre·lee·yaa
Canada	Khanada	*kaa*·naa·daa
New Zealand	eNyuzilendi	e·*nyu*·zee·le·ndee
the UK	eUK	e·*uk'*
the USA	eUSA	e·u·*saa*
I'm (not) married.	(Andi)tshatanga.	(aa·ndee·)*ch'aa*·t'aa·ngaa
Can I take a photo (of you)?	Ndingayithatha ifoto (yakho)?	ndee·ngaa·yee·*taa*·taa ee·*faw*·t'aw (yaa·*kaw*)

eating out

Can you recommend a ...?	Ugakwazi ukukhuthaza ...?	u·ngaa·*k'waa*·zee u·k'u·*ku*·taa·zaa ...
bar	ibhari	ee·*baa*·ree
dish	isitya	ee·see·*ty'aa*
place to eat	indawo yokutya	ee·*ndaa*·waw yaw·k'u·*ty'aa*

I'd like ..., please.	*Ndiyafuna ...*	ndee·yaa·*fu*·naa ...
the bill	*inkcukacha*	ee·*nk!u*·k'aa·!haa
	ngamaxabiso	ngaa·maa·*k¦aa*·b'ee·saw
the menu	*isazisi*	e·saa·*zee*·see
a table for (two)	*itafile*	ee·*t'aa*·fee·le
	(yababini)	(yaa·b'aa·*b'ee*·nee)
that dish	*esasitya*	e·*saa*·see·ty'aa

| Do you have | *Unakho ukutya kwe* | u·*naa*·kaw u·k'u·*ty'aa* k'we |
| vegetarian food? | *vejitheriyeni?* | *ve*·jee·te·ree·ye·nee |

Could you prepare	*Ungalungiselela*	u·ngaa·*lu*·ngee·se·le·laa
a meal without ...?	*isidlo ngaphandle ...?*	ee·see·*dlaw* ngaa·paa·*ndle* ...
eggs	*amaqanda*	aa·maa·*k¦aa*·ndaa
meat stock	*umhluzi*	um·*hlu*·zee

(cup of) coffee ...	*(ikopi) yekofu ...*	(ee·*k'aw*·p'ee) ye·*k'aw*·fu ...
(cup of) tea ...	*(ikopi) yeti ...*	(ee·*kaw*·p'ee) ye·*t'ee* ...
with milk	*nobisi*	naw·*b'ee*·see
without sugar	*ngaphandle*	ngaa·*paa*·ndle
	kweswekile	k'we·*swe*·k'ee·le

| (boiled) water | *amanzi (ashushu)* | aa·*maa*·nzee (aa·*shu*·shu) |

emergencies

| Help! | *Uncedo!* | u·*n!e*·daw |
| I'm lost. | *Ndilahlekile.* | ndee·laa·*hle*·k'ee·le |

Call ...!	*Biza ...!*	*b'ee*·zaa ...
an ambulance	*iambulensi*	ee·aa·*mb'u*·le·nsee
a doctor	*ugqirha*	u·*gjee*·khaa
the police	*amapolisa*	aa·maa·*paw*·lee·saa

Could you help me, please?
Ungandinceda, ndiyakucela? u·ngaa·ndee·*nk!e*·daa ndee·yaa·*k'u*·k!e·laa

Where are the toilets?
Ziphi itoylethi? zee·*pee* ee·*taw*·yee·le·tee

I want to report an offence.
Ndifuna ukuchaza iofensi. ndee·*fu*·naa uk'u·*kh!aa*·zaa ee·*aw*·fe·nsee

I have insurance.
Ndine inshorensi. ndee·ne ee·*nshaw*·re·nsee

I want to contact my consulate/embassy.

	Ndifuna ukhontaktha umzi/	ndee·*fu*·naa u·kaw·*nt'aa*·k'taa um·*zee*/
	kamazakuzaku.	kaa·maa·zaa·k'u·*zaa*·k'u

I've been assaulted. · *Ndibethiwe.* · ndee·be·*tee*·we
I've been raped. · *Ndidlwengulwe.* · ndee·*dlwe*·ngu·lwe
I've been robbed. · *Ndirojiwe.* · ndee·*raw*·jee·we

I've lost my ...	*Ndilahlekelwe ...*	ndee·*laa*·hle·k'e·lwe ...
My ... was/were stolen.	*Eyam ... ibiwe.*	e·*yam* ... ee·*b'ee*·we
bags	*ibhegi*	ee·*be*·gee
credit card	*ikhadi lekhrediti*	ee·*kaa*·dee le·kre·*dee*·tee
handbag	*ibhegi yesandla*	ee·be·*gee* ye·*saa*·ndlaa
jewellery	*ijuwelari*	ee·*ju*·we·laa·ree
money	*imali*	ee·*maa*·lee
passport	*ipaspoti*	ee·*paas*·paw·t'ee
travellers cheques	*iitsheki*	ee·*ch'e*·k'ee
	zabahambi	zaa·b'aa·*haa*·mb'ee
wallet	*iwolethi*	ee·*waw*·le·t'ee

medical needs

Where's the	*Yeyiphi*	ye·*yee*·pee
nearest ...?	*kufutshane ...?*	k'u·*fu*·ch'aa·ne ...
dentist	*ugqirha*	u·*gjee*·khaa
	wamazinyo	waa·maa·*zee*·nyaw
doctor	*ugqirha*	u·*gjee*·khaa
hospital	*isibhedlele*	ee·see·*be*·dle·le
pharmacist	*ifamasi*	ee·*faa*·maa·see

I need a doctor (who speaks English).

Ndifuna ugqirha	ndee·*fu*·naa u·*gjee*·khaa
(othetha isingesi).	(aw·*te*·taa ee·see·*nge*·see)

Could I see a female doctor?

Ndinakho ukubona ugqirha	ndee·naa·*kaw*·u·k'u·*b'aw*·naa u·*gjee*·khaa
obhinqileyo?	aw·*bee*·njee·le·yaw

It hurts here.

Kubuhlungu apha.	k'u·b'u·*hlu*·ngu aa·*paa*

I'm allergic to (penicillin).

Andidibani ne (penisilini).	aa·ndee·*dee*·b'aa·nee ne (*p'e*·nee·see·lee·nee)

english–xhosa dictionary

In this dictionary, words are marked as n (noun), a (adjective), v (verb), sg (singular), pl (plural), inf (informal) and pol (polite) where necessary.

A

accommodation *indawo yokuhlala*
ee-*ndaa*-waw yaw-k'u-*hlaa*-laa
adaptor *iadaptha* ee-aa-*daa*-ptaa
after *emva* e-*mvaa*
airport *isitishi senqwelomoya*
ee-see-*t'ee*-shee se-n!we-law-*maw*-yaa
alcohol *utywala u-tywaa*-laa
all *onke* aw-*nk'e*
and *na* naa
ankle *iqatha* ee-*jaa*-taa
antibiotics *iyeza lokubulala intsholongwane*
ee-ye-zaa law-k'u-b'u-*laa*-laa
ee-*nch'aw*-law-ngwaa-ne
anti-inflammatories *amayeza okukrala*
aa-*maa*-ye-zaa aw-k'u-*kraa*-laa
arm *ingalo* ee-*ngaa*-law
aspirin *iyeza lokudambisa intlungu nefiva*
ee-ye-zaa law-k'u-daa-*mb'ee*-saa ee-*ntlu*-ngu
ne-*fee*-vaa
asthma *umbefu u-mb'e*-fu
ATM *umatshini wokugcina imali*
u-maa-*ch'ee*-nee waw-k'u-*g!ee*-naa ee-*maa*-lee

B

baby *usana u-saa*-naa
back (body) *emva e-mvaa*
backpack *ingxowa oyithwala ngomqolo*
ee-*ngk!aw*-waa aw-yee-*twaa*-laa ngaw-*mjaw*-law
bad *khohlakeleyo* kaw-*hlaa*-k'e-le-yaw
bank *ibhanki* ee-*baa*-nk'ee
bathroom *igumbi lokuhlamba*
ee-*gu*-mb'ee law-k'u-*hlaa*-mb'aa
battery *ibhetri* ee-*bee*-tree
beautiful *hle* hle
bed *ibhedi* ee-*bee*-dee
beer *ibhiya* ee-*bee*-yaa
bees *iinyosi* ee-*nyaw*-see
before *ngaphambili* ngaa-paa-*mb'ee*-lee
bicycle *ibhayisikili* ee-baa-yee-see-*k'ee*-lee
big *khulu* ku-lu
blanket *ingubo* ee-*ngu*-b'aw
blood group *udidi lwegazi u-dee*-dee lwe-*gaa*-zee
bottle *ibhotile* ee-*baw*-t'ee-le

bottle opener *isivuli bhotile* ee-see-vu-lee *baw*-t'ee-le
boy *inkwenkwe* ee-*nkwe*-nkwe
brakes (car) *ibreki zemoto* ee-*bre*-k'ee ze-*maw*-t'aw
breakfast *isidlo sakusasa* ee-see-*dlaw* saa-k'u-saa-*saa*
bronchitis *isifo semibhobho yemiphunga*
ee-see-*faw* se-mee-baw-baw ye-mee-*pu*-ngaa

C

café *ikhefi* ee-ke-fee
cancel *rhoxisa* khaw-*k!ee*-saa
can opener *isivuli kani* ee-see-vu-lee *k'aa*-nee
cash n *imali* ee-*maa*-lee
cell phone *iselifowuni* ee-se-lee-*faw*-wu-nee
centre n *umbindi* u-*mb'ee*-ndee
cheap *tshipu ch'ee*-pu
check (bill) *ibhili* ee-*bee*-lee
check-in n *ikhawuntara yokuzazisa*
ee-kaa-wu-*nt'aa*-raa yaw-k'u-zaa-zee-saa
chest *isifuba* ee-see-*fu*-baa
child *umntwana* um-*nt'waa*-naa
cigarette *isigarethi* ee-see-gaa-re-tee
city *isixeko* ee-see-*k!e*-kaw
clean a *coca k!aw*-klaa
closed *valiwe* vaa-*lee*-we
codeine *ikhowudhini* ee-kaw-wu-dhee-nee
cold a *banda b'aa*-ndaa
collect call *irivesikholi* ee-ree-ve-see-*kaw*-lee
condom *ikhondom* ee-kaw-ndawm
constipation *ukughina kwesisu*
u-k'u-*jhee*-naa k'we-see-su
cough n *ukhohlokhohlo* u-kaw-hlaw-kaw-hlaw
customs (immigration) *indawo yongenelelo*
ee-*ndaa*-waw yaw-nge-ne-le-*law*

D

dairy products *imveliso yasederi*
ee-*mve*-lee-saw yaa-se-de-ree
dangerous *ingozi* ee-*ngaw*-zee
date (time) *ideyithi* ee-de-yee-tee
day *usuku* u-*su*-k'u
diaper *isishuba* ee-see-*shu*-b'aa
diarrhoea *urhudo* u-ru-daw
dinner *isidlo sangokuhlwa*
ee-see-*dlaw* saa-ngaw-k'u-*hlwaa*

dirty *mdaka* mdaa-k'aa
disabled *olimazekileyo* aw-lee-maa-ze-k'ee-le-yaw
double bed *ibhedi eyenzelwe abantu ababini*
ee-be-dee e-ye-nze-lwe a-b'a-nt'u a-b'a-b'ee-nee
drink n *isiselo* ee-see-se-law
drivers licence *isazisi sokuqhuba*
ee-saa-zee-see saw-k'u-jhu-b'aa
drug (illicit) *isiyobisi* ee-see-yaw-b'ee-see

E

ear *indlebe* ee-ndle-b'e
east *mpumalanga* mp'u-maa-laa-ngaa
elevator *ieliveyitha* ee-le-vee-ye-yee-taa
email n *i-imeyili* ee-ee-me-yee-lee
English (language) *ulwimi lwesingesi*
u-lwee-mee lwe-see-nge-see
exchange rate *utshintsho mali u-ch'ee-nch'aw maa-lee*
exit n *indawo yokuphuma*
ee-ndaa-waw yaw-k'u-pu-maa
expensive *duru* du-ru
eye *imehlo* ee-me-hlaw

F

fast *khawuleza* ka-wu-le-zaa
fever *ifiva* ee-fee-vaa
finger *umnwe* um-nwe
first-aid kit *ikiti yoncedo lokuqala*
ee-k'ee-t'ee yaw-nkle-daw law-k'u-kjaa-laa
first class *iklasi yokuqala* ee-k'laa-see yaw-k'u-kjaa-laa
fish n *intlantsi* ee-ntlaa-nts'ee
food *ukutya* u-k'u-ty'aa
foot *unyawo* u-nyaa-waw
fork *ifolokhwe* ee-faw-law-kwe
free (of charge) *simahla* see-maa-hlaa
fruit *isiqhamo* ee-see-kjaa-maw
funny *hlekisayo* hle-k'ee-saa-yaw

G

game park *indawo yokugcina izilwanyana*
ee-ndaa-waw yaw-k'u-glee-naa
ee-zee-lwaa-nyaa-naa
gift *isipho* ee-see-paw
girl *intombi* ee-nt'aw-mb'ee
glass (drinking) *iglasi* ee-glaa-see
glasses *izipeki* ee-zee-p'e-k'ee
gluten *ncangathi* nlaa-ngaa-tee
good *lungileyo* lu-ngee-le-yaw
gram *umlinganiso wobunzima*
um-lee-ngaa-nee-saw waw-b'u-nze-maa
guide n *inkokheli* ee-nk'aw-ke-lee

H

hand *isandla* ee-saa-ndlaa
happy *vuya* vu-yaa
have *ukuba na* u-k'u-baa naa
he *u-(followed by name)* u-
head *intloko* ee-ntlaw-k'aw
headache *intloko ebuhlungu*
ee-ntlaw-k'aw e-bu-hlu-ngu
heart *intliziyo* ee-ntlee-zee-yaw
heart condition *isifo sentliziyo*
ee-see-faw se-ntlee-zee-yaw
heat n *ubushushu* u-b'u-shu-shu
here *apha* aa-paa
high *phezulu* pee-zu-lu
highway *indlela enkulu* ee-ndle-laa e-nk'u-lu
hot *shushu* shu-shu
hungry *lambile* laa-mb'ee-le

I

I *i* ee
identification (card) *ikhadi yelD ee-kaa-dee ye-eed*
ill *gula* gu-laa
important *baluleka* b'aa-lu-le-k'aa
internet *intanethi* ee-nt'aa-ne-tee
interpreter *itoliki* ee-t'aw-lee-k'ee

J

job *umsebenzi* um-se-b'e-nzee

K

key *isitshixo* ee-see-tsee-¦aw
kilogram *ikhilogramu* ee-kee-law-graa-mu
kitchen *ikhitshi* ee-kee-ch'ee
knife *imela* ee-me-laa

L

laundry (place) *indawo yokuhlamba impahla*
ee-ndaa-waw yaw-k'u-hlaa-mb'aa ee-mp'aa-hlaa
lawyer *iqhwetha* ee-khjwe-taa
leg *umlenze* um-le-nze
less *nganeno* ngaa-ne-naw
letter (mail) *ileta* ee-le-t'aa
like v *thanda* taa-ndaa
love v *uthando* u-taa-ndaw
lunch *isidlo sasemini* ee-see-dlaw saa-se-mee-nee

M

man *indoda* ee-ndaw-daa
matches *imatshisi* ee-maa-ch'ee-see
meat *inyama* ee-nyaa-maa
medicine *iyeza* ee-ye-zaa
message *umyalezo* um-yaa-le-zaw
mobile phone *ifowuni onokuhambanayo*
ee-faw-wu-nee aw-naw-k'u-haa-mb'aa-naa-yaw
month *inyanga* ee-nyaa-ngaa
morning *kusasa* k'u-saa-saa
motorcycle *isithuthuthu* ee-see-tu-tu-tu
mouth *umlomo* um-law-maw
MSG *imsg* ee-m-s-g
museum *imuziyam* ee-mu-zee-yam
music *umculo* um-lu-law

N

name n *igama* ee-gaa-maa
napkin *iseviyeti* ee-se-vee-ye-t'ee
nappy *isishuba* ee-see-shu-b'aa
nausea *ubucaphucaphu* u-bu-laa-pu-laa-pu
neck *intamo* ee-nt'aa-maw
new *ntsha* nch'aa
news *indaba* ee-ndaa-b'aa
newspaper *iphephandaba* ee-pe-paa-ndaa-b'aa
night *ubusuku* u-b'u-su-k'u
noisy *ngxolayo* ngj;aw-laa-yaw
nonsmoking *akutshaywa* aa-k'u-ch'aa-ywaa
north *entla* e-ntlaa
nose *impumlo* ee-mp'u-mlaw
now *ngoku* ngaw-k'u
number *inani* ee-naa-nee
nuts *amaqhele* aa-maa-khje-le

O

oil (engine) *ioyile* ee-aw-yee-le
old *ndala* ndaa-laa
open a *vulekileyo* vu-le-k'ee-le-yaw
outside *ngaphandle* ngaa-paa-ndle

P

package *impahla* ee-mp'aa-hlaa
pain *intlungu* ee-ntlu-ngu
palace *ibhotwe* ee-baw-t'we
paper *iphepha* ee-pe-paa
park (car) v *pakisha* p'aa-k'ee-shaa
passport *ipasipoti* ee-p'aa-see-paw-t'ee
pay *umvuzo* u-mvu-zaw

pen *usiba* u-see-b'aa
petrol *ipetroli* ee-p'e-traw-lee
pharmacy *ifamasi* ee-faa-maa-see
plate *ipleyiti* ee-ple-yee-t'ee
postcard *iposikhadi* ee-p'aw-see-kaa-dee
post office *iposi ofisi* ee-p'aw-see aw-fee-see
pregnant *khulelweyo* ku-le-lwe-yaw

R

rain n *imvula* ee-mvu-laa
razor *ireyiza* ee-re-yee-zaa
registered mail *iposi ebhaliswayo*
ee-p'aw-see e-baa-lee-swaa-yaw
rent v *irente* e-re-nt'e
repair v *lungisa* lu-ngee-saa
reservation *isigcinelo* ee-see-glee-ne-law
restaurant *irestyu* ee-re-sty'u
return v *buyela* b'u-ye-laa
road *indlela* ee-ndle-laa
room *igumbi* ee-gu-mb'ee

S

sad *lusizi* lu-see-zee
safe a *gcinakeleyo* glee-naa-k'e-le-yaw
sanitary napkin *iphedi* ee-pe-dee
seafood *ukutya kwaselwandle*
u-k'u-ty'aa k'waa-se-lwaa-ndle
seat *isihlalo* ee-see-hlaa-law
send *thumela* tu-me-laa
sex *isini* ee-see-nee
shampoo *ishampu* ee-shaa-mp'u
share (a dorm, etc) *ukwabelana ngegumbi*
uk'waa-b'e-laa-naa nge-gu-mb'ee
shaving cream *ikhrimu yokusheva*
ee-kree-mu yaw-k'u-she-vaa
she *uno* (followed by name) un-aw
sheet (bed) *ishiti* ee-shee-t'ee
shirt *ihempe* ee-he-mp'e
shoes *izihlangu* ee-zee-hlaa-ngu
shop n *ivenkile* ee-ve-nk'ee-le
shower n *ishawari* ee-shaa-waa-ree
skin *ulusu* u-lu-su
skirt *isiketi* ee-see-k'e-t'ee
sleep v *lala* laa-laa
small *ncinci* nlee-ntee
smoke (cigarettes) v *tshaya* tshaa-yaa
soap *isepha* ee-se-paa
some *inxenye* ee-nj;e-nye
soon *kamsinya* k'aa-msee-nyaa
sore throat *umqala obuhlungu*
um-kjaa-laa aw-b'u-hlu-ngu

M

english-xhosa

197

south *mzantsi mzaa-nts'ee*
souvenir shop *ivenkile ethengisa izikhumbuzo*
ee-ve-nk'ee-le e-te-ngee-saa e-zee-ku-mb'u-zaw
speak *thetha te-taa*
spoon *icephe ee-kle-pe*
stamp n *isitampu ee-see-t'aa-mp'u*
stand-by ticket *itikiti lokulinda*
ee-t'ee-k'ee-t'ee law-k'u-lee-ndaa
station (train) *isitishi ee-see-t'ee-shee*
stomach *isisu ee-see-su*
stop v *ima ee-maa*
stop (bus) n *indawo yokumisa*
ee-ndaa-waw yaw-k'u-mee-saa
street *isitalato ee-see-t'aa-laa-t'aw*
student *umfundi u-mfu-ndee*
sunscreen *ikhrimu yokukhusela ilanga*
ee-kree-mu yaw-k'u-ku-se-laa ee-laa-ngaa
swim v *ukuqubha u-k'u-kju-baa*

T

tampons *iithamponi ee-taa-mp'aw-nee*
teeth *amazinyo aa-maa-zee-nyaw*
telephone n *ifowuni ee-faw-wu-nee*
television *umabonakude u-maa-b'aw-naa-k'u-de*
temperature (weather) *iqondo lobushushu*
ee-kjaw-ndaw law-b'u-shu-shu
tent *intente ee-nt'e-nt'e*
that (one) *leya (inye) le-yaa (e-nyee)*
they *bona b'aw-naa*
thirsty *nxaniwe n!aa-nee-we*
this (one) *le (kanye) le (k'aa-nye)*
throat *umqala um-kjaa-laa*
ticket *itikiti ee-t'ee-k'ee-t'ee*
time *ixesha ee-k!e-shaa*
tired *diniwe dee-nee-we*
tissues *ithishu ee-tee-shu*
today *namhlanje naam-hlaa-nje*
toilet *ithoyilethi ee-taw-yee-le-tee*
tonight *ngokuhlwa ngaw-k'u-hlwaa*
toothache *izinyo elibuhlungu*
ee-zee-nyaw e-lee-b'u-hlu-ngu
toothbrush *ibrashi yokuxukuxa amazinyo*
ee-b'raa-shee yaw-k'u-kju-k'u-k!aa aa-maa-zee-nyaw
toothpaste *intlama yamazinyo*
ee-ntlaa-maa yaa-maa-zee-nyaw
torch (flashlight) *itotshi ee-t'aw-ch'ee*
tourist office *iofisi yabacandi-zwe*
ee-aw-fee-see yaa-b'aa-k!aa-ndee-zwe
towel *itawuli ee-t'aa-wu-lee*
translate *guqula gu-kju-laa*

travel agency *umlungiseleli hambo*
um-lu-ngee-se-le-lee *haa-mb'aw*
travellers cheque *itsheki yabahambi*
ee-ch'e-k'ee yaa-b'aa-haa-mb'ee
trousers *iibhulukhwe ee-bu-lu-kwe*
twin beds *iibhedi ezimbini ezifanayo*
ee-be-dee e-zee-mb'ee-nee e-zee-faa-naa-yaw
tyre *ithayara ee-taa-yaa-raa*

U

underwear *isinxibo sangaphantsi*
ee-see-n!ee-b'aw saa-ngaa-paa-nts'ee
urgent *ngxamiseka ng!aa-mee-se-k'aa*

V

vacant *ngenanto nge-naa-nt'aw*
vegetable n *umfuno um-fu-naw*
vegetarian a *utya izihluma u-ty'aa ee-zee-hlu-maa*
visa *iviza ee-vee-zaa*

W

waiter *iweyita ee-we-yee-t'aa*
walk v *hamba haa-mb'aa*
wallet *isipaji ee-see-p'aa-jee*
warm a *fudumeleyo fu-du-me-le-yaw*
wash (something) *vasa vaa-saa*
watch n *iwotshi ee-waw-ch'ee*
water *amanzi aa-maa-nzee*
we *thina tee-naa*
weekend *impelaveki ee-mp'e-laa-ve-k'ee*
west *ntshona nch'aw-naa*
wheelchair *isitulo esinamavili*
ee-see-t'u-law e-see-naa-maa-vee-lee
when *nini nee-nee*
where *phi pee*
who *bani b'aa-nee*
why *kutheni k'u-te-nee*
window *ifestile ee-fe-st'ee-le*
wine *iwayini ee-waa-yee-nee*
with *na naa*
without *ngaphandle ngaa-paa-ndle*
woman *umfazi um-faa-zee*
write *bhala baa-laa*

Y

you sg inf/pol *wena/nawe we-naa/naa-we*
you pl inf/pol *nina/tina nee-naa/tee-naa*

Yoruba

pronunciation

Vowels		Consonants	
Symbol	English sound	Symbol	English sound
a	act	b	bed
ang	as in 'act', but nasal	d	dog
ay	say	f	fun
e	bet	g	go
eng	as in 'bet', but nasal	gb	rugby
i	hit	h	hat
ing	as in 'hit', but nasal	j	jar
o	pot	k	kit
oh	cold	kp	backpack
ong	as in 'pot', but nasal	l	lot
u	put	m	man
ung	as in 'put', but nasal	n	not
		r	run
		s	sun
		sh	shot
		t	top
		w	win
		y	yes

The Yoruba pronunciation is given in light green after each phrase.

Each syllable is separated by a dot.

For example:

Oṣé.   oh-shay

Yoruba's nasal vowels, indicated with ng after the vowel symbol, are pronounced as if you're trying to force the sound out of your nose.

There are a range of accent marks above and below vowels. You won't need to worry about using these, if you follow the pronunciation guides you'll be understood.

introduction

There's a Yoruba proverb, *Ohun tí o bá gbìn ni wàà ká* o·hung ti o ba gbing ni wa·a ka, which means 'Whatever you sow, you will reap' – and any efforts to speak to locals in Yoruba will be greatly appreciated. Yoruba (*Yorùbá* yoh·ru·ba), a language from the Niger-Congo family, is spoken by around 25 million people in West Africa. The Yoruba nation consists of a number of tribes which trace their origins to a leader called Oduduwa, the founder of the city Ile-Ife in what is now southwestern Nigeria, where Yoruba is primarily spoken. There are also Yoruba speakers in the Benin Republic and eastern Togo, and a variety of the language is spoken in Sierra Leone. Yoruba was one of the first West African languages to have a written grammar and a dictionary in the 1840s. It's also one of the first African languages with a novel published in it, and is the mother tongue of Nobel-prize-winning writer Wole Soyinka.

 yoruba (native language)   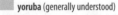 **yoruba** (generally understood)

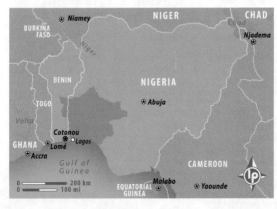

introduction – YORUBA

201

language difficulties

Do you speak English?
Ṣé o ń sọ gẹ̀ẹ́sì?
shay o n so ge-e-si

Do you understand?
Ṣé ó yé ọ?
shay oh yay o

I (don't) understand.
Èmi (kò) gbọ́.
ay-mi (koh) gbo

Could you please ...?	*Jòwó ṣé o lè ...?*	jo-wo shay oh lay ...
repeat that	*tun sọ*	tung so
speak more slowly	*rọra sòrò*	ro-ra so-ro
write it down	*kọ o sílẹ̀*	ko o si-le

time, dates & numbers

What time is it?	*Kí ni aago sọ?*	ki ni a-a-goh so
It's one o'clock.	*Aago kan ni.*	a-a-goh kang ni
It's (two) o'clock.	*Aago (méjì) ni.*	a-a-goh (may-ji) ni
Quarter past (one).	*Aago (kan) kojá ìṣéjú mẹ́ẹ̀dógún.*	a-a-goh (kang) ko-ja i-she-ju me-e-doh-gung
Half past (one).	*Aago (kan) àbọ̀.*	a-a-goh (kang) a-bo
Quarter to (eight).	*Aago (méjo) ku ìṣéjú mẹ́ẹ̀dógún.*	a-a-goh (me-jo) ku i-she-ju me-e-doh-gung
At what time ...?	*Nígbà wo ...?*	ni-gba woh ...
At ...	*Ní ...?*	ni ...
It's (15 December).	*Ní (ojó kẹ̀ẹdógún oṣù dìsẹ́mbà).*	ni (o-jo ke-e-doh-gung oh-shu di-se-m-ba)

yesterday	*àná*	a-na
today	*òní*	oh-ni
tomorrow	*òla*	o-la

Monday	*ojó ajé*	o-jo a-jay
Tuesday	*ojó iṣégun*	o-jo i-she-gung
Wednesday	*ojórú*	o-jo-ru
Thursday	*ojóbò*	o-jo-bo
Friday	*ojó ẹtì*	o-jo e-ti
Saturday	*ojó abámẹ́ta*	o-jo a-ba-me-ta
Sunday	*ojó àìkú*	o-jo a-i-ku

numbers

0	òdo	o·do	16	èrìndìnlógún	e·ring·ding·loh·gung
1	òkan	o·kang	17	ètàdìnlógún	e·ta·ding·loh·gung
2	èjì	ay·ji	18	èjìdìnlógún	ay·ji·ding·loh·gung
3	èta	e·ta	19	òkàndínlógún	o·kang·ding·loh·gung
4	èrin	e·ring	20	ogún	oh·gung
5	àrun	a·rung	21	òkànlélógún	o·kang·lay·loh·gung
6	èfà	e·fa	22	èjìlélógún	ay·ji·lay·loh·gung
7	èje	ay·jay	30	ogbòn	o·gbong
8	èjo	e·jo	40	ogójì	oh·goh·ji
9	èsan	e·sang	50	àádóta	a·a·do·ta
10	èwá	e·wa	60	ogóta	o·go·ta
11	òkànla	o·kang·la	70	àádórin	a·a·do·ring
12	èjìlá	ay·ji·la	80	ogórin	o·go·ring
13	ètàlá	e·ta·la	90	àádòrún	a·a·do·rung
14	èrínlá	e·ring·la	100	ogórùn·ún	o·go·rung·ung
15	èdógún	e·do·gung	1000	egbèrúng	e·gbe·rung

border crossing

I'm here ...	Mo wà níbí ...	moh wa ni·bi ...
in transit	lénu ìrìn-àjò	le·nu i·ring·a·joh
on business	fún iṣé	fung i·she
on holiday	fún ìsimi	fung i·si·mi
I'm here for ...	Mo wà níbí fún ...	moh wa ni·bi fung ...
(10) days	ojó (méwàá)	o·jo (me·wa·a)
(three) weeks	òsè (méta)	o·se (me·ta)
(two) months	oṣù (méjì)	oh·shu (may·ji)

I'm going to (Òyó).
Mò ń lo sí (Òyó).   moh n lo si (o·yo)

I'm staying at the (Premier Hotel).
Mò ń gbé ní (Ilé Ìtura Pírémíà).   moh n gbay ni (i·lay i·tu·ra kpi·re·mi·a)

tickets

A ... ticket	Ìwé ìwọlé ...	i·way i·wo·lay ...
(to Ibàdàn), please.	lọ (sí Ibàdàn).	lo (si i·ba·dang)
one-way	àlọ nìkan	a·lo ni·kang
return	àtàlọ-àtàbọ	a·ta·lo·a·ta·bo
I'd like to ... my	Jòwó mà á fé láti ...	jo·wo ma a fe la·ti ...
ticket, please.	ìwé ìwọlé mi.	i·way i·wo·le mi
cancel	fagilé	fa·gi·lay
change	pààrò	kpa·a·ro
collect	gba	gba
Is there a ...?	Ṣé ... wa?	shay ... wa
air conditioning	èro amúlétutù	e·ro a·mu·lay·tu·tu
toilet	ilé ìgbònsè	i·le i·gbong·se

I'd like a smoking/nonsmoking seat, please.

Jòwó, mà á fé ìjókòó	jo·wo ma a fe i·joh·koh·oh
amusìgá/mámusìgá.	a·mu·si·ga/ma·mu·si·ga

How long does the trip take?

Báwo ni ìrìnàjò yìí ṣe jìnnà sí?	ba·woh ni i·ring·a·joh yi·i shay jing·na si

Is it a direct route?

Ṣé tààràtà ni?	shay ta·a·ra·ta ni

transport

Where does the (Virgin Nigeria) flight arrive/depart?

Ibo ni bàálù (fájínì ti Nàìjíríà)	i·boh ni ba·a·lu (fa·ji·ni ti na·i·ji·ri·a)
yóò ti gbéra/kúrò?	yoh·oh ti gbay·ra/ku·roh

How long will it be delayed?

Fún àkókò wo ni ìdádúró bàálù?	fung a·koh·koh woh ni i·da·du·roh ba·a·lu

Is this the ...	Ṣé èyí ni ...	shay ay·yi ni ...
to (Ekó)?	sí (Ekó)?	si (ay·ko)
boat	ọkò ojú-omi	o·ko oh·ju·oh·mi
bus	bóòsì	bo·o·si
plane	bàálù	ba·a·lu
train	ọkò ojú-irin	o·ko oh·ju·i·ring

How much is it to …?
Èló ni dé …?   ay·loh ni day …

Please take me to (this address).
Jòwó gbé mi lọ sí (àdírésí yìí).   jo·wo gbay mi lo si (a·di·re·si yi·i)

I'd like to hire a car (with air conditioning).
Mà á fé gba ọkọ tí ó   ma a fe gba o·ko ti oh
(ni èrọ amúlétutù).   (ni e·ro a·mu·lay·tu·tu)

How much is it for (three) days/weeks?
Èló ni fún òjó/òsè (méta)?   ay·loh ni fung o·jo/o·se (me·ta)

directions

Where's the   *Ibo ni …*   i·boh ni …
(nearest) …?   *(tí ó súnmọ́ wà)?*   (ti oh sung·mo wa)
   internet café   *búkà ìtàkùn àgbáyé*   bu·ka i·ta·kung a·gba·yay
   market   *ojà*   o·ja

Is this the road to (Ọ̀yọ́)?
Ṣe ọnà (Ọ̀yọ́) nìyí?   shay o·na (o·yo) ni·yi

Can you show me (on the map)?
Ṣé o lè fi hàn mí (lórí àwòrán)?   shay oh lay fi hang mi (loh·ri a·woh·rang)

What's the address?
Kí ni àdíRésì?   ki ni a·di·re·si

How far is it?
Báwo ni ó ṣe jìnnà sí?   ba·woh ni oh shay jing·na si

How do I get there?
Báwo ni mà á ṣe dé ibè?   ba·woh ni ma a shay day i·be

Turn left/right.
Yà sósì/sótùn·ún.   ya soh·si/so·tung·ung

It's …   *Ó wà …*   oh wa …
   behind …   *lé·yìn …*   le·ying …
   in front of …   *níwájú …*   ni·wa·ju …
   near (to …)   *légbèé …*   le·gbe·e …
   next to …   *légbèé …*   le·gbe·e …
   on the corner   *légbèé …*   le·gbe·e …
   opposite …   *níwájú …*   ni·wa·ju …
   straight ahead   *lòkánkán*   lo·kang·kang
   there   *níbè*   ni·be

accommodation

Where's a ...?	Níbo ni ... wà?	ni·boh ni ... wa
camping ground	ilè ìpàgó	i·le i·kpa·go
guesthouse	ilé ìtura	i·lay i·tu·ra
hotel	ilé ìtura	i·lay i·tu·ra
youth hostel	ilé ìtura òdó	i·lay i·tu·ra o·do

Can you recommend somewhere cheap/good?
Şe o lè júwe ibi tí ó ti   shay oh lay ju·way i·bi ti oh ti
dínwo/dára?   ding·woh/da·ra

I'd like to book a room, please.
Jòwó mà á fé gba yàrá kan.   jo·wo ma a fe gba ya·ra kang

I have a reservation.
Mo ti gba yàrá sílè télè.   moh ti gba ya·ra si·le te·le

Do you have a ... room?	Şe e ní yàrá ...?	shay e ni ya·ra ...
single	elénikan	e·le·ni·kang
double	eléniméjì	e·le·ni·may·ji
twin	oníbejì	oh·ni·bay·ji

How much is it per ...?	Èló ni fún ...?	ay·loh ni fung ...
night	alé ojó kan	a·le o·jo kang
person	ẹnì kan	e·ni kang

I'd like to stay for (two) nights.
Mà á fé sun ibí fún ojó (méjì).   ma a fe sung i·bi fung o·jo (may·ji)

What time is check-out?
Ìgbà wo ni kíké rú jáde nínú ilé ìtura?   i·gba woh ni ki·ke ru ja·de ni·nu i·lay i·tu·ra

Am I allowed to camp here?
Şe àyè wà láti pàgó síbí?   shay a·yay wa la·ti kpa·go si·bi

banking & communications

I'd like to ...	Mà á fé ...	ma a fe ...
arrange a transfer	fi owó ránṣẹ́	fi oh-woh rang-she
cash a cheque	fi sòwédowó	fi so-way-doh-woh
	gba owó	gba oh-woh
change a travellers cheque	pàdà sòwédowó arìnrìnàjò	kpa-a-ro so-way-doh-woh a-ring-ring-a-jo
change money	pàdà owó	kpa-a-ro oh-woh
withdraw money	gba owó ní bánkì	gba oh-woh ni bang-ki

I want to ...	Mo fé ...	mo fe ...
buy a phonecard	ra káàdì ìfóònù	ra ka-a-di i-foh-oh-nu
call (Singapore)	pe (Singapore)	kpay (sing-a-po)
reverse the charges	yi owó padà	yi oh-woh kpa-da
use a printer	lo ìtẹ̀wé	loh i-te-way
use the internet	lo itàkùn àgbáyé	loh i-ta-kung a-gba-yay

How much is it per hour?
Èló ni fún wákàtí kan?   ay-loh ni fung wa-ka-ti kang

How much does a (three-minute) call cost?
Èló ni pípè fún (ìṣéjú méta) jé?   ay-loh ni kpi-kpay fung (i-she-ju me-ta) je

(100 naira) per minute/hour.
(Ogórùn-ún náírà) fún ìṣẹjú/   (o-go-rung-ung na-i-ra) fung i-she-ju/
wákàtí kan.   wa-ka-ti kan

tours

When's the next ...?	Ìgbà wo ni ...?	i-gba woh ni ...
day trip	ìrìn-ojó kan	i-ring-o-jo kang
tour	ìrìn-àjò afé	i-ring-a-joh a-fe

Is ... included?	Ṣé ẹ fi ... si?	shay e fi ... si
accommodation	ibùgbé	i-bu-gbay
the admission charge	owó ìgbàwọlé	oh-woh i-gba-wo-lay
food	oúnjẹ	oh-ung-je
transport	ìrìn-àjò	i-ring-a-joh

How long is the tour?
Báwo ni ìrìn-àjò náà se jìnnà sí?   ba·woh ni i·ring·a·joh naa shay jing·na si

What time should we be back?
Ìgbà wo ni ó ye kí á padà?   i·gba woh ni oh ye ki a kpa·da

shopping

I'm looking for ...
Mò ń wá ...   moh n wa ...

I need film for this camera.
Mo fé fíìmù fún èro ayàwòrán yìí.   moh fe fi·i·mu fung e·ro a·ya·woh·rang yi·i

Can I listen to this?
Se mo lè gbó èyí?   shay moh lay gbo ay·yi

Can I have my ... repaired?
Sé mo lè tún ... mi se?   shay moh lay tung ... mi shay

When will it be ready?
Ìgbà wo ni yóò se tán?   i·gba woh ni yoh·oh shay tang

How much is it?
Èló ni?   ay·loh ni

Can you write down the price?
Sé o lè ko iye owó re sílè?   shay oh lay ko i·yay oh·woh re si·le

What's your lowest price?
Èló ni jálè?   ay·loh ni ja·le

I'll give you (800) naira.
Mà á fún o ní (egbèrin) náírà.   ma a fung o ni (e·gbe·ring) na·i·ra

There's a mistake in the bill.
Àsìse wà nínú ìwé owó yìí.   a·shi·she wa ni·nu i·way oh·woh yi·i

It's faulty.
Ó ti bàjé.   o ti ba·je

I'd like a ..., please.   *Jòwò mà á fé gba ...*   jo·wo ma a fe gba ...
  receipt   *rìsíìtì*   ri·si·i·ti
  refund   *owó padà*   oh·woh kpa·da

Do you accept ...?	Ṣé ẹ gba ...?	shay e gba ...
credit cards	káàdì moyáwó	ka·a·di moh·ya·woh
debit cards	káàdì mojẹgbèsè	ka·a·di moh·je·gbay·say
travellers	ìwé sòwédowó	i·way so·way·doh·woh
cheques	arin·rìn·àjò	a·ring·ring·a·joh

Could you ...?	Ṣé o lè ...?	shay oh lay ...
burn a CD from my	da rékòdù yìì kọ	da re·ko·du yi·i ko
memory card	láti inú fón rán	la·ti i·nu fong rang
develop this film	fọ̀ fíìmù	fo fí·i·mu

making conversation

Hello.	Pèlé o.	kpe·le o
Good night.	Ó dààrò.	oh da·a·ro
Goodbye.	Ó dàbò.	oh da·bo

Mr	Ọ̀gbéni	o·gbe·ni
Mrs	Aya	a·ya
Ms/Miss	Omidan	oh·mi·dang

How are you?	Ṣe dáadáa ni?	shay da·a·da·a ni
Fine, and you?	Bééni, iwọ ń kọ́?	be·e·ni i·wo n ko
What's your name?	Kí ni orúkọ rẹ?	ki ni oh·ru·ko re
My name's ...	Orúkọ mi ni ...	oh·ru·ko mi ni ...
I'm pleased to	Inú mi dùn láti	i·nu mi dung la·ti
meet you.	pàde rẹ.	kpa·day re

This is my ...	Èyí ni ... mi.	ay·yi ni ... mi
boyfriend	òrékùnrin	o·re·kung·ring
brother	arakunrin	a·ra·kung·ring
daughter	ọmọ mi obìnrin	o·mo mi oh·bing·ring
father	bàbá	ba·ba
friend	òrẹ́	o·re
girlfriend	òrébinrin	o·re·bing·ring
husband	ọkọ	o·ko
mother	iyá/màmá	i·ya/ma·ma
sister	arábinrin	a·ra·bing·ring
son	ọmọ mi ọkùnrin	o·mo mi o·kung·ring
wife	iyàwó	i·ya·woh

Here's my ...	Eyi ni ...	a-yi ni ...
What's your ...?	Kí ni ... re?	ki ni ... re
address	àdírèsì	a-di-re-si
email address	àdírésì itàkùn	a-di-re-si i-ta-kung
	àgbayé	a-gba-yay
phone number	nómbà fóònù	no-m-ba foh-oh-nu
Where are you from?	Ibo ni ìlú rẹ?	i-boh ni i-lu re
I'm from ...	Ìlú mi ni ...	i-lu mi ni ...
Australia	Ọsirélìà	o-si-ray-li-a
Canada	Kánádà	ka-na-da
New Zealand	Níù sìlandì	ni-u si-la-n-di
the UK	Ìlú òyìnbó	i-lu oh-ying-boh
the USA	Améríkà	a-me-ri-ka
I'm (not) married. m	Mi (ò) tí ì láya.	mi (oh) ti i la-ya
I'm (not) married. f	Mi (ò) tí ì ní oko.	mi (oh) ti i ni o-ko
Can I take a photo (of you)?	Ṣé mo lè yà (ọ) ní fótò?	shay moh lay ya (o) ni fo-toh

eating out

Can you recommend a ...?	Ǹ jé o le júwe ...?	n je oh lay u-way ...
bar	iléọtí	i-lay-o-ti
dish	oúnjẹ	oh-un-je
place to eat	iléoúnjẹ	i-lay-oh-ung-je
I'd like ..., please.	Jòwó, mà á fé ...	jo-wo ma a fe ...
the bill	íwe owó	i-we oh-woh
the menu	àwọn oúnjẹ tí ó wà	a-wong oh-ung-je ti oh wa
a table for (two)	ìjokòó fún (eni méjì)	i-joh-koh-oh fung (e-ni me-ji)
that dish	oúnjẹ yẹn	o-ung-je yeng
Do you have vegetarian food?	Ǹ jé ẹ ní oúnjẹ aláìjẹran?	n je e ni oh-ung-je a-la-i-je-rang
Could you prepare a meal without ...?	Jòwó ba mi se oúnjẹ lai fi ... si?	jo-wo ba mi shay oh-ung-je lai fi ... si
eggs	eyin	e-ying
meat stock	ẹran	e-rang

(cup of) coffee ...	(ife) kọfí ...	(i-fay) ko-fi ...
(cup of) tea ...	(ife) tíì ...	(i-fay) ti-i ...
with milk	pèlú mílíìki	kpe-lu mi-li-i-ki
without sugar	láì sí súgà	la-i si su-ga
(boiled) water	omi (gbígbóná)	oh-mi (gbi-gboh-na)

emergencies

Help!	Ẹ ràn mí lọ́wọ́ o!	e rang mi lo-wo o
Call ...!	Ẹ pe ...!	e kpay ...
an ambulance	ọkọ̀ gbókùúgbokùú	o-ko gboh-ku-u-gboh-ku-u
a doctor	dókítà	doh-ki-ta
the police	ọlópàá	o-lo-kpa-a

Could you help me, please?
Jọ̀wọ́ṣe o lè ràn mí lọ́wọ́? jo-wo-shay oh lay rang mi lo-wo

I'm lost.
Mo ti sọnù. moh ti so-nu

Where are the toilets?
Ibo ni ilé ìgbọ̀nsẹ̀ wà? i-boh ni i-lay i-gbong-se wa

I want to report an offence.
Mo fẹ́ fi ẹjọ́ kan sùn. moh fe fi e-jo kang sung

I have insurance.
Mo ní iwé adójútòfò. moh ni i-way a-do-ju-to-fo

I want to contact my consulate/embassy.
Mo fẹ́ bá aṣojú ilẹ̀ mo fe ba a-shoh-ju i-le
òkèèrè ilú mi sọ̀rọ̀. o-kay-ay-ray i-lu mi so-ro

I've been ...	Wọn ti ...	wong ti ...
assaulted	fiyà jẹ mí	fi-ya je mi
raped	fipá bá mi lò pò	fi-kpa ba mi loh kpo
robbed	jà mí lólè	ja mi loh-lay

I've lost my ...	Mo ju ... nù.	moh ju ... nu
bags	àpò	a·kpoh
credit card	káàdì moyáwó	ka·a·di moh·ya·woh
handbag	àpamówó	a·kpa·mo·wo
jewellery	ohun-oṣo	oh·hung·o·sho
money	owó	oh·woh
passport	ìwé ìrìnnà	i·way i·ring·na
travellers cheques	ìwé sòwédowó	i·way so·way·doh·woh
	arin-rìn-àjò	a·ring·ring·a·joh
wallet	póòsì	kpo·o·si

My (money) was stolen. *(Owó) mi ti sọnu.* (oh·woh) mi ti so·nu

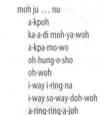

medical needs

Where's the nearest ...?	Ibo ni ... tí ó súnmó ibí?	i·boh ni ... ti oh sung·mo i·bi
dentist	dókítà eléyin	doh·ki·ta ay·lay·ying
doctor	dókítà	doh·ki·ta
hospital	ilé-ìwòsàn	i·lay·i·woh·sang
pharmacist	apògùn	a·kpoh·gung

I need a doctor (who speaks English).
Mo fé dókítà (tí ó lè ṣọ èdè òyìnbó).
moh fe doh·ki·ta (ti oh lay so ay·day oh·ying·boh)

Could I see a female doctor?
Ṣe mo lè rí dókítà obìnrin?
shay moh lay ri doh·ki·ta oh·bing·ring

It hurts here.
O ń dùn mí níbí.
oh n dung mi ni·bi

I'm allergic to (penicillin).
(Ògùn) yìí ṣe owó òdì sí mi.
(oh·gung) yi·i shay o·wo oh·di si mi

english–yoruba dictionary

In this dictionary, words are marked as n (noun), a (adjective), v (verb), sg (singular) and pl (plural) where necessary.

A

accommodation *ibùgbé* i-bu-gbay
adaptor *ìbàdógbà* i-ba-do-gba
after *léyìn* le-ying
airport *ibùdókò òfurufu* i-bu-doh-ko oh-fu-ru-fu
alcohol *otí* o-ti
all *gbogbo* gboh-gboh
allergy *èhun* e-hung
and *àti* a-ti
ankle *orùn-esè* o-rung-e-se
antibiotics *ògùn-èyà wuuru* oh-gung-e-ya wu-u-ru
anti-inflammatories *ògùn-ara wíwú* oh-gung-a-ra wi-wu
arm *apá* a-kpa
aspirin *asipirínìnì* a-si-kpi-ring-ing-ni
asthma *ikó-fèe* i-ko-fay-ay
ATM *èro kàádì agbòwòjàde*
  e-ro ka-a-di a-gboh-woh-ja-de

B

baby *omo-owó* o-mo-o-wo
back (body) *eyìn* e-ying
backpack *apo ìgbérúsíléyìn* a-kpoh i-gbe-ru-si-le-ying
bad *burú* bu-ru
baggage claim *ìbìgbérù* i-bi-i-gbe-ru
bank *ilé-ìfowópamósí* i-lay-i-foh-woh-kpa-mo-si
bathroom *ilé-ìwè* i-lay-i-we
battery *bátìrì* ba-ti-ri
beautiful *dára* da-ra
bed *ìbùsùn* i-bu-sung
beer *bìà* bi-a
bees *oyin* oh-ying
before *télétélè* te-le-te-le
bicycle *kèké* ke-ke
big *tóbi* toh-bi
blanket *aso-ìbora òtútù* asho-i-boh-ra oh-tu-tu
blood group *orísí-èjè* oh-ri-shi-e-je
bottle *ìgò* i-goh
bottle opener *ìsítí* i-shi-ti
boy *omokùnrin* o-mo-kung-ring
brakes (car) *bìréèkì-okò* bi-ray-ay-ki-o-ko
breakfast *oúnje-àárò* oh-ung-je-a-a-ro
bronchitis *òìsàn inú èdòforò* a-i-sang i-n-e-do-foh-roh

C

café *búkà* bu-ka
cancel *fagilè* fa-gi-le
can opener *isí-agolo* i-shi-a-goh-loh
cash n *owó* oh-woh
cell phone *telifóònù aláàgbèkà*
  te-li-foh-oh-nu a-la-a-gbay-ka
centre n *àárin* a-a-ring
cheap *pò* kpo
check (bill) *ìwé sòwèdowó* i-way so-way-doh-wo
check-in n *kérúsókò* ke-ru-so-ko
chest *àyà* a-ya
child *òdómodé* o-do-mo-day
cigarette *sígà* si-ga
city *ìlú* i-lu
clean a *mó* mo
closed *padé* kpa-day
codeine *kodíìnì* koh-di-i-ni
cold a *tútù* tu-tu
condom *kóndóòmù* ko-n-do-o-mo-mu
constipation *inúklkún* i-nu-ki-kung
contact lenses *ìgò-ojú* i-goh-oh-ju
cough n *ikó* i-ko
currency exchange *Isèwó ilè òkèèrè*
  i-she-woh i-le oh-kay-ay-ray
customs (immigration) *asóbodè* a-sho-boh-day

D

dairy products *èròjà wàrà* ay-roh-ja wa-ra
dangerous *léwu* lay-wu
date (time) *àkókò* a-koh-koh
day *ojó* o-jo
diaper *aso-lìèèdì* a-sho-i-lay-ay-di
diarrhoea *ìgbé-gbuuru* i-gbe-gbu-u-ru
dinner *oúnje-alé* oh-ung-je-a-le
dirty *dòtí* do-ti
disabled *abìrùn* a-bi-rung
double bed *ìbùsùn aláàgbèkà* i-bu-sung a-la-a-gbay-ka
drink n *ohun mímu* oh-hung-mi-mu
drivers licence *ìwé èrì awakò* i-way e-ri a-wa-ko
drug (illicit) *ògùn olórò* o-gung oh-loh-roh

E

ear *etí* ay-ti
east *ìlà oòrùn* i-la oh-oh-rung
economy class *ìjòkòò alábòodè*
 i-joh-koh-oh a-la-bo-o-day
elevator *èro-àkàbà* e-ro-a-ka-ba
email n *létà orí ìtàkùn àgbàyé*
 le-ta oh-ri i-ta-kung a-gba-yay
English (language) *èdè gèésì* ay-day ge-e-si
exchange rate *pàsìpààrò owó ilè òkèèrè*
 kpa-shi-kpa-a-ro oh-woh i-le oh-kay-ay-ray
exit n *ònà àbájáde* o-na a-ba-ja-deh
expensive *òwón* o-wong
eye *ojú* oh-ju

F

fast *yá* ya
fever *ibà* i-ba
finger *ìka owó* i-ka o-wo
first-aid kit *àpò ìségùn wàràwèrè*
 a-kpoh i-she-gung wa-ra-way-ray
first class *ìpò kíìní* i-kpoh ki-i-ni
fish n *eja* e-ja
food *oúnje* oh-ung-je
foot *esè* e-se
fork *èmúga* e-mu-ga
free (of charge) *òfé* o-fe
fruit *èso* ay-soh
funny *panilérínín* kpa-ni-le-ring-ing

G

game park *ogba-erankò* o-gba-e-rang-koh
gift *èbùn* e-bung
girl *omobìnrin* o-mo-bing-ring
glass (drinking) *ife-ìmumi* i-fay-i-mu-mi
glasses *dígí-ojú* di-gi-oh-ju
gluten *gulutíínì* gu-lu-ti-i-ni
good *dára* da-ra
gram *gíràámù* gi-ra-a-mu
guide n *amònà* a-mo-na

H

hand *owó* o-wo
happy *ìdùnnú* i-dung-nu
have *ní* ni

he *òun* oh-ung
head *orí* oh-ri
headache *éfórí* e-fo-ri
heart *okàn* o-kang
heart condition *ìpò okàn* i-kpoh o-kang
heat n *ooru* oh-oh-ru
here *ìbí* i-bi
high *gíga* gi-ga
highway *òpópònà* oh-kpoh-kpoh-na
homosexual n&a *okùnrin asebìabo*
 o-kung-ring a-shay-bi-a-boh
hot *gbóná* gboh-na
hungry *ebi* ay-bi

I

I *èmi* ay-mi
identification (card) *kàádì ìdánìmò* ka-a-di i-da-ni-mo
ill *àìsàn* a-i-sang
important *pàtàkì* kpa-ta-ki
internet *ìtàkùn àgbàyé* i-ta-kung a-gba-yay
interpreter *ògbufò* oh-gbu-fo

J

job *isé* i-she

K

key *kókóró* ko-ko-ro
kilogram *kílò* ki-loh
kitchen *ilé ìdáná* i-lay i-da-na
knife *òbe* o-be

L

laundry (place) *ibi ìfoso* i-bi i-fo-sho
lawyer *agbejórò* a-gbe-jo-roh
left-luggage office *òfíìsì ìkérùsí* o-fi-i-si i-ke-ru-si
leg *esè* e-se
lesbian n&a *obìnrin asebiako*
 oh-bing-ring a-shay-bi-a-ko
less *dín* ding
letter (mail) *létà* le-ta
like v *fèràn* fe-rang
lost-property office *òfíìsì ìkérùtònù-sí*
 o-fi-i-si i-ke-ru-toh-nu-si
love v *fé* fe
lunch *oúnje òsán* oh-ung-je o-sang

M

man *okùnrin* o-kung-ring
matches *ìsànà* i-sha-na
meat *eran* e-rang
medicine *ògùn* oh-gung
message *isé* i-she
mobile phone *telifòonù-aláàgbékà* te-li-foh-oh-nu-a-la-a-gbay-ka
month *osù* oh-shu
morning *àárò* a-a-ro
motorcycle *alùkpùkpù* a-lu-kpu-kpu
mouth *enu* e-nu
movie *sinimá* si-ni-ma
MSG *amóbèdùn* a-mo-be-dung
museum *ilé-ìsèmbàyé* i-lay-i-she-m-ba-yay
music *orin* oh-ring

N

name n *orúko* oh-ru-ko
napkin *aso ìnuwó* a-sho i-nu-wo
nappy *aso ìléèdi omodè* a-sho i-lay-ay-di o-mo-day
national park *gbàgede ìgbàfé* gba-gay-day i-gba-fe
nausea *èèbì* ay-ay-bi
neck *orùn* o-rung
new *tuntun* tung-tung
news *ìròyìn* i-roh-ying
newspaper *ìwé-ìròyìn* i-way-i-roh-ying
night *alé* a-le
nightclub *ilé ìgbafé alé* i-lay i-gba-fe a-le
noisy *pariwo* kpa-ri-woh
nonsmoking *màmusìgà* ma-mu-si-ga
north *àarèwà* a-a-ray-wa
nose *imú* i-mu
now *nìsinsìnyí* ni-sing-sing-yi
number *nónbà* no-n-ba
nuts *nóótí* no-o-ti

O

oil (engine) *epo* ay-kpoh
OK *òdàra* oh-da-ra
old *gbó* gboh
open a *sí* shi
outside *ìta* i-ta

P

package *erù* e-ru
pain *irora* i-roh-ra

palace *ààfin* *òba* a-a-fing o-ba
paper *ìwé* i-way
park (car) v *yàrà ìgbókòsí* ya-ra i-gbo-ko-si
passport *ìwé ìrìnnà* i-we i-ring-na
pay *san* sang
pen *kálàmù* ka-la-mu
petrol *epo betiròòlù* ay-kpoh be-ti-roh-oh-lu
pharmacy *ilé ìpòògùn* i-lay kpoh-oh-gung
plate *àwo/abó* a-woh/a-bo
postcard *páálì ìkíni* kpa-a-li i-ki-ni
post office *ilé ìfowópamoòsí* i-lay i-foh-woh-kpa-mo-si
pregnant *oyún* oh-yung

Q

quiet *dàké* da-ke

R

rain n *òjò* oh-joh
razor *abefélé* a-be-fe-le
registered mail *ìwé ìfìrànsé* i-way i-fi-rang-she
rent v *yá lò* ya loh
repair v *tún se* tung shay
reservation *gbà sílè* gba si-le
restaurant *ilé ìtura* i-lay i-tu-ra
return v *padà* kpa-da
road *ònà* o-na
room *yàrà* ya-ra

S

sad *banújé* ba-nu-je
safe a *fi pamó* fi-kpa-mo
sanitary napkin *aso nnkan-osù* a-sho n-n-kang-oh-shu
seafood *àwon-ohun-ijje-inú-òkun* a-wong-oh-hung-ji-je-i-nu-oh-kun
seat *ijokòó* i-joh-koh-oh
send *fi rànsé* fi rang-she
sex *bá sùn* ba sung
shampoo *oseìforun* o-she-i-fo-rung
share (a dorm, etc) *bá pín* ba-kping
shaving cream *oseìfarun* o-she-i-fa-rung
she *òun* oh-ung
sheet (bed) *aso ìbora* a-sho i-boh-ra
shirt *séétì* she-e-ti
shoes *bàtà* ba-ta
shop n *sóòbù* sho-o-bu
shower n *sàwà* sha-wa
skin *awo* a-wo
skirt *aso àwòsòdò obìnrin* a-sho a-wo-soh-doh oh-bing-ring
sleep v *sùn* sung

small *kèrè* kay-ray
smoke (cigarettes) v *mu* mu
soap *ose* o-she
some *dìè* di-e
soon *láìpé* la-i-kpe
sore throat *egbò ôfun* ay-gboh-o-fung
south *gúsù* gu-su
souvenir shop *sóòbù ìtajà* sho-o-bu i-ta-ja
speak *sòrò* so-ro
spoon *síbí* shi-bi
stamp *òòtè* oh-oh-te
stand-by ticket *tíkéètì sì-dúròdìè*
  ti-ke-e-ti si-du-roh-di-e
station (train) *ibudoko rélùwèè*
  i-bu-doh-ko ray-lu-way-ay
stomach *Ìkùn* i-kung
stop v *dúró* du-roh
stop (bus) n *ìbúdòkò* i-bu-doh-ko
street *òpópó* oh-kpoh-kpoh
student *akékòo* a-ke-ko-o
sunscreen *ípara-agbòòrùn* i-kpa-ra-a-gboh-oh-rung
swim v *lúwèé* lu-we-e

T

tampons *aşo nnkan-osù* a-sho n-n-kang-oh-shu
teeth *eyín* ay-ying
telephone n *telifòònù* te-li-foh-oh-nu
television *amóhùnmáwòràn*
  a-moh-hung-ma-woh-rang
temperature (weather) *ojú ojó* oh-ju o-jo
tent *àgó* a-go
that (one) *íyen* i-yeng
they *àwon* a-wong
thirsty *òùngbè* oh-ung-gbe
this (one) *èyí* ay-yi
throat *ôfun* o-fung
ticket *ìwé ìwolé* i-way i-wo-le
time *ìgbà* i-gba
tired *rè* re
tissues *isù ara* i-shu a-ra
today *òní* oh-ni
toilet *ilé ìgbònsè* i-lay i-gbong-se
tonight *alé òní* a-le oh-ni
toothache *akokoro* a-koh-koh-roh
toothbrush *búróòsì ìfoyín* bu-ro-o-shi i-fo-ying
toothpaste *oşe ìfoyín* o-she i-fo-ying
torch (flashlight) *tóòşì* to-o-shi
tourist office *ofíìsì arin-rìn-àjò* o-fi-i-si a-ring-ring-a-joh
towel *tàwèlì* ta-we-li

translate *túmò* tu-mo
travel agency *aşètò arin-rìn-àjò*
  a-she-toh a-ring-ring-a-joh
travellers cheque *ìwé sòwèdowo arin-rìn-àjò*
  i-we so-way-doh-woh a-ring-ring-a-joh
trousers *sòkòtò* shoh-koh-toh
twin beds *béèdì oníbejì* be-e-di oh-ni-bay-ji
tyre *tàyà* ta-ya

U

underwear *àwòtélè* a-wo-te-le
urgent *kíàklà* ki-a-ki-a

V

vacant *sí şìlè* shi si-le
vegetable n *èfó* e-fo
vegetarian a *alàìjeran* a-la-i-je-rang
visa *ìwé àşe ìrìnnà* i-we a-she i-ring-na

W

waiter *agbótí* a-gbo-ti
walk v *rìn* ring
wallet *àpò owó* a-kpoh oh-woh
warm a *ooru* oh-oh-ru
wash (something) *fò* fo
watch n *ìşó* i-sho
water *omi* oh-mi
we *àwa* a-wa
weekend *òpin-òsè* oh-ping-o-se
west *ìwò oòrùn* i-wo oh-oh-rung
wheelchair *kèké abirùn* ke-ke a-bi-rung
when *nígbàwo* ni-gba-woh
where *níbo* ni-boh
who *ta ní* ta ni
why *nítorí kí ni* ni-toh-ri ki ni
window *ferèsè* fay-ray-say
wine *otí fìle* o-ti li-lay
with *pèlú* kpe-lu
without *láìsí* la-i-si
woman *obìnrin* oh-bing-ring
write *ko* ko

Y

you sg *ìwo* i-wo
you pl *èyin* e-ying

Zulu

pronunciation

Vowels		Consonants	
Symbol	**English sound**	**Symbol**	**English sound**
aa	**fa**ther	b	rib-**p**unch
aw	**law**	b'	strong b with air sucked in
e	b**e**t	ch'	as in 'let-**show**' but spat out
ee	s**ee**	d	as in 'ha**rd-t**imes'
u	p**u**t	dl	like a voiced hl
		f	**fun**
		g	as in '**big-k**ick'
		h	**hat**
		hl	as in the Welsh '**ll**ewellyn'
		j	**jar**
		k	**kit**
		k'	k, but spat out
		l	**lot**
		m	**man**
		n	**not**
		ng	fi**ng**er
		ny	ca**ny**on
		p	**pet**
		p'	**popping** p
		r	**run** (rolled)
		s	**sun**
		sh	**shot**
		t	**top**
		t'	**spitting** t
		ts'	as in 'le**ts**', but spat out
		v	**very**
		w	**win**
		y	**yes**
		z	**zero**

In this chapter, the Zulu pronunciation is given in pink after each phrase.

Each syllable is separated by a dot, and the syllable stressed in each word is italicised.

For example:

Uxolo. u-k'|aw·law

Note also that Zulu has no word stress in questions.

The term 'voiced' applied to consonant and clicks in this chapter means 'said with the vocal cords vibrating'.

Zulu's glottalised consonants, simplified as b', ch', k', p', t' and ts' in our pronunciation guide, are made by tightening and releasing the space between the vocal cords when you pronounce the sound, a bit like combining it with the sound in the middle of the word 'uh-oh'. The sound b' has an extra twist – instead of breathing out to make the sound, you breathe in.

For information on Zulu's distinctive click sounds, see the box on page 220.

introduction

The name of the Zulu language (*isiZulu* ee-see-*zu*-lu) comes from the word *izulu* ee-*zu*-lu – literally 'heaven', or, more poetically, 'the people of heaven'. About 10 million Africans speak Zulu as a first language, with the vast majority (more than 95 per cent) in South Africa. Other speakers are in Botswana, Lesotho, Malawi, Mozambique and Swaziland. Zulu, an Nguni language belonging to the Southern Bantu group, is closely related to other Bantu languages in southern Africa, particularly Xhosa. Zulu-speaking people are descendents of the Nguni people who inhabited coastal regions of southeastern Africa from the 16th century. Some linguists believe that during the 16th and 17th centuries, the Nguni dialects acquired their distinctive 'click' sounds, which still feature in Zulu. Another theory claims that Zulu and Xhosa women borrowed the clicks from neighbouring Khoisan languages to disguise taboo words in their own languages. The Zulu Empire was established in the second quarter of the 19th century, a time in which foreign missionaries were recording and documenting the language and culture of the Zulu people. Several spelling systems were in use by 1860, and a standardised writing system was implemented in 1921.

■ **zulu** (native language) ■ **zulu** (generally understood)

language difficulties

Do you speak English?	*Uyasikhuluma isiNgisi?*	u·yaa·see·ku·lu·maa ee·see·ngee·see
Do you understand?	*Uyezwa?*	u·ye·zwaa
I understand.	*Ngiyezwa.*	ngee·*ye*·zwaa
I don't understand.	*Angizwa.*	aa·*ngee*·zwaa
Could you please ...?	*Ake ...?*	aa·ge ...
repeat that	*uphinde*	u·*pee*·nde
speak more slowly	*ukhulume kancane kakhulu*	u·ku·lu·me gaa·nk!aa·ne gaa·ku·lu
write it down	*uyibhale phansi*	u·yee·baa·le paa·nts'ee

click sounds

Zulu has a series of click sounds: some clicks are against the front teeth (like a 'tsk' sound), some are against the roof of the mouth at the front (like a 'tock' sound) and some are against the side teeth (like the chirrup you make to get a horse to start walking).

front teeth	roof of the mouth	side teeth	description
k!	k¡	k¦	voiceless
kh!	kh¡	kh¦	aspirated (with a puff of air)
g!	g¡	g¦	voiced
n!	n¡	n¦	nasalized voiceless
gn!	gn¡	gn¦	nasalised voiced

time, dates & numbers

What time is it?	*Ngubani isikhathi?*	ngu·b'aa·nee ee·see·kaa·tee
It's one o'clock.	*Nguwani.*	ngu·*waa*·nee
It's (two) o'clock.	*Ngu(thu).*	ngu·(*thu*)
It's quarter past (one).	*Yingokhotha-phasi (wani).*	yee·ngaw·kaw·taa·paa·see (*waa*·nee)
Half past (one).	*Ngophasi-(wani).*	ngaw·paa·see·(*waa*·nee)
Quarter to (eight).	*Ngokhotha-thu (eyithi).*	ngaw·kaw·taa·tu (e·*yee*·tee)
At what time ...?	*Ngasikhathi bani ...?*	ngaa·see·kaa·tee b'aa·nee ...
At ...	*Ngo-...*	ngaw·...
It's (17 December).	*Ngumhla ka-(seventini Disemba).*	ngu·*m*·hlaa gaa·(se·ve·*nt'ee*·nee dee·*se*·mbaa)

yesterday	izolo	ee-*zaw*-law
today	namhlanje	naa-m-hlaa-*nje*
tomorrow	kusasa	gu-*saa*-saa

Monday	uMsombuluko	u-m-*saw*-mbu-*lu*-gaw
Tuesday	uLwesibili	u-lwe-see-*b'ee*-lee
Wednesday	uLwesithathu	u-lwe-see-*taa*-tu
Thursday	uLwesine	u-lwe-*see*-ne
Friday	uLwesihlanu	u-lwe-see-*hlaa*-nu
Saturday	uMgqibelo	u-m-gjee-*b'e*-law
Sunday	iSonto	ee-*saw*-nt'aw

numbers

In Zulu, numbers borrowed from English are commonly used and will be understood. They're also given in this chapter, rather than the more complex Zulu forms.
See below for numbers one to 10.

1	uwani	u-*waa*-nee		6	usiksi	u-*seek*-see
2	uthu	u-*tu*		7	usevene	u-se-*ve*-nee
3	uthri	u-*three*		8	u-eyithi	u-e-yeet
4	ufo	u-*faw*		9	unayini	u-*naa*-yee-nee
5	ufayifi	u-*faa*-yee-fee		10	utheni	u-*the*-nee

border crossing

I'm here ...	Ngilapha ...	ngee-*laa*-paa ...
in transit	ngidlula nje	ngee-*dlu*-laa nje
on business	ngebhizinisi	nge-bee-zee-*nee*-see
on holiday	ngeholide	nge-haw-*lee*-de

I'm here for ...	Ngizoba lapha ...	ngee-*zaw*-b'aa *laa*-paa ...
(10) days	amalanga	aa-maa-*lac*-ngaa
	(ayishumi)	(a-yee-*shu*-mee)
(three) weeks	amasonto	aa-maa-*saw*-nt'aw
	(amathathu)	(aa-maa-*taa*-tu)
(two) months	izinyanga	ee-zee-*nyaa*-nga
	(ezimbili)	(e-zee-*mbee*-lee)

I'm going to (the Drakensberg).
Ngiya (oKhahlamba). ngee-yaa (aw-kaa-*hlaa*-mbaa)

I'm staying at the (Durban Sun).
Ngihlala (e-Durban Sun). ngee-*hlaa*-laa (e-de-ben *saa*-nee)

tickets

A one-way ticket to (Eshowe), please.
Ngicela ithikithi elilodwa   ngee-*kle*-laa ee-tee-*gee*-tee e-lee-*law*-dwaa
ukuya (eShowe).   u-gu-yaa (e-*shaw*-we)

A return ticket to (Ulundi), please.
Ngicela ithikithi elilodwa   ngee-*kle*-laa ee-tee-*gee*-tee e-lee-*law*-dwaa
ukuya nokubuya (oLundi).   u-gu-yaa naw-gu-*b'u*-yaa (aw-*lu*-ndee)

I'd like to ... my	*Ngicela uku-...*	ngee-*kle*-laa *u-*gu-...
ticket, please.	*ithikithi lami.*	ee-tee-*gee*-tee *laa*-mee
cancel	*khansela*	kaa-*nts'e*-laa
change	*shintsha*	*shee*-nch'aa
collect	*landa*	*laa*-ndaa

Is there a toilet?
Kukhona ithoyilethi?   gu-kaw-naa ee-taw-yee-le-tee

Is there air conditioning?
Kukhona umoya opholisiwe?   gu-kaw-naa u-maw-yaa aw-paw-lee-see-we

How long does the trip take?
Uhambo luthatha isikhathi   u-haa-mbaw lu-taa-taa ee-see-kaa-tee
esingakanani?   e-see-ngaa-gaa-naa-nee

Is it a direct route?
Yindlela eqondile?   yee-ndle-laa e-kjaw-ndee-le

transport

Where does flight (BA325) arrive/depart?
Lifikela/Lisukekela kuphi   lee-fee-ge-laa /lee-su-ge-ge-laa gu-pee
ibhanoyi u-(BA325)?   ee-ba-naw-yee u-(bee ey three tu faiv)

How long will it be delayed?
Lizomiswa isikhathi   lee-zaw-mee-swaa ee-see-kaa-tee
esingakanani?   e-see-ngaa-gaa-naa-nee

Is this the boat/train to (Cape Town)?
Yiso isikebhe/isitimela   yee-saw ee-see-k'e-be/ee-see-t'ee-me-laa
esiya (eKipi)?   e-see-yaa (e-k'ee-p'ee)

Is this the bus/plane to (Johannesburg)?
Yilo ibhasi/ibhanoyi   yee-law ee-baa-see/ee-baa-naw-yee
eliya (eGoli)?   e-lee-yaa (e-gaw-lee)

I'd like to hire	Ngicela ukuqasha	ngee-k!e-laa u-gu-kjaa-shaa
a ... (with	... (enomoya	... (e-naw-maw-yaa
air conditioning).	opholisiwe).	aw-paw-lee-see-we)
4WD	i-fo-bhayi-fo	ee-faw-baa-yee-faw
car	imoto	ee-maw-t'aw

How much is it for (three) days/weeks?
| Malini amalanga/amasonto | maa-lee-nee aa-maa-laa-ngaa/aa-maa-saw-nt'aw |
| (amathathu)? | (aa-maa-taa-tu) |

How much is it to (Umvoti)?
| Malini ukuya (eMvoti)? | maa-lee-nee u-gu-yaa (em-vaw-tee) |

Please take me to (this address).
| Ake ungise ku-(lelikheli). | aa-ge u-ngee-se gu-(le-lee-ke-lee) |

directions

Where's the	Ingakuphi ...	ee-ngaa-gu-pee ...
(nearest) ...?	(eseduzana)?	(e-se-du-zaa-naa)
internet café	i-Internet café	ee-een-ter-net kaa-fe
market	imakethe	ee-maa-ge-te

Is this the road to (Hluhluwe)?
| Yiyo indlela eya | yee-yaw ee-ndle-laa e-yaa |
| (eHluhluwe)? | (e-hlu-hlu-we) |

Can you show me (on the map)?
| Ungangibonisa (kumephu)? | u-ngaa-ngee-b'aw-nee-saa (gu-me-pu) |

What's the address?
| Lithini ikheli? | lee-tee-nee ee-ke-lee |

How far is it?
| Kukude kangakanani? | gu-gu-de gaa-ngaa-gaa-naa-nee |

How do I get there?
| Ngifika kanjani lapho? | ngee-fee-gaa gaa-njaa-nee laa-paw |

Turn left/right.
| Jikela kwesokunxele/ | jee-ge-laa gwe-saw-gu-n!e-le/ |
| kwesokunene. | gwe-saw-gu-ne-ne |

It's ...	Ku-...	gu·...
behind ...	semva kwa-...	se·mbvaa gwaa·...
in front of ...	phambi kwa-...	paa·mbee gwaa·...
near (to ...)	seduze (na-)...	se·du·ze (naa·)...
next to ...	secaleni kwa-...	se·k!aa·le·nee gwaa·...
on the corner	sekhoneni	se·kaw·ne·nee
opposite ...	bhekene na-...	be·ge·nee naa·...
straight ahead	ngaphambili	ngaa·paa·mbee·lee
there	laphaya	laa·paa·yaa

accommodation

Where's a ...?	Ingakuphi ...?	ee·ngaa·gu·pee ...
camping ground	indawo yokukhempa	ee·ndaa·waw yaw·gu·ke·mpaa
guesthouse	indlu yezivakashi	ee·ndlu ye·zee·vaa·gaa·shee
hotel	ihhotela	ee·haw·t'e·laa
youth hostel	ihostela labasha	ee·haw·st'e·laa laa·b'aa·shaa

Can you recommend somewhere cheap/good?
Ikhona indawo eshibhile/   ee·kaw·naa ee·ndaa·waw e·shee·bee·le/
enhle oyaziyo?   e·ntl'e aw·yaa·zee·yaw

I'd like to book a room, please.
Ngingathanda ukubekisa   ngee·ngaa·taa·ndaa u·gu·b'e·gee·saa
ikamelo.   ee·k'aa·me·law

I have a reservation.
Ngibekelwe indawo.   ngee·b'e·ge·lwe ee·ndaa·waw

Do you have a ... room?	Ninekamelo ...?	nee·ne·k'aa·me·law ...
single	lomuntu oyedwa	law·mu·nt'u aw·ye·dwaa
double	labantu ababili	laa·b'aa·nt'u aa·b'aa·b'ee·lee
twin	elinemibhede emibili	e·lee·ne·mee·be·de e·mee·b'ee·lee

How much is it per ...?	Malini ...?	maa·lee·nee ...
night	ubusuku obubodwa	u·b'u·su·gu aw·b'u·b'aw·dwaa
person	umuntu oyedwa	u·mu·nt'u aw·ye·dwaa

I'd like to stay for (two) nights.
Ngingathanda ukulala   ngee·ngaa·taa·ndaa u·gu·laa·laa
izinsuku (ezimbili).   ee·zee·nts'u·gu (e·zee·mbee·lee)

What time is check-out?
*Kufanele kuphunywe
ngasikhathi bani?*

gu·faa·ne·le gu·pu·nywe
ngaa·see·kaa·tee b'aa·nee

Am I allowed to camp here?
*Kuvunyelwa ukumisa
ikamu lapha?*

gu·vu·nye·lwa u·gu·mee·saa
ee·k'aa·mu laa·paa

banking & communications

I'd like to ...	*Ngicela uku-...*	ngee·k!e·laa u·gu·...
arrange a transfer	*shintshwa*	shee·nch'waa
cash a cheque	*phendula isheke*	pe·ndu·laa i·she·ge
change a travellers cheque	*phendula isheke lesihambi*	phe·ndu·laa ee·she·ge le·see·haa·mbee
change money	*shintsha imali*	shee·nch'aa ee·maa·lee
withdraw money	*khipha imali*	kee·paa ee·maa·lee
I want to ...	*Ngifuna uku-...*	ngee·fu·naa u·gu·...
buy a phonecard	*thenga ikhadi locingo*	te·ngaa ee·kaa·dee law·k!ee·ngaw
call (London)	*fowunela ku(Landani)*	faw·wu·ne·laa gu·(laa·ndaa·nee)
reverse the charges	*buyisela izindleko emuva*	b'u·yee·se·laa ee·zee·ndle·gaw e·mu·vaa
use a printer	*sebenzisa iphrinta*	se·b'e·ndzee·saa ee·phree·nt'aa
use the internet	*sebenzisa i-intanethi*	se·b'e·ndzee·saa ee·ee·nt'aa·ne·tee

How much is it per hour?
Malini nge-awa?

maa·lee·nee nge·aa·waa

How much does a (three-minute) call cost?
*Malini ucingo (lwemizuzu
emithathu)?*

maa·lee·nee u·k!ee·ngaw (lwe·mee·zu·zu
e·mee·taa·tu)

(One rand) per minute/hour.
(Irandi) ngomzuzu/nge-awa.

(ee·raa·ndee) ngaw·m·zu·zu/nge·aa·waa

tours

When's the next ...?	*Luzokuba nini ...?*	lu·zaw·gu·baa nee·nee ...
day trip	*uhambo lwemini*	u·haa·mbaw lwe·mee·nee
	yonke	yaw·nk'e
tour	*uhambo*	u·haa·mbaw
Is ... included?	*Sekuhlangene imali ...?*	se·gu·hlaa·nge·ne ee·maa·lee ...
accommodation	*yokuhlala*	yaw·gu·hlaa·laa
the admission charge	*yokungena*	yaw·gu·nge·naa
food	*yokudla*	yaw·gu·dlaa
transport	*yokuthuthwa*	yaw·gu·tu·twaa

How long is the tour?
Uhambo luthatha isikhathi u·haa·mbaw lu·taa·taa ee·see·kaa·tee
esingakanani? e·see·ngaa·gaa·naa·nee

What time should we be back?
Kufanele sibuye gu·faa·ne·le see·b'u·ye
ngasikhathi bani? ngaa·see·kaa·tee b'aa·nee

shopping

I'm looking for ...
Ngifuna ... ngee·*fu*·naa ...

I need film for this camera.
Ngidinga ifilimu ngee·*dee*·ngaa ee·fee·*lee*·mu
lale khamera. laa·*le* kaa·*me*·raa

Can I listen to this?
Ngingalalela le na? ngee·ngaa·laa·le·laa le naa

Can I have my ... repaired?
Ngingalungiselwa ... na? ngee·ngaa·lu·ngee·se·lwaa ... naa

When will it be ready?
Izobe ilungile nini? ee·zaw·b'e ee·lu·ngee·le nee·nee

How much is it?
Yimalini? yee·maa·lee·nee

Can you write down the price?
Ungangibhalela inani? u·ngaa·ngee·baa·le·la ee·naa·nee

226

What's your lowest price?
  Yini intengo ephansi?   yee·nee ee·nt'e·ngaw e·paa·nts'ee

I'll give you (five) rands.
  Ngizokunika amarandi   ngee·zaw·gu·*nee*·gaa aa·maa·*raa*·ndee
  (amahlanu).   (aa·ma·*hlaa*·nu)

There's a mistake in the bill.
  Kunesiphosiso esikwenetwini.   gu·ne·see·paw·*see*·saw e·see·kwe·ne·*twee*·nee

It's faulty.
  Ayisebenzi kahle.   a·yee·se·*b'e*·ndzee *gaa*·hle

I'd like a receipt, please.
  Ngicela irisidi.   ngee·*k!e*·laa ee·ree·*see*·dee

I'd like a refund, please.
  Ngicela ukubuyiselwa imali.   ngee·*k!e*·laa u·gu·b'u·yee·*se*·lwaa ee·*maa*·lee

Do you accept ...?	*Nithatha ... na?*	nee·taa·taa ... naa
credit cards	*amakhadi ekhrediti*	aa·maa·kaa·dee e·khre·dee·tee
debit cards	*amakhadi edebithi*	aa·maa·kaa·dee e·de·b'ee·tee
travellers cheques	*amasheke esihambi*	aa·maa·she·ge e·see·haa·mbee

Could you ...?	*Unga-... na?*	u·ngaa-... naa
burn a CD from	*wathatha amafayili*	waa·taa·taa aa·maa·faa·yee·lee
my memory	*ekhadini lami*	e·kaa·dee·nee laa·mee
card	*le-memory*	le·me·maw·ree
	uwabhale ku-CD	u·waa·baa·le gu·see·dee
develop this film	*khulisa leli filimu*	ku·lee·saa le·lee fee·lee·mu

making conversation

Hello.	*Sawubona.* sg	saa·wu·*b'aw*·naa
Hello.	*Sanibonani.* pl	saa·nee·b'aw·*naa*·nee
Good night.	*Lala/Lalani kahle.* sg/pl	laa·laa/laa·laa·nee *gaa*·hle
Goodbye (stay well).	*Sala/Salani kahle.* sg/pl	saa·laa/saa·laa·nee *gaa*·hle
Goodbye (go well).	*Hamba/Hambani*	haa·mbaa/haa·mbaa·nee
	kahle. sg/pl	*gaa*·hle
Mr	*(u)Mnumzane*	(u)·m·nu·m·*zaa*·ne
Mrs	*(u)Nkosikazi*	(u)·nk'aw·see·*gaa*·zee
Ms/Miss	*(u)Nkosazana*	(u)·nk'aw·saa·*zaa*·naa

(the *u* in the Zulu title is omitted when you actually address someone)

How are you?	*Unjani?/Ninjani?* sg/pl	u·njaa·nee/nee·njaa·nee
Fine. And you?	*Sikhona. Nawe/Nani?* sg/pl	see·*kaw*·naa naa·we/naa·nee
What's your name?	*Ngubani igama lakho?*	ngu·*b'*aa·nee ee·gaa·maa laa·kaw
My name's ...	*Igama lami ngu-...*	ee·gaa·maa *laa*·mee ngu-...
I'm pleased to meet you.	*Ngiyajabula ukukwazi/ukunazi.* sg/pl	ngee·yaa·jaa·*b'u*·laa u·gu·*gwaa*·zee/u·gu·*naa*·zee

This is my ...	*Lo ... wami.*	law ... *waa*·mee
brother	*ngumfowethu*	ngu·m·faw·*we*·tu
father	*ngubaba*	ngu·*b'*aa·*b'*aa
friend	*ngumngane*	ngu·m·*ngaa*·ne
husband	*ngumyeni*	ngu·m·*ye*·nee
mother	*ngumama*	ngu·*maa*·maa
sister	*udadewethu*	u·daa·de·*we*·tu
wife	*ngunkosikazi*	ngu·nk'aw·see·*gaa*·zee

Here's my ...	*Nayi ...*	naa·yee ...
What's your ...?	*Lithini ... lakho?*	lee·tee·nee ... laa·kaw
address	*ikheli*	ee·ke·lee
email address	*ikheli le-email*	ee·ke·lee le·e·me·yee·lee

| Where are you from? | *Uvelaphi?* | u·ve·laa·pee |
| I'm from (Australia). | *Ngivela (e-Ostrelia).* | ngee·*ve*·laa (e·aw·stre·*lee*·yaa) |

I'm married.	*Ngishadile.*	ngee·shaa·*dee*·le
I'm not married.	*Angishadanga.*	aa·ngee·shaa·*daa*·ngaa
Can I take a photo (of you)?	*Ngicela uku(ku)-thatha isithombe.*	ngee·*k!e*·laa u·gu·(gu)-*taa*·taa ee·see·*taw*·mbe

eating out

Can you recommend a ...?	*Ungasitshela ... na?*	u·ngaa·see·ch'e·laa ... naa
bar	*ngendawo yokuphuza oyithandayo*	nge·ndaa·waw yaw·gu·pu·zaa aw·yee·taa·ndaa·yaw
dish	*ngesidlo osithandayo*	nge·see·dlaw aw·see·taa·ndaa·yaw
place to eat	*ngendawo yokudla oyithandayo*	nge·ndaa·waw yaw·gu·dlaa aw·yee·taa·ndaa·yaw

I'd like ..., please.	Ngicela ...	ngee-*k!e*-laa ...
the bill	irisidi lokukhokha	ee-ree-*see*-dee law-gu-*kaw*-kaa
the menu	imenyu	ee-*me*-nyu
a table (for two)	itafula (yabantu ababili)	ee-t'aa-*fu*-laa (yaa-*b'aa*-nt'u aa-b'aa-*b'ee*-lee)
that dish	leso sidlo	le-saw *see*-dlaw

Do you have vegetarian food?	Ninokudla kwabangadli nyama?	nee-naw-gu-dlaa gwaa-b'aa-ngaa-dlee nyaa-maa

Could you prepare a meal without ...?	Ungakupheka ukudla ngaphandle kokusebenzisa ... na?	u-ngaa-gu-pe-gaa u-gu-dlaa ngaa-paa-ndle gaw-gu-se-*b'e*-ndzee-saa ... naa
eggs	amaqanda	aa-maa-*kjaa*-ndaa
meat stock	isobho lenyama	ee-*saw*-baw le-nyaa-maa

(cup of) coffee/tea ...	ikhofi/itiye ...	ee-*kaw*-fee/ee-*t'ee*-ye ...
with milk	elinobisi	e-lee-naw-*b'ee*-see
without sugar	elingenashukela	e-lee-nge-naa-shu-*ge*-laa

(boiled) water	amanzi (abilisiweyo)	aa-*maa*-ndzee (aa-b'ee-lee-see-*we*-yaw)

emergencies

Call ...!	Biza ...!	*b'ee*-zaa ...
an ambulance	i-ambulense	ee-aa-mbu-*le*-nts'e
a doctor	udokotela	u-daw-gaw-*t'e*-laa
the police	amaphoyisa	aa-maa-paw-*yee*-saa

Could you help me, please?
Ake ungisize/ningisize. sg/pl   aa-ge u-ngee-*see*-ze/nee-ngee-*see*-ze

I'm lost.
Ngilahlekile.   ngee-laa-hle-*gee*-le

Where are the toilets?
Ziphi izindlu zangasese?   zee-pee ee-zee-ndlu zaa-ngaa-se-se

I want to report an offence.
Ngifuna ukubika icala.   ngee-*fu*-naa u-gu-*b'ee*-gaa ee-*k!aa*-laa

I have insurance.
Nginomshwayilense.   ngee-naw-m-shwaa-yee-*le*-nts'e

I've been assaulted.	Ngilinyaziwe.	ngee·lee·nyaa·*zee*·we
I've been raped.	Ngidlwenguliwe.	ngee·dlwe·ngu·*lee*·we
I've been robbed.	Ngigetshengiwe.	ngee·ge·ch'e·*ngee*·we

I've lost my ...
Ngilahlekelwe yi-...   ngee·laa·hle·ge·*lwe* yee·...

My bags were stolen.
Amapotimende ami ebiwe.   aa·maa·p'aw·tee·*me*·nde *aa*·mee e·*b*·*ee*·we

My passport was stolen.
Iphasiphothi lami lebiwe.   ee·paa·see·*paw*·tee *laa*·mee le·*b*·*ee*·we

My wallet was stolen.
Isikhwama sami semali sebiwe.   ee·see·*kwaa*·maa *saa*·mee se·*maa*·lee se·*b*·*ee*·we

I want to contact my consulate/embassy.
Ngifuna ukuthintana   ngee·*fu*·naa u·gu·tee·*nt'aa*·naa
ne-consulate/ne-embassy.   ne·kaw·nsu·*laa*·tee/ne·e·*mbaa*·see

medical needs

Where's the nearest ...?	Ikuphi indawo ... eseduzane?	ee·gu·pee ee·ndaa·*waw* ... e·se·du·*zaa*·ne
dentist	kadokotela wamazinyo	gaa·daw·gaw·*te*·laa waa·maa·*zee*·nyaw
doctor	kadokotela	gaa·daw·gaw·*te*·laa

Where's the nearest hospital?
Sikuphi isibhedlela esiseduzane?   see·gu·pee ee·see·be·*dle*·laa e·see·se·du·*zaa*·ne

Where's the nearest pharmacist?
Likuphi ikhemisi eliseduzane?   lee·gu·pee ee·ke·mee·see e·lee·se·du·*zaa*·ne

I need a doctor (who speaks English).
Ngidinga udokotela (okwazi   ngee·*dee*·ngaa u·daw·gaw·*te*·laa (aw·*gwaa*·zee
ukukhuluma isiNgisi).   u·gu·ku·*lu*·maa ee·see·*ngee*·see)

Could I see a female doctor?
Ngingabona udokotela   ngee·ngaa·b'aw·naa u·daw·gaw·*te*·laa
wesifazane na?   we·see·faa·*zaa*·ne naa

It hurts here.
Kubuhlungu lapha.   gu·b'u·*hlu*·ngu *laa*·paa

I'm allergic to (penicillin).
Angizwani na-(nephenisilini).   aa·ngee·*zwaa*·nee naa·(ne·pe·nee·see·*lee*·nee)

english–zulu dictionary

In this dictionary, words are marked as n (noun), a (adjective), v (verb), sg (singular) and pl (plural) where necessary. Note that in Zulu the pronouns are prefixes attached to the beginning of a verb, as indicated with hyphens in this dictionary. Zulu adjectives usually come after the noun and the form of the adjective changes according to the class of the noun. Just use the form of the adjective given in this dictionary and remember to have it after the noun – it won't be completely correct grammatically, but you should be understood.

A

accommodation *indawo yokulala*
  ee-*ndaa*-waw yaw-gu-*laa*-laa
after *emva kwa-* e-mbvaa gwaa-
airport *isikhumulo samabhanoyi*
  ee-see-ku-mu-law saa-maa-baa-*naw*-yee
alcohol *utshwala u-ch'waa*-laa
all *-onke -aw*-nk'e
and (joins nouns) *na-* naa-
and (joins sentences) *futhi fu*-tee
ankle *iqakala ee-kjaa-gaa*-laa
arm *ingalo* ee-*ngaa*-law
aspirin *i-aspirin* ee-es-pee-*ree*-nee
asthma *umbefu* u-m-b'e-fu
ATM *i-ATM* ee-e-yee-tee-*em*

B

baby *usana* u-*saa*-naa
back (body) *umhlane* u-m-*hlaa*-ne
backpack *unxazisuka* u-n'jaa-zee-su-gaa
bad *-bi -b'ee*
baggage claim *ithikithi yempahla*
  ee-tee-*gee*-tee ye-*mp'aa*-hlaa
bank *ibhange* ee-baa-nge
bathroom *ibhavulumu* ee-baa-vu-lu-mu
battery *ibhetri* ee-be-tree
beautiful *-hle* -hle
bed *umbhede* u-m-be-te
beer *ubhiya* u-bee-ya
bees *izinyosi* ee-zee-*nyaw*-see
before *phambi kwa-* paa-mbee gwaa-
bicycle *ibhayisikili* ee-baa-yee-see-*gee*-lee
big *-khulu -ku*-lu
blanket *ingubo* ee-ngu-b'aw
blood group *uhlobo lwegazi* u-*hlaw*-b'aw lwe-*gaa*-zee
bottle *ibhodlela* ee-baw-*dle*-laa
bottle opener *isivulo sebhodlela*
  ee-see-*vu*-law se-baw-*dle*-laa
boy *umfana* u-m-*faa*-naa
brakes (car) *amabhuleki* aa-maa-bu-*le*-gee

breakfast *ibhulakufesi* ee-bu-laa-gu-*fe*-see
bronchitis *ukucinana kwesifuba*
  u-gu-k!ee-*naa*-naa gwe-see-*fu*-b'aa

C

café *ikhefi* ee-*ke*-fee
cancel *-khansela* -kaa-*nts'e*-laa
can opener *isivulo sethini* ee-see-*vu*-law se-*tee*-nee
cash n *ukheshe* u-*ke*-she
cell phone *isele* ee-se-le
centre n *iphakathi* ee-paa-*gaa*-tee
cheap *-shibhile* -shee-*bee*-le
check (bill) *irisidi lokukhokha*
  ee-ree-see-dee law-gu-*kaw*-kaa
check-in n *ukubhalisa* u-gu-baa-*lee*-saa
chest *isifuba* ee-see-*fu*-b'aa
child *umntwana* u-m-nt'*waa*-naa
cigarette *usikilidi* u-see-gee-*lee*-dee
city *idolobha* ee-daw-*law*-baa
clean a *-hlanzekile* -hlaa-ndze-*gee*-le
closed *-valiwe* -vaa-*lee*-we
codeine *i-codeine* ee-kaw-*dee*-nee
cold a *-bandayo* -b'aa-*ndaa*-yaw
collect call *ucingo olukhokhelwa ngolutholayo*
  u-k!ee-ngaw aw-lu-kaw-ke-lwaa ngaw-lu-taw-*laa*-yaw
condom *ikhondomu* ee-kaw-*ndaw*-mu
constipation *ukuqunjelwa* u-gu-kju-*nje*-lwaa
contact lenses *ama-contact lens* aa-maa-kawn-tekt *lens*
cough n *umkhuhlane* u-m-ku-*hlaa*-ne
currency exchange *ukushintshwa kwezimali*
  u-gu-*shee*-nch'waa gwe-zee-*maa*-lee

D

dairy products *imikhiqizo yobisi*
  ee-mee-kee-*kjee*-zaw yaw-b'ee-see
dangerous *-nengozi* -ne-*ngaw*-zee
date (time) *usuku* u-su-gu
day *ilanga* ee-*laa*-ngaa
diaper *inabukeni* ee-naa-b'u-*k'e*-nee
diarrhoea *uhudo* u-hu-daw
dinner *idina* ee-dee-naa

dirty *-ngcolile* -ng!aw-*lee*-le
disabled *-nobulima* -naw-b'u-*lee*-maa
double bed *umbhede wedabuli* u-m-*be*-de we-daa-*b'u*-lee
drink n *isiphuzo* ee-see-*pu*-zaw
drivers licence *ilayisense lokuqhuba*
ee-laa-yee-se-nts'e yaw-gu-*k!hu*-b'aa
drugs (illicit) *izidakamizwa* ee-zee-daa-gaa-*mee*-zwaa

E

ear *indlebe* ee-*ndle*-b'e
east *impumalanga* ee-mp'u-maa-*laa*-ngaa
economy class *iklasi elishibhile*
ee-*klaa*-see e-lee-shee-*bee*-le
elevator (lift) *ikheshi* ee-*ke*-shee
email n *i-e-mail* ee-ee-me-*yee*-lee
English (language) *isiNgisi* ee-see-*ngee*-see
exchange rate *izinga loshintsho lwezimali*
ee-zee-ngaa law-*shee*-nch'aw lwe-zee-*maa*-lee
exit n *umnyango wokuphuma*
u-m-*nyaa*-ngaw waw-gu-*pu*-maa
expensive *-dulile* -du-*lee*-le
eye *iso* ee-*saw*

F

fast *ngokusheshisa* ngaw-gu-she-*shee*-saa
fever *imfiva* ee-*mpf*ee-vaa
finger *umunwe* u-*mu*-nwe
first-aid kit *ibhokisi losizo lokuqala*
ee-baw-*gee*-see law-*see*-zaw law-gu-*k!aa*-laa
first class *ufesi* u-*fe*-see
fish n *inhlanzi* ee-*ntl'aa*-ndzee
food *ukudla* u-gu-*dlaa*
foot *unyawo* u-*nyaa*-waw
fork *imfologo* ee-mpf*aw*-*law*-gaw
free (of charge) *mahhala* maa-*haa*-laa
fruit *isithelo* ee-see-*te*-law
funny *-hlekisayo* -hle-gee-*saa*-yaw

G

game park *indawo yezilwane zasendle*
ee-*ndaa*-waw ye-zee-*lwaa*-ne zaa-se-ndle
gift *isipho* ee-see-*paw*
girl (older) *intombi* ee-*nt'aw*-mbee
girl (young) *intombazana* ee-nt'aw-mbaa-*zaa*-naa
glass (drinking) *ingilazi* ee-ngee-*laa*-zee
glasses *izibuko* ee-zee-*b'u*-gaw
good *-hle* -hle
gram *igramu* ee-*graa*-mu
guide n *umphelezeli* u-m-pe-le-*ze*-lee

H

hand *isandla* ee-*saa*-ndlaa
happy *-jabule* -jaa-*b'u*-le
have *-na-* -*naa*-
he *u-* u-
head *ikhanda* ee-*kaa*-ndaa
headache *ikhanda* ee-*kaa*-ndaa
heart *inhliziyo* ee-ntlee-zee-*yaw*
heart condition *isifo senhliziyo*
ee-see-faw se-ntl'ee-zee-yaw
heat n *ukushisa* u-gu-*shee*-saa
here *lapha* *laa*-paa
high *-phakamileyo* -paa-gaa-mee-*le*-yaw
highway *umgwaqomkhulu* u-m-gwaa-k!aw-m-*ku*-lu
homosexual n *inkonkoni* ee-nk'aw-*nk'aw*-nee
hot *-shisa* -*shee*-saa
hungry *-lambile* -laa-*mbee*-le

I

I *ngi-* ngee-
identification (card) *i-ID* ee-aa-yee-*dee*
(be) ill *-gula* -gu-laa
important *-balulekile* -b'aa-lu-le-*gee*-le
internet *i-intanethi* ee-ee-nt'aa-*ne*-tee
interpreter *ihumusha* ee-hu-*mu*-shaa

J

job *umsebenzi* u-m-se-*b'e*-ndzee

K

key *isikhiye* ee-see-*kee*-ye
kilogram *ikhilogramu* ee-kee-law-*graa*-mu
kitchen *ikhishi* ee-*kee*-shee
knife *umese* u-*me*-se

L

laundry (place) *ilondolo* ee-law-*ndaw*-law
lawyer *ummeli* u-m-*me*-lee
leg *umlenze* u-m-*le*-ndze
lesbian n *inkonkoni yesifazane*
ee-nk'aw-nk'aw-nee ye-see-faa-*zaa*-ne
less a *-ncane* -*nk!aa*-ne
letter (mail) *incwadi* ee-*nk!waa*-dee
like v *-thanda* -*taa*-ndaa
love v *-thanda* -*taa*-ndaa
lunch *ilantshi* ee-laa-*nch'*ee

M

man *indoda* ee-ndaw-daa
matches *umentshisi* u-m*e-nch'ee*-see
meat *inyama* ee-*nyaa*-maa
medicine *umuthi* u-*mu*-tee
message *umlayezo* u-m-laa-*ye*-zaw
mobile phone *isele* ee-se-le
month *inyanga* ee-*nyaa*-ngaa
morning *intsasa* ee-nts'aa-saa
(in the) morning *ekuseni* e-gu-se-nee
motorcycle *isithuthuthu* ee-see-tu-tu-tu
mouth *umlomo* u-m-*law*-maw
movie *ibhayisikobho* ee-baa-yee-see-k'aw-baw
MSG *i-MSG* ee-em-es-jee
museum *imnyuziyamu* ee-m-nyu-zee-*yaa*-mu
music *umculo* u-m-*kju*-law

N

name *igama* ee-*gaa*-maa
napkin (serviette) *iseviyethe* ee-se-vee-ye-te
nappy *inabukeni* ee-naa-b'u-ge-nee
national park *iphaki elivikelwe lezwe lonke*
  ee-*paa*-gee e-lee-vee-ge-lwe le-zwe *law*-nk'e
nausea *isicasucasu* ee-see-k!aa-su-k!aa-su
neck *intamo* ee-nt'aa-maw
new *-sha* -shaa
news *izindaba* ee-zee-ndaa-b'aa
newspaper *iphephandaba* ee-pe-paa-ndaa-b'aa
night *ubusuku* u-b'u-su-gu
nightclub *iklabhu yasebusuku*
  ee-*klaa*-bu yaa-se-b'u-su-gu
noisy *-nomsindo* -naw-m-*see*-ndaw
nonsmoking *lapho kungebhenywe khona*
  laa-paw gu-nge-be-nywe *kaw*-naa
north *inyakatho* ee-nyaa-*gaa*-taw
nose *impumulo* ee-mp'u-*mu*-law
now *manje* maa-nje
number (numeral) *inombolo* ee-naw-*mbaw*-law
number (quantity) *inani* ee-*naa*-nee
nuts *amantongomane* aa-maa-nt'aw-ngaw-*maa*-ne

O

oil (engine) *uwoyela* u-waw-ye-laa
OK *kulungile* gu-lu-*ngee*-le
old (objects) *-dala* -daa-laa
old (people) *-khulile* -ku-*lee*-le
open a *-vuliwe* -vu-*lee*-we
outside *ngaphandle* ngaa-*paa*-ndle

P

package *iphasela* ee-paa-se-laa
pain *ubuhlungu* u-b'u-*hlu*-ngu
paper *iphepha* ee-*pe*-paa
park (car) v *-paka* -*paa*-gaa
passport *iphasiphothi* ee-paa-see-*paw*-tee
pay v *-khokha* -*kaw*-kaa
pen *ipeni* ee-*pe*-nee
petrol *uphethilolo* u-pe-tee-*law*-law
pharmacy *ikhemisi* ee-ke-*mee*-see
plate *isitsha* ee-see-ch'aa
postcard *iposikhadi* ee-p'aw-see-*kaa*-dee
post office *iposi* ee-*paw*-see
pregnant *-khulelwe* -ku-*le*-lwe

R

rain n *imvula* ee-*mbvu*-laa
razor *ireza* ee-re-zaa
registered mail *iposi elirejistiwe*
  ee-*p'aw*-see e-lee-re-jee-st'ee-we
rent v *-qashisa* -kjaa-*shee*-saa
repair v *-lungisa* -lu-*ngee*-saa
reservation (place) *indawo ebhukiwe*
  ee-ndaa-waw e-bu-*gee*-we
reservation (table) *itafula elibhukiwe*
  ee-t'aa-fu-laa e-lee-bu-*gee*-we
restaurant *ikhefi* ee-ke-fee
return (come back) *-buya* -b'u-yaa
return (give back) *-buyisa* -b'u-*yee*-saa
road *indlela* ee-ndle-laa
room *ikamelo* ee-k'aa-*me*-law

S

sad *-dabukile* -daa-b'u-*gee*-le
safe a *-ngenangozi* -nge-naa-*ngaw*-zee
sanitary napkins *amaphede* aa-maa-*pe*-te
seafood *ukudla okuvela olwandle*
  u-gu-dlaa aw-gu-ve-laa aw-*lwaa*-ndle
seat *isihlalo* ee-see-*hlaa*-law
send (someone) *-thuma* -tu-maa
send (something) *-thumela* -tu-*me*-laa
sex *ukulalana* u-gu-laa-*laa*-naa
shampoo *ishampu* ee-shaa-mp'u
share (a dorm, etc) *ukulala sibaningi ekamelweni*
  u-gu-*laa*-laa see-b'aa-*nee*-ngee e-k'a-me-*lwe*-nee
shaving cream *umuthi wokushefa*
  u-*mu*-tee waw-gu-she-faa
she *u-* u-
sheet (bed) *ishidi* ee-shee-dee

shirt *iyembe* ee-*ye*-mbe
shoes *izicathulo* ee-zee-klaa-*tu*-law
shop n *ivenkile* ee-ve-*nk*'ee-le
shower n *ishawa* ee-*shaa*-waa
skin *isikhumba* ee-see-*ku*-mbaa
skirt *isiketi* ee-see-*k'e*-tee
sleep v *-lala* -*laa*-laa
small *-ncane* -*nk!aa*-ne
smoke (cigarettes) v *-bhema* -*be*-maa
smoking a *lapho kungabhenywa khona*
  laa-paw gu-ngaa-*be*-nywaa *kaw*-naa
soap *insipho* ee-*nts'ee*-paw
some *-nye* -*nye*
soon *masinyane* maa-see-*nyaa*-ne
sore throat *umphimbo obuhlungu*
  u-m-*pee*-mbaw aw-b'u-*hlu*-ngu
south *iningizimu* ee-nee-ngee-*zee*-mu
speak *-khuluma* -ku-*lu*-maa
spoon *ukhezo* u-*ke*-zaw
stamp *isitembu* ee-see-*t'e*-mbu
station (train) *isiteshi* ee-see-*t'e*-shee
stomach *isisu* ee-*see*-su
stop v *-ma* -*maa*
stop (bus) n *isitobhi (sebhasi)*
  ee-see-*t'aw*-bee (se-*baa*-see)
street *umgwaqo* u-m-*gwaa*-kjaw
student *umfundi* u-m-*fu*-ndee
sunscreen *i-sunscreen* ee-saan-*skree*-nee
swim v *-bhukuda* -bu-gu-daa

T

tampons *amathemponi* aa-maa-te-*mp'aw*-nee
teeth *amazinyo* aa-maa-*zee*-nyaw
telephone n *ucingo* u-*klee*-ngaw
television *umabonakude* u-maa-b'aw-naa-*gu*-de
temperature (weather) *izinga lokushisa*
  ee-zee-ngaa law-gu-*shee*-saa
tent *itende* ee-*t'e*-nde
that (one near you) *leyo* *le*-yaw
that (one in the distance) *leya* le-*yaa*
they (animals & objects) *zi-* zee-
they (people) *ba-* b'aa-
thirsty *-omile* -aw-*mee*-le
this (one) *le* le
throat *umphimbo* u-m-*pee*-mbaw
ticket *ithikithi* ee-tee-*gee*-tee
time *isikhathi* ee-see-*kaa*-tee
tired *-khathele* -kaa-*te*-le
today *namhlanje* naa-m-hlaa-*nje*

toilet *indlu yangasese* ee-ndlu yaa-ngaa-*se*-se
tonight *namhlanje ebusuku* naa-m-hlaa-*nje* e-b'u-*su*-gu
toothbrush *isixubho* ee-see-*k'ju*-baw
toothpaste *umuthi wokugeza amazinyo*
  u-*mu*-tee waw-gu-ge-*zaa* aa-maa-*zee*-nyaw
torch (flashlight) *ithoshi* ee-*taw*-shee
towel *ithawula* ee-taa-*wu*-laa
translate *-humusha* -hu-*mu*-sha
travellers cheque *isheke lezihambi*
  ee-*she*-ge le-zee-*haa*-mbee
trousers *ibhulukwe* ee-bu-*lu*-gwe
tyre *ithaya* ee-*taa*-yaa

vacant *-ngenamuntu* -nge-naa-*mu*-nt'u
vegetable n *umfino* u-m-*fee*-naw
vegetarian a *okungenanyama* aw-gu-nge-na-*nyaa*-maa
visa *iviza* ee-*vee*-zaa

W

waiter *uweta* u-*we*-t'aa
walk v *-hamba ngezinyawo*
  -*haa*-mbaa nge-zee-*nyaa*-waw
wallet *isikhwama* ee-see-*kwaa*-maa
warm a *-fudumele* -fu-du-*me*-le
wash (something) *-geza* -ge-zaa
watch n *iwashi* ee-*waa*-shee
water *amanzi* aa-*maa*-ndzee
weekend *impelasonto* ee-mp'e-laa-*saw*-nt'aw
west *intshonalanga* ee-nch'aw-naa-*laa*-ngaa
wheelchair *isitulo esinamasondo*
  ee-see-*t'u*-law e-see-naa-maa-*saw*-ndaw
when *nini* nee-nee
where *kuphi* gu-pee
who sg *ubani* u-b'aa-nee
who pl *obani* aw-b'aa-nee
why *yini* yee-nee
window *ifasitela* ee-faa-see-*t'e*-laa
wine *iwayini* ee-waa-*yee*-nee
with *na-* naa-
without (someone) *engekho* e-*nge*-kaw
without (something – eg milk, sugar)
  -ngena -nge-naa-
woman *inkosikazi* ee-nk'aw-see-*gaa*-zee
write *-bhala* -*baa*-laa

Y

you sg *u-* u-
you pl *ni-* nee-

Culture

The glory of Africa is the sheer diversity of its myriad cultures – from rich **histories** and varied **cuisines** to colourful **festivals**, Africa has it all.
Here we present you with a cultural snapshot of the region and give you the tools to communicate and travel in an exciting, respectful and **sustainable** way.

history timeline

Take a wander through the rich history of Africa ...

1 million – 10,000 BC	The evolution and rise of *Homo sapiens* (modern man), who, most scientists agree, originated in Africa and then spread around the world.
9000 – 3000 BC	Agricultural development begins in the Sahel, the Sahara desert and North Africa, which were home to lakes, rainforests and a pleasant Mediterranean climate.
5000 BC	Global climate change initiates the long process of turning the Sahara into a desert, and people begin migrating south towards the Gulf of Guinea.
4000 – 3000 BC	West Africa's peoples forsake nomadic life and settle in communities, domesticating cattle and cultivating native plants.
2000 BC	The Bantu people begin migrating from West Africa, eventually reaching East Africa by 100 BC and Southern Africa by AD 300.
1000 BC	The Askum Empire is established in Ethiopia by the son of the Queen of Sheba. It lasts until 1974, when the 237th emperor, Haile Selassie, is deposed.
800 BC	Phoenicians from Tyre in modern-day Lebanon establish the colony of Carthage in Tunisia.
6th century BC	At this point, the Phoenicians control much of the trade taking place in the Mediterranean.
500 – 400 BC	Iron smelting has been established in Nigeria, central Niger and southern Mali.
AD 300	The Ghana Empire is founded. By the 8th century it has profited from its control of trans-Saharan trade and from its legendary gold deposits.
333	The Askum Empire's King Ezana adopts Christianity as the official religion of his kingdom.
639	Islam sweeps through North Africa, largely displacing Christianity. By AD 1000, traders from the north have introduced it to West Africa via the Saharan trade routes.
750	The Swahili civilisation – a rich mixture of Bantu, Arabic, Persian and Asian influences – begins to flourish in East Africa.

11th century	Great Zimbabwe attains power and wealth by trading gold and ivory with Swahili traders. It triumphs for 400 years, but collapses by the 16th century.
late 11th century	The Ghana Empire is defeated by the Muslim Berbers of the Almoravid Empire from Mauritania and Morocco.
13th century	Eleven rock-hewn churches are built in Lalibela, Ethiopia. Stunning examples of monolithic architecture, they are cut straight from the bedrock, with their roofs at ground level.
early 1235	The Mali Empire has expanded to control almost all trans-Saharan trade. This brings great wealth to its rulers, who enthusiastically embrace Islam.
1235	Sundiata Keita, the leader of the Malinké people, establishes the Mali Empire. He adopts the 'Charter of Kurukanfuga', which includes a clause prohibiting slavery.
14th century	The Dogon people first move into central Mali, where they build unique rock and mud villages consisting of buildings for each sex and a central square where most ceremonies are held.
1325	The Arab architect Abu Ishap Es-Saheli Altouwaidjin constructs Timbuktu's oldest mosque, Dyingerey Ber Mosque.
early 15th century	The Sankoré Mosque is built in Timbuktu. Also functioning as a university, it becomes one of the largest schools of Arabic learning in the Muslim world by the 16th century.
1443	The Portuguese, while seeking to exploit the Arab and Muslim-dominated gold trade, reach the mouth of the Senegal River.
1444	The first slaves are brought to Portugal from Mauritania.
mid-15th century	The power of the Mali Empire has declined. The Songhaï Empire, also established in Mali, is at the height of its powers and rules over much of West Africa.
1482	The Portuguese build St George's Castle – the earliest European structure in Sub-Saharan Africa – at Elmina, Ghana.
1487	The Portuguese explorer Bartholomeu Dias successfully navigates the Cape of Good Hope in Southern Africa.
1490	The first Christian missionaries come to Sub-Saharan Africa at the request of King Nzinga of Kongo (also known as the Manikongo) and rebuild the capital in stone at Mbanza Kongo.
1510	The Spanish start shipping the first African slaves to their colonies in South America .

CULTURE

AFRICA – history timeline

17th century	Islam becomes the Sahel's dominant religion. The Tofinu in Benin flee from slave hunters to the swampy Ganvié region, and establish Africa's only village of bamboo huts on stilts.
1699	Tulbagh in South Africa is first settled. It is famous for Church Street, one of the most complete examples of an 18th- and 19th-century Cape Dutch village in South Africa.
1728	East Africa's first known Swahili manuscript, an epic poem written in Arabic script, is penned.
early 19th century	Bioko Island in Equatorial Guinea becomes an important slave-trading base for many European nations.
1813	One of the earliest written accounts of the highly-symbolic mural art (*litema*) of the Basotho people of southern Africa appears. The art's bright colours and geometric shapes were originally painted on houses as a plea for rain and good fortune.
1816	Shaka Zulu becomes chief of the Zulu kingdom in southern Africa, sparking the *difaqane* (or forced migration) that accelerates the formation of Sotho (Lesotho) and Swazi (Swaziland).
1850–80s	The 'Marabout Wars' are fought between Islam's holy warriors and Europeans in Senegal.
1860	Livingstone House – which was later used a base by many European missionaries, including David Livingstone – is built in Zanzibar for Sultan Majid.
1870	The slave trade is officially abolished.
1871	Anthropologist EB Tylor coins the term 'animism'. It can be used to describe almost all traditional African religions, which attribute life or consciousness to natural objects or phenomena.
1881	Adventurer and explorer Henry Morgan Stanley allegedly utters the famous words 'Dr Livingstone, I presume' after he journeys into Congo (Zaïre) in search of the good doctor Livingstone.
1884–85	Africa is split into French, British, German, Portuguese, Italian, Spanish and Belgian colonies at the Berlin Conference.
1893	The Grande Mosquée is built in Burkina Faso. Designed in the Sahel mud-brick style, it consists of conical towers and wooden struts that support the structure.
1907	The Djenné Mosque, another classic of Sahel mud-brick architecture, is built in Mali. It is based on the design of an older mosque (built in 1280) that once stood on the site.
1910	Union of South Africa created, with no voting rights for blacks.

238

1913	Theologian, philosopher and musician Albert Schweitzer moves to Lambaréné, Gabon, and builds a hospital to serve humanity in what is regarded as the heart of 'darkest, savage' Africa.
1948	Apartheid is institutionalised in South Africa.
1951	Libya becomes the first African country to win independence.
1960	Independence is granted to a host of African nations, including Mali, Senegal, Madagascar, Niger, Nigeria and Mauritania.
1970s	Oil is discovered in Gabon. The discovery helps make the central African nation one of the richest in Sub-Saharan Africa.
1974	The Askum empire ends when Emperor Haile Selassie is deposed..
1975	The Portuguese exit their colony at São Tomé & Príncipe, leaving it with virtually no skilled labour, a 90 per cent illiteracy rate, only one doctor and many derelict cocoa plantations.
1976	The Soweto uprising, which protests against the use of the Afrikaans language in black schools, begins in South Africa.
1977	Central African Republic dictator Jean-Bédel Bokassa has himself crowned 'emperor' of a renamed Central African Empire. France pays most of the US$20 million coronation bill.
1990–91	The legal apparatus of apartheid is abolished in South Africa.
1994	Nelson Mandela, president of the African National Congress, is elected president in South Africa's first democratic elections.
1996	Voodoo (or vodou) is formally recognised as a religion in Benin. Its followers believe in a supreme god, and a host of lesser spirits that are ethnically specific to them and their ancestors.
1999	South African novelist JM Coetzee is awarded the Booker Prize for a second time for Disgrace..
2001	Kenya's Lamu Old Town, the oldest and best-preserved Swahili settlement in East Africa, becomes a Unesco World Heritage Site.

food

Africa, the second-largest landmass on Earth, is home to hundreds of tribes, ethnic and social groups with traditions that have been influenced by Arab, European and Asian colonisers. From desert areas to verdant coasts, it's also a land of extremes that affect the range of ingredients available to its inhabitants. Still, as you travel through this great continent, you are sure to encounter staples peculiar to the region you are in.

Starch forms the basis of all African meals and has many regional variations. *Ugali* is generally made from maize (corn) flour and has a consistency varying from porridge to a stiff dough. Also referred to as *posho* (Uganda), *nshima* (Zambia), *nsima* (Mali), *sadza* (Zimbabwe), *mealie pap* (South Africa) and *chakula* (Tanzania), *ugali* is an important part of the diet of east and southern Africans, as the crops that produce corn flour grow well in poor conditions. Millet and rice are both popular in West Africa, as is *foufou*, a thick paste (a bit like mashed potatoes mixed with gelatine) made with root vegetables like yam or cassava. To eat *ugali* or *foufou* local-style, grab a portion and roll it into a ball before dipping it with your right hand into the accompanying sauce or vegetable or meat stew. If you can, try *sauce arachide*, a thick brown paste made from groundnuts (peanuts) – it may stain your fingers, but the taste is well worth it!

Couscous is ubiquitous in North Africa, particularly in Morocco, where it's the national dish. It's both an ingredient (a semolina native in varying forms in North Africa) and the name of a dish (the semolina topped with a rich stew). The holy grail is Moroccan couscous, a perfumed, spicy and fragrant concoction that includes any number of elements such as meat, seasonal vegetables, dried fruit and nuts. Another delectable Moroccan speciality is *pastilla*, a rich savoury-sweet dish with a filling made from pigeon meat and lemon-flavoured eggs plus almonds, cinnamon, saffron and sugar, encased in layers of paper-fine pastry.

Once famously mistaken by an American tourist for the tablecloth, *injera* is a large, thin, slightly bitter pancake that forms the base of almost every Ethiopian meal. Quite a clever invention, *injera* does away with the need for plates, bowls and even utensils: it's either wrapped around small pieces of food or simply heaped with the food. Good-quality *injera* is pale (the paler the better), regular in thickness, smooth and always made with the cereal *tef*, native to the Ethiopian highlands. The favourite companion of *injera* is *wat*, Ethiopia's version of stew. Most commonly made with *bege* (lamb), *wat* can also consist of *bure* (beef), *figel* (goat) or *doro* (chicken). It can also be boiled in a spicy sauce made with oodles of *berbere*, a red powder containing up to 16 spices.

Chillies or *jaxatu* (similar to a green or yellow tomato but extremely bitter) are used to flavour dishes in Nigeria and other coastal regions of West Africa, where seafood is abundant. Okra, which is native to Africa, is also popular – the cooked result is a slimy green concoction that tastes a whole lot better than it looks – as are black-eyed peas. These ingredients feature in dishes widely available in West Africa, including the ubiquitous *jollof* (rice and vegetables with meat or fish), *kedjenou* (Côte d'Ivoire's national dish of slowly simmered chicken or fish with peppers and tomatoes) and *poulet yassa* (a Senegalese dish of rice baked in a thick sauce of fish and vegetables.

In South Africa, you will not only encounter the unusual *biltong* (dried meat), but a fusion of culinary influences: the hearty meat-and-vegetable stews dating from the early days of Dutch settlement, spicy curries from India, and the melange of local produce and Asian spices that is Cape (Malay) cuisine. Cape dishes to watch out for include *bobotie* (a curried mince pie topped with egg custard, usually served with rice and chutney), *waterblommetjie bredie* (lamb stew mixed with water-hyacinth flowers and white wine) and *malva* (a delicious sponge dessert with apricot jam and vinegar).

Tea and coffee are standard drinks throughout the continent, but there are some interesting variations. These include Swahili tea or coffee spiced with lemongrass or cardamom in East Africa, coffee flavoured with a woody leaf called *kinkiliba* in West Africa, and a marriage of black tea with mint in Morocco. In Ethiopia, where coffee was discovered between the 5th and 10th centuries, the coffee ceremony elevates coffee drinking to an art form. After a meal, the host invokes nature by sprinkling freshly cut grass on the ground, then roasts coffee beans in a pan over a tiny charcoal stove. The roasted beans are ground up with a mortar and pestle before being brewed, and the coffee is served in tiny china cups. The guest is obliged to accept at least three cups – the third in particular is considered to bestow a blessing upon the drinker.

While imported alcoholic drinks are available in most African countries, it's worth trying the local brew. *Tej*, the Ethiopian honey mead, used to be the drink of Ethiopian kings. It's a delicious and pretty powerful drink, fermented using a local shrub known as *gesho*. In the Sahel region of West Africa, locals make a rough, brown, gritty beer (called *chakalow* or *kojo*) using millet. However, the most popular drink in West Africa is palm wine, a milky-white low-strength brew made from the sap from palm trees.

Argungu Fishing Festival (Argungu, Nigeria)

First held in 1934 to mark peace between the former Sokoto Caliphate and the Kebbi kingdom, the Argungu Fishing Festival is the climax of an annual four-day cultural event held in Nigeria's Kebbi state. Thanks to a fishing ban along a one-mile stretch of the Sokoto River, a plentiful bounty of fish is ensured for the thousands of local fisherman who, armed with nets and gourds, compete to find the biggest fish. The event begins with the competitors leaping into the Sokoto River at the sound of a starting gun. As the men madly scramble to find the 'catch of the day', drummers move through the surging water on canoes, providing a soundtrack to the proceedings. After an hour, the men stagger up stone steps with their fish for the verdict. One year the winning fish weighed 75 kilos, for which the fisherman was awarded a brand new bus and one million *naira* (about $US7000).

Cape Town New Year Karnaval (South Africa)

On 2 January each year from the early 19th century, Cape Town slaves celebrated a day of freedom they christened *Tweede Nuwe Jaar* (Second New Year), a kind of independence day for the coloured community. Today, each 31 December and 2 Jan-uary, Capetonians honour this tradition with noisy, joyous and disorganised parades of marching troupes made up of members from a particular neighbourhood of the city and decked out in make-up and colourful costumes in every colour of satin, sequin and glitter. Throughout January and early February these troupes also participate in a minstrel competition, where they perform ribald song-and-dance routines inspired by American minstrels who visited the Cape in the early 20th century. Even if they don't emerge victorious, they are still winners in the eyes of their local communities, who provide them with booze and an array of delicious Cape cuisine.

Djenné Festival (Djenné, Mali)

Each spring, members of Djenné's community work together to maintain the city's Great Mosque. It's a festive occasion accompanied by music, food and fun for all involved. The focus of the renovations is the replastering of the mosque – but first the plaster, which cures for days in large vats, has to be prepared. During this time, boys caked with mud from head to toe stir the mixture by playing barefoot in the vats. The actual plastering work begins before dawn, and is heralded with chanting, drumming and flute playing. Young women carry buckets of water to the mosque on their head, while one group of men carries plaster from the pits to other men who climb onto the mosque's built-in scaffolding to smear the plaster on its walls. This all happens under the gaze of elderly community members, who sit in a place of honor in the town's market square.

Festival au Désert (Essakane, Mali)

Held in the desert oasis of Essakane, 65 kilometres from Timbuktu, the Festival au Désert focuses on the culture of the Tuareg nomads of the Sahara, who traditionally held festivals to race camels, stage sword fights, settle scores, make policy and play music. The Festival au Désert allows outsiders, including Westerners and other tribes, to experience these customs for the first time. The festival straddles the traditional and modern, with daytime cultural events (including dancing, swordplay, camel races and artisans' exhibits) and electrifying music after the sun goes down. Western artists like Robert Plant and Damon Albarn (of the band Blur) have played at the festival, but with their gourd guitars plugged into amps and screaming against a hypnotising backdrop of indigenous rhythms supplied by tom-toms, bongos, tindé drums and water drums, the traditional Saharan and African musicians are the real stars of the show.

Fez Sacred Music Festival (Fez, Morocco)

Sufi whirling dervishes, Berber trance music, Arab-Andalusian music, Hindustani chants, Celtic sacred music, Christian gospel, flamenco, and the Philharmonic Orchestra of Morocco: all have featured at the Fez Sacred Music Festival. Renowned as one of the world's greatest music festivals, the Fez Festival brings together the musical traditions of religions from across the globe in a fitting setting – the ancient holy city of Fez, where Christian, Jewish and Islamic communities have coexisted peacefully for centuries. The festival is held each June/July and features both paid and free performances . The paid performances are held under a majestic Barbary oak in the gardens of the 100-year-old Hispano-Moorish Batha Museum, and in the courtyard of the splendid Bab Makina palace, while the free performances are staged in the grand Bab Bou Jeloud Square and Dar Tazi Gardens.

Imilchil Marriage Feast (Marrakech, Morocco)

According to legend, a man and a woman from two local Moroccan tribes once fell in love, but were forbidden to marry by their families. The man and woman cried themselves to death, creating the neighbouring lakes of Issly and Tisslit near Imilchil in the Middle-High Atlas Mountains. The devastated families honoured the anniversary of the lovers' deaths by establishing a day on which members of the two tribes could marry each other. On this day – the Imilchil Marriage Feast – potential husbands survey the single women done up in traditional dress by their families (their pointed head apparel gives them away). Once a man has found a suitor, he makes his proposal. The woman can either refuse the offer, or accept it by uttering the words, 'You have captured my liver.' And so with these immortal words, the pair joins the 40 other couples tying the knot on this festive day.

La Cure Salée (In-Gall, Niger)

La Cure Salée (The Salt Cure) is a sort of homecoming for the nomadic Fula and Tuareg peoples, who bring their animals to the area around In-Gall during the rainy season. Supervised by their owners – who sit on camels, catching up with old friends and frequently camel racing – the animals partake in the 'salt cure', slurping up a healthy dose of minerals to sustain them during the dry months ahead. For the Wodaabé sect of the Fulani, it is also the time of the Gerewol festival, an event in which Wodaabé men aim to impress eligible women by participating in a 'beauty contest' featuring a dance intended to display their beauty, charisma and charm. The women are looking for tall lean bodies, long slender noses, white even teeth and bright eyes – the men oblige by preening themselves for hours in an effort to highlight their assets. The prize? A highly-sought-after marriage proposal.

The Maitisong Festival (Gaborone, Botswana)

Back in the 1980s, when officials of the Maru-a-Pula School were planning to build a hall, they decided it should be available to the whole community of Gaborone, which at the time had nowhere to stage professional performances. The hall was completed at the beginning of 1987, and was introduced to the public with the Maitisong Festival shortly after. Testament to the saying, 'From little things big things grow', the festival is now the largest arts festival in Botswana, and attracts big names from all over the nation and region. Featuring a range of films, dance troupes, drama and music, the festival is renowned for the huge gospel and pop performances to which thousands of locals flock. Locals also get in on the act themselves – to keep everyone happy during the intervals of free outdoor concerts, they get up on stage and perform impromptu music, dance and comedy acts!

Rustler's Easter One World Unity Party (Ficksburg, South Africa)

Held in the famous Rustler's Valley Retreat, South Africa's original hippy hangout, the One World Unity Party is an eclectic event held over four days over Easter each year. According to organisers, Rustler's events are 'eco-friendly and natural celebrations blended with modern music and dance'. Consider the 'Futures Field' chill-out space, which has a sound rig driven by solar panels and bicycle power. Together with the 'Sweat Hut' and the nearby game reserve featuring animals in their natural habitat, the 'Futures Field' offers a respite from the World Stage, which hosts nonstop performances by international musicians and DJs, and the Comet Stage, which features jam sessions, comedy sketches and more DJs. Children are warmly welcomed (although management kindly request that, due to the sensitive ecological nature of the valley, punters leave their dogs at home).

The Serengeti-Masai Mara Wildebeest Migration (Tanzania-Kenya)

According to African legend, the curious-looking wildebeest was created using left-over parts. Still he is the undeniable star of one of nature's most stunning spectacles. It is difficult to pinpoint when the wildebeest – who are accompanied by small numbers of zebras, elands and Thompson's gazelles – will begin their exodus from the dry plains of Serengeti National Park to the nutrient-rich grassy landscape of Kenya's Masai-Mara region, but the best time to see the migration is usually between June and August, when the animals congregate and prepare to cross the Grumeti River enroute to the Masai-Mara. Here gigantic crocodiles await their prey and the animals try not to stumble as they cross the teeming waters. Witnessing animals fall victim to the hungry crocodiles can be upsetting, but being in the Masai-Mara area as up to one and a half million animals pour in is truly mind-blowing.

Timkat (Feast of Epiphany) Festival (Ethiopia)

Held on 19 January each year, Timkat commemorates John the Baptist's blessing of Jesus Christ. On the eve of Timkat, *ketera* (priests) remove the *tabot* (symbolizing the Ark of the Covenant containing the Ten Commandments) from each church and cover it in layers of rich cloth to protect it from impious eyes. Accompanied by men, women and children dressed in dazzling white traditional dress – a dramatic contrast to the jewelled colours of the priests' ceremonial robes and sequinned velvet umbrellas – the *tabot* is carried to a pool of water or river to be blessed for the next day's celebration. People camp here throughout the night, eating and drinking by fire- and torch-light. Towards dawn, members of the congregation gather around the blessed water, and are symbolically baptised by the priest. The *tabots* are then taken back to their respective churches and the festivities ramp up.

Umhlanga (Reed) Dance (Lombaba, Swaziland)

In August or September each year, young maidens from all parts of Swaziland gather in the nation's royal heartland. They come voluntarily in their thousands to learn skills that will help them to handle married life in a dignified manner, and to perform a traditional 'reed dance' for the Swazi King. From this performance, the King, who typically takes over 400 wives during his lifetime, chooses a bride. For their big moment, the women wear a traditional costume of *ligcebesha* (a beaded necklace with colours of the Swazi flag), *umgaco* (colourful beads with wooly tassels that hang from the left shoulder to the right hip) and *indlamu* (short beaded skirts) and perform with reeds they have hand-picked. The dance attracts many tourists and, when it is over, the reeds are taken to the royal village where they are used to make wind breakers for the queen mother's house.

sustainable travel

What is sustainable travel and responsible tourism?

Being a responsible tourist in Africa means acknowledging that travel inevitably impacts on the host communities and environment you visit – when you travel, you're not only embracing the diversity of this big, wide wonderful world, but you're adding your footprints to those left by some of the 700-million-plus people who travel internationally each year. This runaway juggernaut affects wilderness, native species and traditional cultures. The goal is to make the impact as positive as possible by giving back to local communities and acting to minimise negative outcomes. In doing so, you are helping to make your steps lighter, greener and friendlier.

How can travel to Africa have a positive effect on local African industries and wildlife?

A land of stunning geography, all-night partying and wondrous architecture, Africa is also the ultimate destination to observe the 'Big Five' (elephant, rhinoceros, leopard, lion and Cape buffalo) in their natural habitat. However, with the global inequities of wealth distribution so pronounced in Africa, it's particularly important to ensure that your travel enjoyment is not at the expense of locals and their environment.

At one level, the impact of tourism can be positive – it can provide an incentive for locals to preserve environments and wildlife by generating employment, while enabling them to maintain their traditional lifestyles. However, the negative impacts of tourism can be substantial and contribute to the gradual erosion of traditional life. You can try to keep your impact as low as possible by considering the following tips:

- Support local enterprise. Use locally owned hotels and restaurants and buy souvenirs directly from the tradespeople and craftspeople who make them.
- Don't buy items made from natural materials such as ivory, skins and shells.
- Choose safari and trekking operators that treat local communities as equal partners, and that are committed to protecting local ecosystems.
- Question any so-called eco-tourism operators for specifics about what they're really doing to protect the environment and the people who live there.
- Instead of giving cash, food or medicines to locals, make a donation to a recognised project such as a health centre or school.
- Try to get a balanced view of life in developed countries, and focus on the strong points of local culture.
- Resist the local tendency to be indifferent to littering. On treks, in parks or when camping, carry out your litter and leave areas cleaner than you found them.
- In order to help minimise land degradation, keep to the tracks when walking or when on safari, or encourage your driver to do so.

safari

What are the main safari regions in Africa?

East and Southern Africa have a clutch of popular parks showcasing some of the greatest wildlife spectacles on earth. Highlights in East Africa, where Swahili is commonly spoken, are the magnificent Serengeti–Masai Mara ecosystem; the wildlife-packed Ngorongoro Crater and Tarangire National Park in Tanzania; Parc National de Volcans, Rwanda's original *Gorillas in the Mist* backdrop; and the hippo-, crocodile- and elephant-filled Murchison Falls and Budongo Central Forest Reserve with its chimpanzees and dense forest, in Uganda. In Southern Africa, where Afrikaans, Xhosa and Zulu are the most common languages, you'll find world-class wildlife watching at South Africa's Madikwe Game Reserve, Pilanesberg National Park, and its safari showpiece Kruger National Park; in Swaziland, there's the wildlife-rich Mkhaya Game Reserve, noted for its black rhinos, and the evocative Phinda Resource Reserve.

In the following, we give you the vocabulary you need to communicate effectively and respectfully in the two main languages spoken in these popular safari areas. The symbol ⓐ indicates Afrikaans and ⓢ indicates Swahili.

safari animals		
buffalo	*buffel* ⓐ	bi·fil
	mbogo ⓢ	m·*boh*·goh
camel	*kameel* ⓐ	ka·*meyl*
	ngamia ⓢ	ngaa·*mee*·aa
crocodile	*krokodil* ⓐ	kraw·ku·*dil*
	mamba ⓢ	*maam*·baa
elephant	*olifant* ⓐ	*oo*·lee·fant
	ndovu/tembo ⓢ	n·*doh*·voo/*teym*·boh
giraffe	*kameelperd* ⓐ	ka·*meyl*·pert
	twiga ⓢ	*twee*·gaa
leopard	*luiperd* ⓐ	*lay*·pirt
	chui ⓢ	*choo*·ee
lion	*leeu* ⓐ	*ley*·u
	simba ⓢ	*seem*·baa
monkey	*tumbili* ⓐ	toom·*bee*·lee
	apie ⓢ	*aa*·pi
rhinoceros	*renoster* ⓐ	ri·*naws*·tir
	kifaru ⓢ	kee·*faa*·roo
zebra	*sebra* ⓐ	*sey*·bra
	punda milia ⓢ	*poon*·daa mee·*lee*·aa

I'd like to stay at a locally run safari park.

Ek wil in 'n safaripark bly wat deur　ek vil in i sa-*faa*-ree-park blay vat deyr
plaaslike mense bestuur word. ⓐ　*plaas*-li-ki *men*-si bi-*stewr* vort

I'd like to visit a native-style tourist station.

Ningependa kufikia kwenye　neen-gey-*peyn*-daa koo-*fee*-kaa *kweyn*-yey
kituo cha kitalii cha　kee-*too*-oh chaa kee-taa-*lee* chaa
kienyeji. ⓢ　kee-eyn-*yey*-jee

Are there any eco-lodges at the park?

Is daar enige eko-hutte in die park? ⓐ　is daar ee-ni-khi *ee*-ku-hi-ti in dee park

Are there any local-style guesthouses in the park?

Kuna nyumba za wageni za　koo-naa *nyoom*-baa zaa waa-*gey*-nee zaa
kienyeji ndani ya hifadhi? ⓢ　kee-eyn-*yey*-jee n-*daa*-nee yaa hee-*faa*-dhee

Are there fair working standards at this park?

Is die werksomstandighede　is dee *verks*-om-*stan*-dikh-hee-di
in hierdie park billik? ⓐ　in *heer*-dee park *bi*-lik
Kuna viwango vya kazi za　koo-naa vee-*waan*-goh vyaa *kaa*-zee zaa
kistaarabu ndani ya　kee-staa-*raa*-boo n-*daa*-nee yaa
hifadhi? ⓢ　hee-*faa*-dhee

Does your business have responsible tourism policies?

Het julle besigheid 'n　het *ji*-li *bey*-sikh-hayt i
verantwoordelike toerismebeleid? ⓐ　fir-ant-*voor*-di-li-ki tu-*ris*-mi-bi-*layt*

Is your business involved in tourism activities that protect the environment?

Biashara yako　bee-aa-*shaa*-raa *yaa*-koh
inajihusisha na shughuli　ee-naa-jee-hoo-*see*-shaa naa shoo-*goo*-lee
za kitalii kuhifadhi　zaa kee-taa-*lee* koo-hee-*faa*-dhee
mazingira? ⓢ　maa-zeen-*gee*-raa

I'd like to hire a local guide.

Ek wil 'n plaaslike gids huur. ⓐ　ek vil i *plaas*-li-ki khits hewr
Nataka kuajiri kiongozi　naa-*taa*-kaa koo-aa-*jee*-ree kee-ohn-*goh*-zee
kutoka hapo jirani. ⓢ　koo-*toh*-kaa *haa*-poh jee-*raa*-nee

I'd like to go somewhere off the beaten track.

Ek wil êrens anders as na — ek vil *e*·rins an·dirs as naa
die gewone plekke toe gaan. ⓐ — dee khi·*voo*·ni *ple*·ki tu khaan
Nataka kuenda mahali — naa·*taa*·kaa koo·*eyn*·daa maa·*haa*·lee
ambapo siyo kawaida — aam·*baa*·poh *see*·yoh kaa·waa·*ee*·daa
kwa watalii. ⓢ — kwaa waa·taa·*lee*

Is it safe to walk around this section of the park?

Is dit veilig om in hierdie deel — is dit *fay*·likh om in *heer*·dee deyl
van die park rond te loop? ⓐ — fan dee park ront ti loop
Ni salama nikitembea kwa — nee saa·*la*·maa nee·kee·teym·*bey*·aa kwaa
miguu katika sehemu hii ya — mee·*goo* kaa·*tee*·kaa sey·*hey*·moo hee yaa
hifadhi? ⓢ — hee·*faa*·dhee

Do you have information about the preservation of wildlife at this park?

Het julle inligting oor die — het *ji*·li *in*·likh·ting oor dee
bewaring van wild in hierdie park? ⓐ — bi·*vaa*·ring fan vilt in *heer*·dee park
Je, unazo taarifa — jey oo·*naa*·zoh taa·*ree*·faa
zinazohusiana na — zee·naa·zoh·hoo·see·*aa*·naa naa
utunzaji wa wanyama — oo·toon·*zaa*·jee waa waan·*yaa*·maa
pori ndani ya hifadhi hii? ⓢ — *poh*·ree n·*daa*·nee yaa hee·*faa*·dhee hee

Do you have any endangered species at this park?

Het julle enige bedreigde — het *ji*·li ey·ni·khi bi·*draykh*·di
spesies in hierdie park? ⓐ — *spey*·sees in *heer*·dee park
Je, unao viumbe — jey oo·*naa*·oh vee·*oom*·bey
walioko hatarini katika — waa·lee·*oh*·koh haa·taa·*ree*·nee kaa·*tee*·kaa
hifadhi? ⓢ — hee·*faa*·dhee hee

Do you have the Big Five animals at this park?

Het julle die Groot Vyf in — het *ji*·li dee khroot fayf in
hierdie park? ⓐ — *heer*·dee park
Je, unao wanyama wakuu — jey oo·*naa*·oh waan·*yaa*·maa waa·*koo*
watano katika hifadhi hii? ⓢ — waa·*taa*·noh kaa·*tee*·kaa hee·*faa*·dhee hii

Can you recommend a company that organises safaris?

Kan julle 'n maatskappy aanbeveel — kan *ji*·li i maat·ska·*pay* aan·bi·feyl
wat safari's organiseer? ⓐ — vat sa·*faa*·rees awr·kha·nee·*seer*
Unaweza kupendekeza — oo·naa·*wey*·zaa koo·peyn·dey·*key*·zaa
kampuni ya safari kwa miguu? ⓢ — kaam·*poo*·nee yaa sa·*faa*·ree kwaa mee·*goo*

Can you recommend a 4WD/walking safari?

Kan julle 'n vier-by-vier/ — kan *ji*·li i feer bay feer/
stapsafari aanbeveel? ⓐ — stap·sa·*faa*·ree *aan*·bi·feyl

Can you recommend a camel/walking safari?
Unajua safari ya ngamia/ kutembea nzuri? ⓢ
oo·naa·*joo*·aa saa·*faa*·ree yaa n·gaa·*mee*·aa/ koo·teym·*bey*·aa n·*zoo*·ree

When's the next safari?
Wanneer is die volgende safari? ⓐ
va·nir is dee *fol*·khin·di sa·*faa*·ree
Safari ijayo itakuwa lini? ⓢ
saa·*faa*·ree ee·*jaa*·yoh ee·taa·*koo*·waa *lee*·nee

Are park fees included?
Is parkfooie ingesluit? ⓐ
is *park*·foy·i *in*·khi·slayt
Inazingatia ada za hifadhi? ⓢ
ee·naa·zeen·gaa·*tee*·aa *aa*·daa zaa hee·*faa*·dhee

How many people will be in the group?
Hoeveel mense sal in die groep wees? ⓐ
hu·fil *men*·si sal in dee khrup veys
Kundi itakuwa na watu wangapi? ⓢ
koon·dee ee·taa·*koo*·waa naa *waa*·too waan·*gaa*·pee

We'd like to go wildlife spotting.
Ons wil gaan diere kyk. ⓐ
awns vil khaan *dee*·ri kayk
Tunataka kwenda kutafuta wanyama pori. ⓢ
too·naa·*taa*·kaa *kweyn*·daa koo·taa·*foo*·taa waa·*nyaa*·maa *poh*·ree

What animals are we likely to see?
Watter diere gaan ons sien? ⓐ
va·tir *dee*·ri khaan ons seen
Tutegemee kuona wanyama gani? ⓢ
too·tey·gey·*mey* koo·*oh*·naa waa·*nyaa*·maa *gaa*·nee

We're very keen to see (elephants).
Ons wil graag (olifante) sien. ⓐ
awns vil khraakh (*oo*·lee·fan·ti) seen
Tunataka sana kuona (tembo). ⓢ
too·naa·*taa*·kaa *saa*·naa koo·*oh*·naa (*teym*·bo)

What animal is that?
Watter dier is dit? ⓐ
va·tir deer is dit
Ni mnyama gani? ⓢ
nee m·*nyaa*·maa *gaa*·nee

Is it a protected park/species?
Is dit 'n beskermde park/spesie? ⓐ
is dit a bi·*ske*·rim·di park/*spey*·see
Mbuga/Spishi inahifadhiwa? ⓢ
m·*boo*·gaa/*spee*·shee ee·naa·hee·faa·*dhee*·waa